D0126404

Unamuno

JOSÉ RUBIA BARCIA is Professor of Spanish and Chairman of the Department of Spanish and Portuguese, University of California, Los Angeles.

M. A. ZEITLIN is Professor Emeritus of Spanish and Portuguese in the same department.

MIGUEL DE UNAMUNO
SELF-PORTRAIT

Unamuno

Creator and Creation

Edited by José Rubia Barcia
and M. A. Zeitlin

Berkeley and Los Angeles 1967
UNIVERSITY OF CALIFORNIA PRESS

LIBRARY

SEP 10 1968

UNIVERSITY OF THE PACIFIC

187677

University of California Press
Berkeley and Los Angeles, California

Cambridge University Press
London, England

© 1967 by The Regents of the University of California
Library of Congress Catalog Card Number: 67–22249
Designed by W. H. Snyder
Printed in the United States of America

PREFACE

From October 22 to November 6, 1964, the Department of Spanish and Portuguese, University of California, Los Angeles, in cooperation with the Committee on Public Lectures, the Center of Latin American Studies, and the Del Amo Foundation, presented a program of events commemorating the centennial of the birth of Miguel de Unamuno. Among these events was a series of lectures under the general title "Unamuno: The Man and His Work." Reprints of these lectures constitute the major portion of this volume; but also included are essays contributed by Professors Gullón, Meregalli, and Ferrater Mora who, although invited to participate in the celebration, were unable to attend. The commemoration concluded with a symposium on Unamuno under the chairmanship of Professor Américo Castro. His opening remarks are published here "in lieu of prologue," and Professor Walter Starkie graciously agreed to contribute the epilogue.

Each contributor was given complete freedom to approach the many-faceted Spaniard from any aspect he chose. In spite of the resulting apparent variety, almost all these essays share one underlying theme: the poignant relevancy of Unamuno's achievement as a human being and as a writer to our own time. This relevancy is, of course, the main reason for the celebration of the centenary of Unamuno's birth in more than a hundred universities throughout the world.

The essays have been arranged to follow, insofar as possible in a collection of this kind, a logical pattern. Presented first are those on Unamuno as man and thinker; second, those dealing primarily with Unamuno as novelist and playwright; third, essays comparing Unamuno with other writers and evaluating him as a literary critic and a politician; and, finally, an essay studying specifically his importance to our day and age.

As editors, we have been particularly concerned with making this volume useful to present and future readers, reducing references to common and, when possible, easily available sources in

Spanish and English, and striving toward a basic uniformity in matters of style and form, without undue interference with personal approaches. In matters involving controversial opinions and interpretations, or idiosyncrasies of expression, our role has been merely advisory; in instances of disagreement, the wishes of the contributors have been uniformly respected.

Special thanks are due Professor Aníbal Sánchez-Reulet for substantial preparatory work on several of the essays; to Frances J. Kirschenbaum for valued editorial suggestions and aid; to Armando Grant, Curtiss Millner, and Agnes Moncy for translating into English the essays by Professors Meregalli, Ferrater Mora, and Gullón, respectively; to Martin H. Sable for assistance in preparing the bibliography; to Margarita Nieto for preparing the index; and to the members of the staff of the Reference Department of the UCLA Research Library for cheerful and painstaking help on numerous occasions.

Finally, we are deeply grateful to the University of California, Los Angeles, for the understanding and generosity that have made possible the publication of this volume.

J. R. B.
M. A. Z.

CONTRIBUTORS

CARLOS BLANCO-AGUINAGA, Professor of Spanish Literature at the University of California, San Diego. His works include *Unamuno: Teórico del lenguaje* and *El Unamuno contemplativo.* Guggenheim Fellow, 1957.

AMÉRICO CASTRO, indisputably the main exponent of Hispanic scholarship in the United States, now Professor Emeritus in Residence at the University of California, San Diego. His works include studies on a wide variety of literary, historical, and philological subjects, among them the epoch-making *The Structure of Spanish History.* Recipient of countless national and international honors.

JOSÉ FERRATER MORA, Professor of Philosophy at Bryn Mawr College, Bryn Mawr, Pennsylvania. His works include *Unamuno: A Philosophy of Tragedy.* Guggenheim Fellow, 1946.

RICARDO GULLÓN, Professor of Spanish Literature at the University of Texas. His works include studies on modern and contemporary Spanish writers, among them *Autobiografías de Unamuno.*

PAUL ILIE, Associate Professor of Spanish at the University of Michigan. His works include studies on modern and contemporary Spanish writers, among them *La novelística de Camilo José Cela.* Guggenheim Fellow, 1965.

LEON LIVINGSTONE, Professor of Spanish Literature at the University of Buffalo. His works include studies on Azorín, Ortega, and Unamuno. Visiting Professor at the University of California, Los Angeles, 1964–65.

FRANCO MEREGALLI, Director of Hispanic Studies at the Facoltá di Lingue e Letterature Straniere di Ca'Foscari (Venice, Italy).

His works include studies on the literary interinfluences between Italy and Spain. Visiting Professor of Spanish at the University of California, Los Angeles, 1964–65.

C. P. OTERO, Associate Professor of Spanish at the University of California, Los Angeles. His works include studies on a variety of subjects, from linguistics to contemporary literature.

ALEXANDER A. PARKER, Director of Hispanic Studies at the University of Edinburgh. His works include studies on Cervantes, Quevedo, Calderón, Garcilaso de la Vega, and Góngora. Visiting Mellon Professor at the University of Pittsburgh, 1964–65.

STANLEY PAYNE, Associate Professor of History at the University of California, Los Angeles. His works include *Falange: A History of Spanish Fascism*. Guggenheim Fellow, 1962.

JOSÉ RUBIA BARCIA, Chairman of the Department of Spanish and Portuguese at the University of California, Los Angeles. His works include creative writing and studies on the modern and contemporary periods of Spanish literature. Guggenheim Fellow, 1962.

ANÍBAL SÁNCHEZ-REULET, Professor of Spanish-American Literature at the University of California, Los Angeles. His works include studies on the history of thought and ideas in Spanish America. Guggenheim Fellow, 1947.

WALTER STARKIE, Professor in Residence at the University of California, Los Angeles. Internationally known Hispanist. Translator of Cervantes. His works include studies on a number of the most significant Spanish authors and various aspects of Spanish life.

ALFRED STERN, Professor of Philosophy and Languages at the California Institute of Technology, Pasadena. His works include *Sartre: His Philosophy and Psychoanalysis*, and many other studies on philosophical and literary subjects.

CONTENTS

ix

MAJOR WORKS OF UNAMUNO CITED
(IN ORDER OF DATE OF ORIGINAL PUBLICATION)

1895   *En torno al casticismo* (included among collected essays in *Ensayos*, 7 vols., 1916–1918)

1897   *Paz en la guerra*

1902   *Amor y pedagogía*

1905   *Vida de don Quijote y Sancho* (2d aug. ed., 1914)

1907   "Mi religión" (included in *Mi religión y otros ensayos breves*, 1910)

1912   *Contra esto y aquello* (collected articles on literary themes published mainly in the Buenos Aires newspaper *La Nación* between 1907 and 1911)

1913   *Del sentimiento trágico de la vida*

1914   *Niebla*

1916   *Nada menos que todo un hombre* (included in *Tres novelas ejemplares y un prólogo*, 1920)

1917   *Abel Sánchez*

1921   *La tía Tula*

1925   *De Fuerteventura a París*

1925   *L'agonie du christianisme* (Spanish version: *La agonía del cristianismo*, 1931)

1927   *Cómo se hace una novela*

1931   *San Manuel Bueno, mártir* (included in *San Manuel Bueno, mártir y tres historias más*, 1933)

1932   *El Otro*

1933   *La Novela de don Sandalio, jugador de ajedrez*

1934   *El hermano Juan*

ABBREVIATIONS OF UNAMUNO'S WORKS*

Obras   *Obras completas.* Madrid: Afrodisio Aguado, 1959–1964. 16 vols.

ABS   *Abel Sanchez and Other Stories.* Trans. with introduction by Anthony Kerrigan. Chicago: Regnery, 1956.

AGC   *The Agony of Christianity.* Trans. with introduction by Kurt Reinhardt. New York: Ungar, 1960.

ESS   *Essays and Soliloquies.* Trans. with introductory essay by J. E. Crawford Flitch. New York: Knopf, 1925.

LDQ   *The Life of Don Quixote and Sancho According to Miguel de Cervantes Saavedra Expounded with Comment by Miguel de Unamuno.* Trans. Homer P. Earle. New York: Knopf, 1927.

MST   *Mist (Niebla): A Tragicomic Novel.* Trans. Warner Fite. New York: Knopf, 1928.

PEP   *Perplexities and Paradoxes.* Trans. Stuart Gross. New York: Philosophical Library, 1945.

SMB   *Saint Emmanuel the Good, Martyr.* See *ABS*, pp. 167–216.

TEN   *Three Exemplary Novels*, with an introduction by Angel del Río. Trans. Angel Flores. New York: Grove Press, 1956.

TSL   *Tragic Sense of Life.* Trans. J. E. Crawford Flitch. Introductory essay by S. de Madariaga. 2d ed. New York: Dover, 1954.

---

*References are usually to the Spanish text of Unamuno's writings. When published translations are available, the corresponding passages are indicated in parentheses. When primary references are to a translated version, the order is reversed, with corresponding passages in the original being given in parentheses.

1

IN LIEU OF PROLOGUE
Américo Castro

With this symposium[1] the events at the University of California, Los Angeles, in commemoration of Miguel de Unamuno, born a century ago, come to an end. In the series of lectures that constituted the major part of the celebration, eminent Unamuno scholars have examined in one way or another almost every aspect of his life and works. The task is now to explore what is, what will be, what should be Unamuno's contribution to twentieth-century culture. On this score the distinguished participants here with me on this platform are better prepared to answer than I. Nevertheless, I do have a deep interest in our common problem, and perhaps the best way to get our discussion started will be for me simply to tell you some of the questions I have been asking myself without finding clear-cut answers to them.

First of all, is Unamuno going to survive as a thinker, or as a purely literary writer? Intellectual intent and the purely artistic coexist in his works, though in most of them it becomes apparent at first sight that the former prevails over the latter. Witness the nature of the books written on Unamuno, most of which emphasize the intellectual, the reasoning quality, rather than the poetic or novelistic dimensions and the artistic form. Ferrater Mora and François Meyer have written on Unamuno's philosophy. Unamuno's *Obras escogidas* are prefaced by a philosopher, Julián Marías. Carlos Blanco's substantial work *Unamuno contemplativo* is primarily a penetrating biography of the deep per-

[1] The celebration at the University of California, Los Angeles, of the centenary of Unamuno's birth was concluded by a symposium held on November 6, 1964. Professor Castro presided, and his opening remarks are embodied in this prologue.

1

sonality of a thinker. It is evident, on the other hand, that much
has been written on Unamuno as poet and novelist. Hence, I ask
myself this question: How should these highly different aspects
be blended or harmonized? Or, should one of them be played
against the other?

Another direction for our meditations could be to delve into
the possibility of a relationship between Unamuno's idea of man's
personality and the present-day conflict in which man struggles
between the "impersonal" world and his awareness of self. It
seems, at times, that the dazzling strides taken by technology
are alienating man from his inner self, leaving him at the mercy
of a world that, although inhabited by man, is becoming an extension of the cosmic world, whose silence and nonhumanness
terrify him.

In Unamuno's philosophical poetry we definitely should not
look for any pragmatic or practical virtue, or any poetic philosophy of human existence. I am just wondering whether Unamuno
is not closer today to our human worries than he was fifty years
ago when many regarded him as an intellectual eccentric, primarily interested in confusing his readers with paradoxes and
contradictions. In saying *human* worries, I am not thinking of
science, politics, business, social status, or of such forms of ex-
ternalized human activity. I am merely referring to what a human
being finds within his human loneliness when, after having been
busy with one thing and another, he returns to the home of his
soul and asks himself a good number of what's and what-for's.
According to a medieval legend, King Alfonso the Wise in the
thirteenth century, by dint of looking at the stars, lost sight of
himself and found himself on the verge of losing his kingdom.

Let us now ask whether this *self* of man is something to be
minimized, to be dealt with as a leftover of the scientist, the
businessman, the politician, the priest, the gangster? This is the
kind of problem Unamuno—and the same is true, in a different
way, of Ortega y Gasset also—forces us to come to grips with.
Unamuno's humanism has nothing in common with mysticism
or with psychoanalysis. As every student of Unamuno knows,
the ideal spatial realm for his quest is not objective, neutral
reality, but *agony*—"struggle" in Greek. His is a living dialectic,

a sustained dialogue that moves between the hope of eternity and the terror of nothingness, midway between lofty poetry and flat reality.

I do not know why but, while I was involved in thoughts and *feelings* about Unamuno and the problems that swarm around his historical figure, something written by Albert Camus in 1957 came to my mind. It is a statement in connection with Lope de Vega's play *El caballero de Olmedo* ("The Knight of Olmedo"):

> To our Europe in ashes, Lope de Vega and the Spanish theater can bring their inexhaustible light, their remarkable youth; they can help us to bring back to our stages the spirit of grandeur.

The knight—who actually was killed rather prosaically, and appears in the dirge as already dead—was brought back to life by the combined efforts of poetry and love. As a dramatic character, the knight was torn apart by the contradictory obligation of surviving lyrically as a lover or dying tragically as a hero. This struggle between the actual person's earthly transitoriness and the poetic character's earthly perenniality would have fascinated Unamuno, although he was not particularly fond of Lope de Vega's theater.

This notwithstanding, some of Unamuno's works, some of his literary situations, call to mind certain aspects of Lope de Vega's artistry, what Lope de Vega sometimes achieved through sheer poetical instinct, through, may I add, his "Spanishness." Low reality was raised to a sort of third poetical power. In Unamuno's *The Living Poem of Love* we read:

> A look which, by diffusing its light over the forms of things around it, spread a steady quietness over them all.

Gentlemen, *symposium* etymologically meant "drinking together." Allow me to give you, symbolically, Miguel de Unamuno.

2

UNAMUNO THE MAN
José Rubia Barcia

The title chosen for this essay, "Unamuno the Man," may perhaps be misleading, especially if it disposes the reader to expect a characterization of Unamuno the author based on a résumé of human traits and qualities as prerequisites for an understanding of his work. It might have been more appropriate to have selected the quasi synonym *person*, instead of *man*. The word *person*, it may be recalled, derives from the Latin word *persona*, which, in turn, came from the verb *personare*, "to sound or resound, to shout." *Persona* was first applied to indicate the resounding mask used by Roman actors on the stage. A step further and the object became the character himself, or personage.

It is a fact that even a superficial reading of Unamuno's work gives the impression of a man shouting at the top of his lungs through a mask that hides the flesh-and-bone identity of the shouter. And it is in what he says, and in how and when he says or does things, that we will discover the identity of the real author —an author who, at least in appearance, is always subordinated to the actor in Unamuno. It is as if Unamuno wanted to imply that it is the actor, not the author, who ought to monopolize our attention. It would be a mistake to attribute to frivolity or other superficial reasons this preference of Unamuno's for the actor. The privacy of an actor is irrelevant to the lines assigned to him, and furthermore, an actor is, by his own nature, a social, public creature functioning outside himself, but with an impact on others far superior to that possible for an ordinary person, no matter how sincere he may be.

4

It is this extraordinary, tragic, and meaningful actor known as Miguel de Unamuno who is here examined. His configuration is derived mainly from his own words and actions, and also from the testimony of his contemporaries, from the imagination of his readers, and from the set of circumstances in which he lived, without, by any means, excluding from the total composition of the resultant image, the man Unamuno himself.

Miguel de Unamuno y Jugo was born on September 29, 1864, in the Spanish Basque country and of Basque ancestry. The fact that he was a Basque predisposed the boy to look upon the rest of Spain with peculiar eyes, and the fact that he was born close to the revolution of 1868 gave him an ideologically liberal background. When Unamuno was six years old his father died, and he was raised by his mother. His father had been an immigrant in Mexico and had retired to Spain with enough money to marry, raise a family, and die leaving his wife and children with sufficient means to live comfortably. During Unamuno's childhood, Spain went through its second civil war of the nineteenth century, and he himself remembered all his life the bombardment of his native city of Bilbao by the forces of the Carlists, who were, in today's language, the extreme rightists of their time. From 1874 on, there was in Spain a period called the Restauración (or Restoration), which ensured more than two decades of peace and relative prosperity and which was interrupted only by the Cuban conflict and the short-lived Spanish-American War.

In 1880, when he was only sixteen, Unamuno was sent by his family to Madrid to study humanities at Madrid University. He arrived with somewhat more than the usual Catholic background of a Spanish youth, having been affiliated to the San Luis Gonzaga brotherhood in his native town. In Madrid he became a frequent visitor to the Ateneo, a sort of walled-in Hyde Park, where every idea could be exposed and every system of thought explained and divulged. The young Unamuno listened, read voraciously, and began to change. In the process he suffered the first crisis in his religious faith. He decided to be reborn but this time as a creature made of paper and ink, not flesh and blood, for he had discovered the creative magic of the written word, or had become convinced, in the words of another great Spaniard, the famous painter Picasso, that "art is a lie that makes us realize truth."[1]

A dual and simultaneous process now began to take place. Life for Unamuno continued to be lived in everyday terms, but at the same time, in the exalted and selective way of the imagination in order to create for others the image of what *ought to be*, which was sometimes similar but most often contrary to what *was*. The main motivations in this new life were two: a feeling of terror at the fatal prospect of death, and a tremendous thirst for immortality. This newly created alter ego, the first of several successive ones Unamuno was to create, put on his mask and was baptized Pachico Zabalbide.

Pachico's conception and gestation took a long time but finally he was presented to the public in 1897 under the soft covers of a book entitled *Paz en la guerra*. Its author, Unamuno the man, was at the time thirty-three years old and already a fairly well-known professor of Greek at the University of Salamanca and a frequent contributor to newspapers and literary magazines. He had arrived in Salamanca six years before accompanied by his wife Concha and the first of eight children that would be born to them. Pachico Zabalbide appears in the novel *Paz en la guerra* as being twenty-six at the time of the Carlist bombardment of Bilbao, and therefore sixteen years older than Unamuno himself had been. He is the opposite of another young man in the novel, called Ignacio, who is the prototype of the antiliberal Spaniard under the traditional motto of "God, Fatherland, and King." In the mocking opinion of the narrator, Ignacio's God was "an immense power spread over everything; his Fatherland, a burning field full of the clattering of armor; and the King was God's arm and the trunk of the Fatherland."[2] He was attracted to Pachico because of his reputation of being "strange."[3]

Pachico had been orphaned at seven, had been a weak child, and in his adolescence had gone through a period of "childish

[1] See Alfred H. Barr, Jr., *Picasso: Fifty Years of His Art* (New York, 1946), p. 270.
[2] *Obras*, II, 126–127.
[3] *Ibid.*, p. 128.

mysticism and intellectual voracity."[4] At eighteen, his uncle sent him to Madrid to study at the university. At this time the Spanish capital was going through the Krausist philosophical fashion with its emphasis on rationalism, and Pachico found himself "in the middle of a tumult of new ideas."[5] As a consequence, he suffered an inner crisis that culminated in his abandonment of his Catholic faith.

Back in Bilbao, out of respect for the memory of his mother and under the pressure of his uncle, Pachico went for a time through the motions of being a firm believer. He experienced, on his own and for the first time, the possibility of a double life, in which the outside did not correspond to the inside. Within his inner self the dominant emotion was the confrontation with the idea of death. In his own words, he "was crushed by the thought that one day he was to fall asleep and not awaken." He also felt "an irrational terror at the idea of nothingness, of finding himself alone in empty time."[6] But outwardly Pachico used to talk a lot, "irking many of his listeners with his tiresome and pedantic conversation."[7] His interminable monologues were filled with the "greatest paradoxes and exaggerated ideas."[8] One day he said to two of his best friends, without caring at all whether he was understood or not, "that everybody was right, and nobody was; that it made no difference to him if you were a white piece or a black, because you were moved from square to square like chessmen moved by invisible players; that he was not a Carlist, nor a Liberal, nor a Monarchist, nor a Republican, but everything at the same time."[9]

The Civil War, on the one hand, and his inner life, on the other, gave Pachico the pretext for further consideration of the meaning and importance of what the French have called *la grande histoire* and *la petite histoire*, with his preference going toward the latter, or to what he later on would like to call the *intrahistoria*, a mixture of everyday occurrences and individual reactions. The

---

[4] *Ibid.*, p. 129.
[5] *Ibid.*, p. 131.
[6] *Ibid.*, p. 134.
[7] *Ibid.*
[8] *Ibid.*
[9] *Ibid.*, p. 135.

same trend of thought would diminish the importance of wars among nations or among factions if compared with the wars that rage within each individual's conscience. Pachico Zabalbide feels "that his inner life has great variety, that he never gets tired of it."[10] And he asks himself, implying a negative answer, if "all this business of the war that everybody else is worrying about can really compare with the inner battles of a soul . . . of his soul."[11] He concludes by saying that true peace can be found even in the middle of an objective war.

In spite of the fact that the first spiritual crisis that Unamuno suffered did not coincide with any outside or objective war, he placed Pachico in the midst of the Carlist War in order to intensify his own ideas. The truth of the matter is that when Unamuno published *Paz en la guerra*, he was coming out of his second serious spiritual crisis, and thus the one he attributes to Pachico was made up of two of his own experiences.[12] For quite a few years Unamuno had been living under the apprehension of having a weak heart and with a great fear of sudden death. He was a definite hypochondriac. His condition was aggravated around 1895. The following year, on January 7, 1896, his son Raimundo Jenaro was born and a short time later an attack of what was probably meningitis left the child permanently afflicted with hydrocephaly, from which he died in 1902 after a prolonged agony. About the time when Unamuno found out how bad his son's condition was, his second important spiritual crisis took place. He broke down one night, and the following day left his home and went to spend a few days in a Dominican convent to try to recover his childhood faith and pray to God for help in his sorrow. He even went to see a priest friend of his, looking for religious consolation and advice in the faraway town of Alcalá de Henares.

The depth and spontaneity of his sorrow cannot be denied, but the duration and permanent consequences of the crisis were

[10] *Ibid.*, p. 354.
[11] *Ibid.*
[12] For the documentation of Unamuno's spiritual crisis, the basic works are Antonio Sánchez Barbudo, *Estudios sobre Unamuno y Machado* (Madrid: Guadarrama, 1959), pp. 43–79; Armando F. Zubizarreta, *Tras las huellas de Unamuno* (Madrid: Taurus, 1960), pp. 33–45, 111–195.

quite another matter. How can one explain the fact that Unamuno was able to keep a diary of all his emotions and thoughts during those nightmarish days? That he was neither reticent nor bashful in communicating the contents of the diary to several friends and even acquaintances? A friend of his, Timoteo Orbe, in a letter of November 25, 1897, shows his reaction in these words: "There is no denial, you are an aesthete, the most charming passages of your diary are those where you appear as a continuer of our beautiful Castilian mysticism; literature, my dear Unamuno, pure literature."[13] Unamuno himself confesses to another friend, Juan Arzadún, that he has in his diary material for many articles.[14] The tendency to convert every human experience into literary material was too strong in Unamuno to be resisted.

Much has been written, especially in today's Spain, about the return of Unamuno, if not to Catholicism, at least to Christian belief, using as proof the crisis of 1897. What is apparently forgotten is that he never renounced Christ in the first place, before, during, or after any of his crises. But it is also true that he did permanently renounce, after his adolescence, with the single exception of a few days during the crisis of 1897, all the sacraments, mysteries, and rituals of the Catholic church, for lack of true religious faith. As early as 1899, he writes: "But faith is not a matter of will; it comes with grace, and if I do not have it, what can I do?"[15] The Catholic church recognized from the very beginning the heretical teachings of Unamuno and down to this day has kept on the *Index* two of the most important books that Unamuno wrote: *Del sentimiento trágico de la vida* and *La agonía del cristianismo*.

As soon as Unamuno started to rework his experiences into literature, he no doubt noticed how there were inevitable discrepancies between fact and fiction, and how once a public image has been established, a person finds himself bound to a certain pattern of behavior. In other words, he would in the future be forced either to fight, or to accept, the inner logic both of his own

---

[13] Quoted by Zubizarreta, *op. cit.*, p. 120.

[14] See "Cartas de Miguel de Unamuno," *Sur*, no. 119 (Sept., 1944), p. 57.

[15] *Obras*, III, 130.

self and of the image; and if he had to sacrifice one or the other, he would always choose fiction over fact, the image over the self. As can easily be guessed, this self-image conflict raised the problem of personal sincerity, and may perhaps explain the number of writings left unpublished by Unamuno, among them his *Filosofía lógica*, part of his memoirs, his novel *Nuevo mundo*, his diary, and, especially, a considerable number of poems. As early as the time he wrote *Nuevo mundo* (it was probably finished by the end of 1895), he expressed his consciousness of the problem. "Men care more," he wrote, "about how they appear in other people's minds than how they really are inside themselves."[16] In 1900, in a letter written to his friend, Pedro Corominas, he added: "Regarding sincerity lots could be said; I myself think it is not possible, or—to put it better—my opinion is that all sincerity is somewhat affected and that all affectation is in great part sincere."[17] From the same letter comes this thought: "My destiny as a man is to be a writer, because when I shall be no longer, there is the possibility that my work will remain. I am an instrument, and I cultivate myself and work like a performer tuning his instrument."[18]

It is amazing that in this, as well as in some other aspects, one finds so many similarities between Unamuno and Sartre, not all of them explainable by their common heritage of Kierkegaard's doctrines. In *Les mots*, the latest work of the famous French writer, an autobiography of a sort, Sartre poses the problem of the origin of the self, of himself as self-creation. Like Unamuno he was raised without a father and soon learned "to regard teaching as a priesthood and literature as a passion."[19] Life was for both full of worn-out beliefs, and each man had to create himself and his values in a void. Sartre also questions his own sincerity and confesses having perpetrated an immense deception: "I was almost nothing, at most an activity without content, but that was

---

[16] Quoted from *Nuevo mundo* in a letter to Unamuno written by Leopoldo Gutiérrez dated March 28, 1896, and reproduced in part by Zubizarreta, *op. cit.*, p. 76.

[17] Quoted from part of letter reproduced by Zubizarreta, *op. cit.*, p. 182.

[18] *Loc. cit.*

[19] See Jean-Paul Sartre, *The Words*, trans. from French by Bernard Frechtman (New York: George Braziller, 1964), p. 44.

all that was needed. I was escaping from play-acting. I was not yet working, but I had already stopped playing. The liar was finding his truth in the elaboration of his lies."[20] Similarly, Unamuno had written: "Yes, I confess that in my work there is some playacting. In a few years more, if my dreams are realized and if the faith I have in myself gives me strength to move the mountain against which I am struggling, when I no longer need to dress my convictions in paradoxical attire, nor to shout to be listened to, the real, tranquil, simple, and, above all, sensible Unamuno will come forth."[21]

In the meantime, Unamuno continues the elaboration of his "lies" and reappears in a second important configuration of his alter ego in *Niebla*, published in 1914, a book that he calls not a *novela*, a "novel," but, in a play on the word, a *nivola*. By then he was already well known throughout the Spanish-speaking world, and his fame was beginning to cross non-Spanish borders. In Salamanca, the city where he continued to live, he not only became the most important intellectual figure of the university, to the point of being its president from 1901 to 1914, but he was also a popular figure with the townspeople, who even elected him as one of their city councilmen. Politically, he had been known as a socialist and an anarchist, having contributed articles to newspapers of these tendencies, and was generally considered as belonging to the progressive spectrum of political thought. The pre–First World War years of this century saw the publication of seventeen of his books, and the completion of several plays and a considerable number of articles and short stories not gathered in volumes. Among his books were volumes of essays, novels, poetry, and impressions of landscapes and places he visited on his travels. The best-known and most successful ones were: *Amor y pedagogía, Vida de don Quijote y Sancho, Contra esto y aquello, Del sentimiento trágico de la vida,* and the previously mentioned *Niebla*.

Niebla was Unamuno's third book of published narrative fiction. It is divided into thirty-three short chapters, preceded by a

---

[20] *Ibid.,* p. 153.
[21] Quoted from a letter to Unamuno's friend Pedro Corominas, written on May 17, 1900, and reproduced in part by Zubizarreta, *op. cit.,* p. 180.

prologue and a postprologue, and followed by an epilogue made up mostly of the thoughts of a dog called Orfeo. The prologue is signed by a secondary character of the novel who says that the author insisted on his writing it. The postprologue bears the initials M. de U., which stand for Miguel de Unamuno himself. Prologue and postprologue are the first sign, a kind of threshold, of a world of interchangeable reality and fiction, in recognition and reinforcement of a traditional trend in Spanish plastic arts, thought, and literature which can be illustrated almost from the dawn of Spanish culture. In sculpture, there is the example, at least in legend if not in fact, of the twelfth-century creator of that unique masterpiece of Romanesque art, in the Santiago de Compostela cathedral, known as the Pórtico de la Gloria, kneeling in prayer and becoming part of the breathtaking group of his own sculptures. In painting everyone is familiar with Velázquez' *Las Meninas*, where the painter appears in the act of painting the very picture that the spectator has in front of him. In literature the examples are more abundant: the Arcipreste de Hita, Cervantes, Lope, and others, have re-created themselves to be able to enter the still and durable world of the imagination and escape from the perishable society of human beings. Common to all of them is the implicit desire to overcome the eventual disappearance of their physical bodies and to assure for themselves a place in the memory of future human beings.

On the other hand, so-called reality has never had for the inhabitants of the Iberian Peninsula the same firmness or consistency as for the rest of Europe. For Spaniards things are not always what they appear to be, but what at a certain moment one needs them to be, as if the nature of reality were determined by its functionality in relation to men. Genial Don Quixote transforms windmills into ferocious giants or sheep into soldiers because this is the only way for him to prove his immense valor; he changes an unattractive and crude peasant girl into a delicate beauty to make good use of his extraordinary capacity for love, or he transforms the old shaving dish of a barber into a warrior's helmet, insisting that no transformation has taken place, to protect his head from the blows of possible enemies. There are innumerable paths from reality to fantasy and from fantasy to reality, and one must keep in mind that reality for men is always temporary and frequently deceptive. Unamuno went very deep into the meaning of Don Quixote and was the first to realize his superiority over his creator Cervantes. Therefore, he aspired to be a mortal creator himself, but, at the same time and even more, he aspired to be an immortal creature, with the thirst for immortality of a nonbeliever in the world of the hereafter. There is no doubt that he understood and was attracted by the figure of Erostratus, in the same way that Sartre was to be thirty years later.[22] In spite of the great length of time that separated both Unamuno and Sartre from the young Ephesian, the three shared common motivations rooted in the deepest levels of human nature. Erostratus, as is well known, was a nobody who set fire to the temple of Diana to immortalize his name in history. The fact that we still remember him today is proof he succeeded, much against the wishes of his countrymen, who, in order to defeat his purpose, forbade his name ever to be mentioned, but to no avail.

Chapter xxxi of *Niebla* is entirely devoted to a visit paid by Augusto Pérez, the protagonist, to Miguel de Unamuno, the author, in his study in Salamanca. Augusto Pérez, overwhelmed by misfortunes, has decided to commit suicide; but before doing so, he wants to talk to Unamuno, who now plays the triple role of narrator, author, and character. Once we accept the entrance of Unamuno into the magic realm of the book, he becomes as fictional or as real as the rest of the characters, with the assurance of coming back to life any time that a reader puts his imagination into play in contact with the written words. Unamuno tries to convince Augusto of his nonexistence, or of his existence only in Unamuno's fantasy, and assures him that he can do only what the whim of Unamuno allows him to do. To this Augusto answers that it is not so, that "even the so-called fictional beings have their inner logic"[23] and that "novelists and playwrights can by no means make of a character that they create anything that

---

[22] Unamuno used the word *erostratismo* as a synonym for "thirst for immortality" in *Amor y pedagogía* (1902) (see *Obras*, II, 542–543). Sartre paid homage to the meaning of Erostratus by writing a short story under that name.

[23] *Obras*, II, 977 (*MST*, p. 297).

occurs to them; a fictional character in a novel cannot do, in accordance with good artistic rules, things that a reader would not expect him to do."[24] The only logical solution to the predicament in which Augusto finds himself is, in his judgment, to commit suicide. Unamuno becomes irritated by his character's arguments and, not knowing what else to make him do, decides right then and there that Augusto is not going to commit suicide, but instead that he, Unamuno, is going to make him die. Unamuno's decision awakens in Augusto the will to live, and he cries, and kneels and begs Unamuno to spare his life. Then, seeing that Unamuno will not change his mind, he explodes: "The answer is no? You will not allow me to be myself, to emerge from the mist, to live, live, live, to see myself, to listen to my voice, to touch myself, to feel myself, to pity myself, to come into myself. Is your decision final? Will I have to die a fictional being? Well then, my lord and creator Don Miguel, you will also die, you too, and return to the nothingness from which you came! God will cease to dream you! You will die, yes, you will die, whether you want to or not; you and every person that reads my story will die, each and every one of you without exception! You are all fictional beings like me; exactly like me!"[25] Unamuno ends the chapter with this paragraph: "I pushed him out of the door. He walked away crestfallen. He touched himself as if he were already doubting his own existence. And I raised my hand to brush away a furtive tear."[26]

Unamuno, whose first name, Miguel, is a biblical one meaning in Hebrew "Who is like God?"[27] had earlier (in chapter xxv of *Niebla*) interrupted a conversation between Augusto Pérez and Víctor Goti, writing in a parenthesis: "While Augusto and Víctor were having this *nivolistic* conversation, I, the author of this *nivola* that you, reader, have in your hands and are reading, was smiling enigmatically to notice that my *nivolistic* characters were

[24] *Ibid.*, pp. 977–978 (*MST*, pp. 297–298).
[25] *Ibid.*, p. 982 (*MST*, p. 304).
[26] *Ibid.* (*MST*, p. 305).
[27] Unamuno was of course conscious of this meaning. In a footnote to Sonnet XXIX in his book *De Fuerteventura a París*, he says: "Miguel is a Hebrew name meaning "Who is like God?" (see *Obras*, XIV, 505). The same meaning is attached to the name in the four-line poem, "Etimologías" (*Obras*, XV, 329).

advocating my case and justifying my procedures, and I told myself: How far these poor wretches are from realizing that they are only trying to justify what I am doing to them! Thus when a man looks for reasons to justify himself, all he really does is to justify God. And I am the God of these two poor *nivolistic* devils."[28]

If Miguel de Unamuno felt like a god when in the act of creating his literary reality, in conscious or unconscious tribute to the meaning of his first name, he undoubtedly felt like the incarnation of Spain itself when he decided to add his ancestor's name Larraza to his other surnames Unamuno y Jugo ("Unamuno" inherited from his father and "Jugo" from his mother, in the Spanish tradition), to make up U. Jugo de la Raza, which suggests to the Spanish ear the meaning of "Unamuno, the essence of his race." He gave this intentionally meaningful name to a third alter ego who was to appear in 1927 as the shadowy protagonist of his book *Cómo se hace una novela*, a title that may be translated to mean "How a Novel Is Made," "How One Writes a Novel," "How a Novel Is Written," or "How a Novel Writes Itself," this last being my choice.

For the explanation of this third mask or what is behind it, it is necessary to take into account not only what happened in Unamuno's life before 1914 but especially any new experiences he had between 1914 and the time he conceived and wrote the book. It may suffice to mention the most important factors, beginning with the year 1914 itself. This year saw the explosion of the First World War with the resulting shattering of the nineteenth-century dream of mankind in uninterrupted moral and material progress based on the conquests of science. That war was the outward confirmation of a slowly appearing and, since then, ever-increasing feeling of deep crisis in the traditional values of Western civilization. Unamuno, never remiss in becoming *engagé*, or taking sides, chose to place his antipathy with the Germans in that conflict, underlining once more his deep-seated liberal convictions. Noticing the authoritarian leanings of King Alfonso XIII, he began to attack him in the press. The year 1917

[28] *Obras*, II, 950 (*MST*, p. 252).

saw the Russian Revolution and in Spain the first general strike, followed by a harsh repression on the part of the government. Many of Unamuno's friends went to jail as a consequence, and after that he himself was under legal indictment several times. In September of 1921, he was condemned to sixteen years in prison, but soon afterward he was pardoned and even restored to the position of vice-president of his university. On September 12, 1923, a general by the name of Primo de Rivera, in connivance with the King, headed an uprising against the constitutional government and established a military dictatorship. Unamuno protested immediately, both publicly and privately; and on February 20, 1924, the Dictator gave orders to expel him from the university and to exile him to the Canary Islands. Before leaving Salamanca accompanied by a policeman, he said to a small crowd that had gathered at the railroad station: "I will come back. . . . I will come back, not with my freedom, but with yours."[29] Einstein, from Germany, and D'Annunzio, from Italy, were two of the many world-known figures who wrote to Unamuno to express their sympathy. His name and, in part, his work became more widely known because of all the publicity. On July 9, after approximately five months of confinement on the island of Fuerteventura, he escaped to Las Palmas and from there to France. From the island of Fuerteventura he wrote that he had carried there with him the *personality* of Spain, and he himself underlined the word *personality*.[30] From then on he lived the role of the newly acquired symbol thoroughly and passionately. In the last days of August, 1925, he moved from Paris to the French border city of Hendaye, impatient at the durability, in spite of his attacks, of the dictatorship which he mistakenly thought would fall much sooner than it did. He still had to wait several years before he was able—or willing—to enter his country again.

From 1914 to 1927, he added to his published literary output two *nivolas*, three books of poetry, a volume of three short stories,

---

29 See Francisco Madrid, *Genio e ingenio de don Miguel de Unamuno* (Buenos Aires: Aniceto López, 1943), p. 74.

30 *Obras*, XIV, 520 (footnote to Sonnet XLII from the book *Sonetos de Fuerteventura*).

one play, eight volumes of a combination of previously published
and unpublished essays, the first version of *La agonía del cristianismo*, published in French, and, last but not least, the book
Cómo se hace una novela. Unamuno began to write this last-
named work as he was reaching his sixties, and in a state of de-
pression and bitterness brought on by his exile. The idea that
death was threatening, closing in on him, pushed him on to complete it. He had to turn his anguish into literary material, much
as he had done before in 1897 when he wrote his first diary; but
this time there were some new exterior, objective factors and
the will to re-create and enrich his image. He had been thinking
about a new meaning for the terms "novel" and "autobiography."
He was more than ever aware that words always create a social
reality and that this reality is the only one that counts because of
the fact that it transcends the individual. Sincerity per se cannot
be conveyed into words and has no social value. Man functions
and acquires his full dimension only in society with other men.
A true novel has to be, therefore, the result of social acts and/or
words with social impact in order to form the social image of a
person. Every life is like a novel written by life itself, and every
man is living his own novel during every minute of his lifetime.
The idea of an autobiography implies a contradiction and defeats
itself. One cannot write—put into words—his novel: at most,
one can aspire only to set down some ideas about how his novel
is progressing, how his life is being lived, that is to say, *how his
novel is getting itself written*. Any meaningful fictional life (or
novel) is the result of a prior condensation of time and space
and the elimination of the superfluous elements and details that
are so abundant in ordinary life. What remains after this indispensable reduction and selection is what Unamuno calls "the
legend." He writes: "There is a legend of reality, which is the
substance, the intimate reality of reality itself . . . and this legend,
this history is devouring me, and when it ends I shall be ended
with it."[31] Again he says: "The Unamuno of my legend, of my

---

[31] *Obras*, X, 863–864. Some extracts from *Cómo se hace una novela*
were translated into English from a then unpublished manuscript by
Samuel Putnam in the anthology *The European Caravan* (New York:
Brewer, Warren and Putnam, 1931), pp. 310–320.

novel, the Unamuno that my friendly I and my unfriendly I, and everybody else, both my friends and my enemies, have all of us together made, it is this Unamuno who gives me life and death, creates me and destroys me, keeps me afloat and drowns me. He is my agony. Am I as I think I am, or am I as others think I am?"[32]

It is not amiss to surmise that Unamuno, taking stock during the Parisian days of his past life, saw more clearly than ever before that the image of himself he presented to others, his "legend," was becoming more rigid, less flexible, and that through inner logic it was already possible to trace its ultimate configuration. At sixty he felt as if his life was over, his novel written. When Unamuno makes the character U. Jugo de la Raza supposedly pick up a novel in one of the bookstalls along the banks of the river Seine in Paris, this novel will be symbolically the finished novel of his own life. The following paragraph has to be read with this in mind:

> U. Jugo de la Raza, wandering on the banks of the Seine, along the docks and among the stalls of secondhand books, found a novel in which he had hardly begun to browse when he felt tremendously absorbed by it, drawn outside himself, thrust into the character of the novel (the novel of an autobiographic-romantic confession), identified with the character. In short, endowed with a history. The coarse world of everyday reality disappeared from his eyes. When, for an instant, he took them from the pages of the book to look at the water of the river, it seemed to him that the water was not flowing, that the river was still, like a mirror. He could not stand the feeling and turned his horrified eyes back to the pages of the book, of the novel, to find himself in them, to come back to life in them. And his eyes fell upon this passage, an eternal passage, which contained these prophetic words: "When the reader reaches the end of this painful history, he will die with me." At that moment, Jugo de la Raza felt that his vision blurred . . .[33]

If one goes back to the words used by Unamuno, it will be noticed that he does not say that Jugo de la Raza *picked up* the book but instead, in a context full of ambiguity, that he *found it.*

[32] *Obras*, X, 865.
[33] *Ibid.*, pp. 866–867.

This leaves open the possible symbolical interpretation that he found it inside himself, in his own memory. The river as an image of life is a traditional one, and if its water is *still*, it then becomes an anticipation of death. This explains the horrified look of the character. The final prophecy makes very clear the identification and fusion of both characters into a single one: Jugo de la Raza the reader, on the one hand, and Jugo de la Raza the protagonist of the novel, on the other. Needless to say, as many others have already observed, the book *Cómo se hace una novela* is perhaps the most complex and enigmatic of Unamuno's books. Jugo de la Raza appears only at six unrelated points in the book. The unifying factor, if any, is the author himself (with his confessions, reflections, memories, etc.) whom we watch in the act of writing, of creating the novel, and, at the same time, of creating himself, in a conscious but hopeless effort to separate his historical and accepted image from his inner self. There is no plot and the ingredients lack any kind of continuity and uniformity, as if the author wanted to destroy any appearance of fiction and to substitute for it the feeling of a bare and pure reality.

After *Cómo se hace una novela* no way seemed to be left for the further cultivation of the genre; but the crisis that had originated the book—like others before in Unamuno's life—was finally overcome, and Unamuno was still to write such revealing *nivolas* as *San Manuel Bueno, mártir* and *La novela de don Sandalio, jugador de ajedrez* ("The Novel of Don Sandalio, Chess Player"). In *San Manuel Bueno, mártir*, Unamuno goes back to dramatizing the idea that each human life acquires its maximum dimension in contact with other human lives. The story of Don Manuel, a rural parish priest, is told by a woman, Ángela Carballino. Don Manuel is all activity; he never stops doing what is good and right. The inhabitants of the small village where he has his church are convinced that he is a saint. A brother of Ángela, Lázaro by name, arrives from America full of progressive ideas, but a complete agnostic. Don Manuel puts into play all his capacity of persuasion in an effort to change Lázaro's mind and reconvert him to Catholicism. When Don Manuel realizes that he is unable to accomplish his aim, he begs Lázaro to pretend that he believes, so as not to set a bad example for others. At

the same time, he lets him share a secret: "I am here," he confesses to Lázaro, "to give life to the souls of my parishioners, to
make them happy, to make them dream that they are immortal.
Not to kill them. What they need is to live a wholesome life, a life
with unanimity of purpose. With the truth, with my truth, they
would not be able to live. Let them live. And this is the Church's
function, to give them life. Is there truth in my religion? All re-
ligions are true insofar as they make their followers live spiri-
tually, insofar as they bring them consolation for having had to be
born to die, and for each people the truest religion is their own,
the one that has made them what they are. What is my religion?
Mine is to find consolation for myself in consoling others, even
if the consolation I give them cannot be mine."[34] It is unimportant
whether Don Manuel was or was not an atheist. The important
thing is that after his death the unanimous opinion in his small
town was that he was a saint, that nobody dared doubt his sainthood, the *novel* of his sainthood.

La novela de don Sandalio even goes a step farther. Whereas
the determining factors for the novel about Don Manuel were
his words and his actions as lived by the people of the small town,
for Don Sandalio there is only one determining factor: his presence, and even this is limited to a single witness. Unamuno uses
the scheme of an unknown person going to a small town to relax,
and from there writing to a friend of his that at the casino he had
seen a number of persons, among them, but only from a distance,
a chess player by the name of Don Sandalio. The correspondent
writes: "I have not been able to make out a single thing about
his life, and I do not really care. I much prefer to imagine it."[35]
From then on, he does just that, and Don Sandalio becomes somebody different from what he is through the imagination of another person, for whom, however, the Don Sandalio he has created is the only one that counts.

From 1927 to the end of Unamuno's life there were yet to appear, in separate volumes, one more book of poetry, his *Ro-
mancero del destierro*, three plays, a book of public speeches and

---

[34] *Ibid.*, XVI, 605 (*SMB*, pp. 192–193).
[35] *Ibid.*, p. 637.

articles, the Spanish version of *La agonía del cristianismo*, and the book *San Manuel Bueno, mártir y tres historias más*.

On January 28, 1930, King Alfonso XIII replaced General Primo de Rivera with another general. The end of the dictatorship was in sight. Unamuno went back to Spain on February 9. He wrote, spoke, and acted against the Monarchy in every conceivable way. Finally on April 14, 1931, the Republic was proclaimed after the most exemplary and democratic elections ever held in that country. The new regime recognized in Unamuno one of its most illustrious grand old men and conferred upon him all kinds of honors. He was given a life appointment as president of the University of Salamanca and was elected a member of the Academy and of the Cortes. He was the first Spaniard to receive the newly created title of Honored Citizen and he was proposed for the Nobel Prize in literature.

In the summer of 1934, I had the opportunity of meeting Unamuno and seeing him frequently for a few weeks while I was a student at the International University of Santander in Spain. This university was a very interesting and meaningful experiment organized by the government of the Spanish Republic. Its faculty was composed of famous scholars drawn from different foreign and national universities. The student body was made up of graduate students, also from different countries. Among the foreign celebrities present that year, I particularly recall Jacques Maritain, the French philosopher, and Erwin Schrödinger, the famous scientist and winner of the Nobel Prize in physics. The Spanish were represented by the philosophers Ortega y Gasset, Zubiri, and José Gaos; the poet Pedro Salinas, who was president of the university; Jorge Guillén, also an internationally famous poet; Gerardo Diego, another poet; Palacios, the physicist; Zulueta, the entomologist; Recassens Siches, Fernando de los Ríos, Salvador Madariaga, and many, many others of equal renown. The students could choose any number of courses and attend any of a wide selection of lectures offered every day. Students and faculty shared the same dormitories, the same food in the same dining rooms, the same concerts, and the same shows, among which there were presentations of classical Spanish plays arranged and directed by García Lorca and his company of student actors. The university was established in the summer palace of the Spanish kings, an imposing building with a private beach, set in the middle of a forest of pine trees. At night after dinner you could see in the different halls groups of teachers, personalities, and students discussing various topics.

The theme of every university course and lecture, whether given in German, French, English, Spanish, or Italian, was one and the same. It was, symbolically enough, "Crisis in the Twentieth Century," which was explained and studied in relation to every field: crisis in the different sciences, crisis in philosophy, crisis in national and international law, crisis in literature (in the novel, in the theater, in poetry). In fact, it seemed that the feeling of crisis was an all-pervading one, affecting every human endeavor. Nevertheless, the atmosphere of the university and relations among its members evidenced no pessimistic features. On the contrary, everyone seemed to be overflowing with *joie de vivre*, a contradiction that nobody felt called upon to explain in the innumerable courses and lectures.

Unamuno came to Santander that summer as a special guest of the university and even agreed to read one of his latest works in the main auditorium, a play called *El hermano Juan* ("Brother Juan"), his personal and controversial version of the myth of Don Juan. Unamuno, as I remember him, could easily be mistaken for a respectable Protestant minister. He was an average-sized man, but considered tall by Spanish standards, strongly built, always dressed in black with a white shirt collar over a black sweater (he never wore a tie), bareheaded, and with a sort of crew cut, a well-kept moustache, and a small and pointed beard. He wore glasses, although one did not notice them at first glance because of the intensity of his piercing eyes. Caricaturists often drew his head like that of an owl; in fact, he did look like one, but he moved like a leopard, with youthful and nervous movements that belied his almost seventy years. He entered the main auditorium with a handful of papers and a copy of his play and went directly to the platform. The whole international audience gave him a long standing ovation which he seemed to enjoy considerably. He waited until all the noise had ceased and then began to speak. His voice was high-pitched. He began by saying that he was forced to read his own play because there were no actors on the Spanish stage capable of delivering his lines. He asked forgiveness for acting out not only the male but also the female roles, at the same time citing historical precedents in justification of doing so. Then he went on to discuss briefly the meaning of his play. At this point, he noticed the presence in the first row of the head of the insignificant feminist movement in Spain, and greeted her—a charming woman—with complimentary remarks for being the first "masculinist" of the country. Seated at the lady's side was a well-known literary critic, and Unamuno, referring to him, said that he did not mind his presence because he was not afraid of the entomologists of literature, implying that all literary criticism is the equivalent of counting the feet of insects, or something like that. People laughed, even the feminist and the critic, and Unamuno began to read, at first naming the characters in each scene and then without naming them. At that time I had already developed a certain weakness for the theater in general, and I listened very attentively. It was not long before it began to seem to me that all the different characters, in spite of the obvious theatrical talent of the reader, had the same voice and the same personality even though their thoughts were different, a phenomenon I did not think much about at the time.

During the following days, I saw Unamuno regularly. I saw him in the dining room eating and talking simultaneously and, at the end of the meal, picking up with his index finger, after wetting it in his mouth, little crumbs of bread and mechanically putting them in his mouth. I saw him making, while he talked, his famous paper birds and other animals, an art at which he was a real expert, to the point of having written a long essay on the subject. I even learned from him to make some myself. I saw him always in the center of a group, in the halls or sometimes sitting on the grass, talking and very seldom listening. I recall him one day saying to a group of students that their main duty was to go to the small villages and farms, as they were already doing, and bring unhappiness, not amusement, to the peasants. Spanish students were very active in those days in an organization called Pedagogi-

cal Missions, created by the government for the purpose of helping to raise the cultural standards of the peasants and villagers.

During Unamuno's stay in Santander, the newspaper *Ahora* of
Madrid was publishing a series of articles of his about Spanish
youth and their political activities. European young men—and
Spanish young men were no exception—were organized at the
time in groups of every shade of political thought; and Unamuno
wrote one week against one group, the following week against
another, and so on, never in favor and always against each and
every one of the different groups: Catholics, Socialists, Anarchists, Communists, Monarchists, Republicans, and so on. It so
happens that I was a member of one of these groups and, when
our turn arrived, it seemed to me that the attack was especially
harsh and arbitrary, so I decided to talk to him about it. I found
out that he used to get up very early in the morning and take a
stroll through the forest. The following morning I was waiting
for him in the forest with the apprehension and nervousness
natural in a Spanish student, not knowing how he would react or
if I would know how to approach the subject. Very timidly I said:
"Good morning, Don Miguel." He looked at me over his glasses
and said: "Good morning, young man, do you want to talk to
me?" I answered: "Yes, sir." "About what?" came his reply.
"Well," I started, "yesterday I read your article in *Ahora* and . . ."
"And you don't agree with what I said, isn't that so?" Making a
tremendous effort that required all my courage, I mumbled,
"Well, sir, to tell you the truth, no." I do not remember whether
he smiled or not, but I do know that the subject was dropped
right then and there, when he answered, "I don't either." He then
asked me if I would like to listen to some poems he had just
finished. I said that I would love to. We both sat down under a
tree and he read, one after another, twenty compositions dedi-
cated to the memory of his wife, who had died six months before
and whom he had loved dearly and faithfully for almost half a
century. He was at moments very moved and so was I. When he
finished, he tried to hide his emotion, or overcome mine, I don't
know which, by asking if I thought that those poems were worth
a penny each because he was thinking of publishing them and
charging twenty pennies for the book.

Those days in Santander were probably the last peaceful days for most of the people present there, including Unamuno. In October of that year, the turmoil began which was to culminate two years later in the tragic, badly named, and frequently misunderstood Spanish Civil War. Those last two years saw Unamuno attacking the Republic almost in the same way that he had attacked the Monarchy and the military dictatorship of General Primo de Rivera. During his long life he had systematically been against everything and everybody, but always intelligently and forcefully. It is ironic that, at the beginning of the Civil War, he had to be present at the inauguration of a new academic year in his Salamanca University, where, after some controversial speeches, one of the most prominent generals of the group who had rebelled against the legal government shouted, having him in mind, "Muera la inteligencia" ("Death to intelligence"). That day Unamuno went to his house, resolved never to leave it again. He was seventy-two years old.

A couple of months later, on December 31, 1936, on a cold afternoon Unamuno was seated at a round table that had a lighted charcoal brazier underneath. A friend and colleague from the university was paying him a visit and had left him alone for a few minutes. Upon returning he noticed some smoke and saw that one of Unamuno's feet was on fire. He was dead. A symbolical interpretation is possible here: the fire may be viewed as a symbol of the inner fire that had tried to consume Unamuno throughout his lifetime and had finally broken loose. It could also be a symbol of the inquisitorial fire that had burned so many heretics in the past and was again being lighted on Spanish soil.

3

UNAMUNO:
PIONEER OF EXISTENTIALISM
Alfred Stern

A pioneer is a person who opens up new roads through the thicket of unexplored territories, or, at least, through territories that have previously been accessible only to a few isolated, daring minds. Unamuno was a pioneer of existentialism in the second sense. The few daring minds that had preceded him in this inhospitable territory during the last three centuries were, above all, Pascal, Kierkegaard, and Nietzsche.

Many attempts have been made to define existentialism. It is, however, not a definite doctrine, but rather a mental attitude, an approach to human existence and to philosophy, so that some thinkers have been existentialists without realizing it and without carrying that fashionable label. While the traditional thinker's approach to philosophy is that of an objective, detached observer who proudly pretends to a throne outside and above the world—this is also partly the meaning of "transcendental philosophy"—the existentialist philosophizes as an *actor* in the human drama. While the traditional thinker, the classical philosopher, philosophizes only with his *reason*, the existentialist philosophizes with his *whole personality*—with his feelings, his will, his passions, his sufferings, his endeavors, with his most secret personal longings, fears, and hopes. This is perhaps the main reason existentialism finds so strong a resonance among nonphilosophers. In reading existentialist philosophy or literature, the average educated person realizes the meaning of Horace's words, "De te fabula narratur" ("It is your story that is told").

It is in *this* way that Unamuno philosophized—like all authentic existentialists, whatever the names they used to designate their enterprises. Some of them were aware of this peculiar character of their philosophizing. At the end of the nineteenth century, Friedrich Nietzsche wrote: "I always wrote my books with my whole body and life. . . . I am speaking only of things I have experienced and do not present only processes in the head."[1]

At the beginning of the twentieth century Unamuno, who had only a superficial, secondhand knowledge of Nietzsche and was certainly not influenced by this thinker he disliked so deeply, wrote: "Philosophy is a human product of each philosopher, and each philosopher is a man of flesh and bone who addresses himself to other men of flesh and bone like himself. And, whatever he may do, he does not philosophize with his reason alone but with his will, his feeling, with his flesh and bones, with his whole soul, and his whole body. It is the *man* who philosophizes."[2] And by *man* Unamuno did not mean the abstract timeless and spaceless man of the Stoics and the rationalistic Enlightenment, nor the even more abstract transcendental Ego of Kant, which is nothing but the completely disindividualized and disembodied consciousness in general (*Bewusztsein überhaupt*). Unamuno likewise did not mean Fichte's theoretical Ego, but—as he repeats time and again—the man of flesh and bone, who suffers from toothache and has no other certainty than his personal death.

Thus, Unamuno's Ego is a concrete Ego, an individual existing in space and time, which is much more than a mutilated species, for the individual exists, while the species does not. Unamuno's man is also much more than Descartes's *res cogitans,* "the thinking thing." He is an intellect incarnated in a body and disharmoniously united with many nonintellectual, anti-intellectual, irrational functions, incompatible with one another. Therefore, Unamuno also rejected Descartes's principle *cogito, ergo sum* ("I think, therefore I am"), for to the Spanish existentialist the fact of existing, of living, was more fundamental than the fact of

---

[1] "Ich habe meine Schriften jederzeit mit meinem ganzen Leib und Leben geschrieben. . . . Ich rede nur von erlebten Dingen und präsentiere nicht nur Kopfvorgänge" (Friedrich Nietzsche, *Gesammelte Werke* [Munich: Musarion Verlag, *ca.* 1922–1929], XXI, 81 f.).

[2] *Obras,* XVI, 155–156 (*TSL,* p. 28).

thinking, since there are beings that live without thinking. Are we not also aware of our existence by feeling and willing, so that the man of flesh and blood who truly philosophizes could also say: "I feel, therefore I am," or "I will, therefore I am"? The main character in Unamuno's philosophical novel *Niebla* says, "Amo, ergo sum" ("I love, therefore I am"), and even, "Edo, ergo sum" ("I eat, therefore I am").[3] If one philosophizes with one's whole embodied personality and not just with one's reason, then the functions of feeling, willing, loving, and even eating also have their say.

We see here one of the many justifications for calling Unamuno a pioneer of existentialism: This philosophizing with one's whole existing personality, which was an isolated, strictly individual case in Nietzsche, and which is one of the characteristics of existentialism, was generalized by Unamuno and elevated by him to the rank of a principle. It led him also to a new approach to the history of philosophy. To Unamuno, the different philosophers who followed one another in time were not just names standing for certain possibilities of thought, inherent in the very structure of the mind, which, with inner logical necessity, must appear at a certain moment of history, when certain scientific, social, and psychological conditions are fulfilled. In my opinion, this is a legitimate approach to the history of philosophy, but it was not Unamuno's. What he sought *behind* a philosopher's thought was the man of flesh and bone, who existed in a certain time, in a definite cultural and social surrounding, and who had certain specific individual psychological and even physiological problems. Thus, Spinoza did not mean to Unamuno the solution of the inner contradictions of Descartes's dualism; he could not simply be equated with monistic rationalism or psychophysical parallelism. Spinoza was to Unamuno *el trágico judío portugués de Amsterdam,* "the tragic Portuguese Jew of Amsterdam," whose *Ethica* was, in spite of being *ordine geometrico demonstrata,* only a "desperate elegiac poem" of a man haunted by the idea of death, written in a vain attempt to free himself from this thought.[4]

3 *Ibid.,* II, 837 (*MST,* p. 74), 985 (*MST,* p. 310).
4 *Ibid.,* XVI, 167, 158 (*TSL,* pp. 40, 31).

We see here another tendency of existentialism, applied to the history of philosophy. Existentialism emphasizes the fact that man always exists at a certain place and at a certain time, that he is a "man-in-the-world," a *concrete* man, "situated historically, geographically, culturally, and socially. He is not, in Heidegger's terms, a *weltloses Subjekt*, a "subject without a world," like the subject of traditional idealism. It was thus in the true spirit of existentialism that Unamuno changed Terentius' famous sentence, "Homo sum; nihil humani a me alienum puto" ("I am a man and consider nothing human to be strange to me"), to conclude, "nullum hominem a me alienum puto" ("no other man do I deem a stranger"). Unamuno was not concerned with the abstract principle called "the human," and was even suspicious of the concept of "humanity," another abstraction that allows us to escape from concrete existing realities and their problems.

It was Søren Kierkegaard, the Danish Protestant thinker who died in 1855 and is considered the founder of existentialism, who most strongly insisted on the necessity for philosophy to move away from abstractions and empty generalities, in order to face the real issues of concrete human existence. Therefore, he fought Hegel, the most influential thinker of the first half of the nineteenth century, who, while pretending to offer a philosophy of "concrete concepts," completely absorbed the individual's particular existence into the abstraction of the "absolute Idea" and its dialectical unfolding in time (i.e., in history). The existing individual "does not count," Hegel wrote, and the study of philosophy has the main purpose of making us indifferent toward questions of existence or nonexistence.[5]

Kierkegaard's writings were a violent protest against this kind of idealistic evasion of the real issues of human existence into impersonal, objective, timeless schemes of eternal truths. Having gone through all the tragic antinomies and grim oppositions of individual existence with the terrifying "either-or" decisions it imposes, Kierkegaard rejected Hegel's solvent "mediation" of these oppositions by means of an almost automatic dialectical

[5] Georg Wilhelm Friedrich Hegel, *Die Vernunft in der Geschichte* (Hamburg: Ausg. Hoffmeister, 1955), p. 113; also, *The Logic of Hegel* (2d ed., rev. and aug.; Oxford: Clarendon Press, 1892), p. 164.

process that deals with timeless ideas and hollow generalities. Throwing the acid of his irony against Hegel's system, Kierkegaard wrote:

> Can the principle of mediation also help the existing individual while still remaining in existence himself to become the mediating principle, which is *sub specie aeterni*, whereas the poor existing individual is confined to the strait-jacket of existence? Surely, it cannot do any good to mock man, luring him on by dangling before his eyes the identity of subject and object, when his situation prevents him from making use of this identity, since he is in process of becoming in consequence of being an existing individual. How can it help to explain to a man how the eternal truth is to be understood eternally, when the supposed user of the explanation is prevented from so understanding it through being an existing individual, and merely becomes fantastic when he imagines himself to be *sub specie aeterni*? What such a man needs instead is precisely an explanation of how the eternal truth is to be understood in determinations of time by one who as existing is himself in time, which even the worshipful Herr Professor concedes, if not always, at least once a quarter when he draws his salary.[6]

Attacks of this type caused a sharpening of the antithesis between *being* and *existence*, two concepts that in earlier philosophy had been used interchangeably. In my book on *Sartre: His Philosophy and Psychoanalysis*, I state that we may today characterize this opposition between being and existence in the following way:

> *Being* is universal, abstract, timeless, and unlimited by space. *Existence* is individual, concrete, limited to a definite, very short time, and confined to a restricted spatial environment.
>
> *Being* is "everywhere" and "always." *Existence* is only "here and now" (*hic et nunc*).
>
> *Being* embraces everything and everyone. *Existence* is always one's own—my own, your own.
>
> *Being* is unaware of itself. *Existence* is self-conscious and understands itself.
>
> *Being* is objective, determined, and logically necessary; for whatever I think I have to think its being, at least as a possible

[6] Søren Kierkegaard, *Concluding Unscientific Postscript* (Princeton: Princeton University Press for American-Scandinavian Foundation, 1941), pp. 171–172.

thought. *Existence* is subjective, completely fortuitous, sheer fact, free, without any necessity.

Being is the synthesis and identity of the subject and the object; thus it represents fullness. *Existence* is the insurmountable separation of the subject from the object, the permanent non-coincidence and tension between subject and object, even when this object is the subject's own personality; *existence* is the unbridgeable abyss between knowing and being, [which Rationalism had in vain tried to bridge in the words of Parmenides: τὸ γὰρ αὐτὸ νοεῖν ἐστίν τε καὶ εἶναι,[7] "thinking is the same as being." Existence is also the separation] between the lack [which provokes] the subject's wishes, and the objectives which would satisfy [those wishes]. Thus, existence is characterized by "a lack of being," a kind of emptiness.[8]

Although none of the existentialists formulated the oppositions between being and existence in such definite terms, they all were aware of them and defended the rights of existence against being. Existentialism may be defined as a phenomenological description and interpretation of human existence, Heidegger's *Dasein*.

Kierkegaard's attack on Hegel, which I quoted earlier, was written in Copenhagen in 1846, fifteen years after Hegel, professor at the University of Berlin, had died of cholera. At that time Hegel's reputation was still bathed in glory, and Kierkegaard's protests found little echo. Outside his hometown he was unknown, and in Copenhagen he was considered as only a quarrelsome crackpot. But fifty years after his death, at the beginning of the twentieth century, Kierkegaard's works were discovered by Miguel de Unamuno, who immediately realized that here he had found a spiritual brother. Unamuno, who mastered at least nine languages, read Kierkegaard's works passionately in the Danish original, at a time when they were hardly known outside the author's homeland. Several of Unamuno's biographers say that this Spanish Catholic thinker learned Danish only in order to be able to read the works of the Scandinavian Protestant, a fact that Jesús-Antonio Collado designates as "not entirely exact." But it is at least very probable, for one can hardly imagine

[7] Hermann Diels, *Die Fragmente der Vorsokratiker* (6th ed.; Berlin: Weidmann, 1951), I, 231, Fragment no. 3.

[8] Alfred Stern, *Sartre: His Philosophy and Psychoanalysis* (New York: Liberal Arts Press, 1953), p. 6.

any other reason Unamuno, who never went to Denmark, should have learned the language of that small Nordic country. Collado is the author of *Kierkegaard y Unamuno*, a very learned, very thorough treatise of 571 pages, published in Madrid in 1962. Collado tried to present to the Spanish reader the religious existential conception of Kierkegaard and to determine its influence on Unamuno. This influence has sometimes been overrated, and some critics have considered Unamuno a kind of reincarnation of Kierkegaard. Unamuno himself once said jokingly that in a previous existence he had lived in Copenhagen. Yet Collado, who also analyzed the very illuminating marginal annotations Unamuno made in his copies of Kierkegaard's works, comes to the conclusion that, although Unamuno had been influenced by Kierkegaard to a certain extent, we must rather speak of a *parallelism* of their ideas. But this parallelism has different origins and different aims, so that their ideas are sometimes antithetic. This parallelism reveals a "constitutional affinity" between the Spanish Catholic and the Danish Protestant thinker.[9]

Certainly, Unamuno did not owe his religious inquietudes to Kierkegaard. They were rooted in his own character. What he found in the Danish thinker was more a corroboration of his own ideas and, to some extent, a fertilization. When Unamuno started reading Kierkegaard, the foundation of his own philosophy was already established.

Collado's study is mainly concerned with problems of theology and religious metaphysics—he gave his book the subtitle *La existencia religiosa*—while my modest attempt is strictly philosophical, although one can hardly speak of either Unamuno or Kierkegaard without bringing religion into the picture. Besides, the purpose of my analysis is not a comparison between Kierkegaard and Unamuno, but a study of Unamuno's existentialism. Therefore, I shall only mention—independently of Collado's valuable book—a few typically existential attitudes one can find in both Unamuno and Kierkegaard.

I have already spoken of the Spanish thinker's rejection of Descartes's principle *cogito, ergo sum* ("I think, therefore I

[9] Jesús-Antonio Collado, *Kierkegaard y Unamuno: la existencia religiosa* (Madrid: Gredos, 1962), p. 15.

am"). But Unamuno's critique of this principle was not purely negative, for he reversed it and thus gave existentialism its clearest expression. "Sum, ergo cogito, soy, luego pienso" ("I am, therefore I think"),[10] he wrote, and with this idea he established the basic existential principle of the primacy of human existence over cognition. Fifteen years after Unamuno, Martin Heidegger, the leader of German existentialism, came to a similar formulation,[11] of course without mentioning his Spanish predecessor. Cognition, Heidegger added, is only a mode of existence as being-in-the-world.[12]

From the primacy of existence over cognition, over thought, follows the extreme subjectivity of existentialism; for while thought is an attempt at objectivizing our subjective impressions, of constituting an objective reality detached from our subjective impressions, existence can be grasped only in pure subjectivity. This subjectivity of existence places it almost beyond the reach of philosophy. While being is always objective, existence is subjective in so exclusive a way that it can never become object, not even to itself. This is, in my opinion, one of the stumbling blocks of existentialism as a philosophy of existence; for by its very nature philosophy is conceptualization, and concepts are objective or, at least, intersubjective. In trying to objectivize existence, concepts denature it, thus changing it into something else, namely another variety of abstract being.

Existentialist philosophers, then, find themselves somehow in the situation of St. Augustine, who, when asked "What is time?" answered, "Si nemo ex me quaerat scio; si quaerenti explicare velim nescio" ("If nobody asks me, I know; but if I wished to explain it to one who should ask me, I do not know").[13]

Fortunately, all of us are existing beings and thus know, from our own inner experience, what existence is. Only by this appeal to our ineffable subjective inwardness are we able to understand what the existentialists mean by existence. Thus, our understanding of their philosophy rests on an irrational basis.

---

[10] *Obras*, XVI, 163 (*TSL*, p. 35).
[11] Martin Heidegger, *Sein und Zeit* (Halle a.d.S.: M. Niemeyer, 1935), pp. 24, 211.
[12] *Ibid.*, p. 61.
[13] *S. Augustini Confessionum* Liber XI, Cap. XIV.

Both Kierkegaard and Unamuno fought for the rights of subjectivity in forming our philosophies; but, in my opinion, Unamuno did so with more moderation than his Nordic predecessor, with more respect for the rights of the objective approach of reason, which he himself was unable to miss. Against the dispassionate thought which philosophers had been preaching since the days of the ancient Greeks and which triumphed in modern science, Kierkegaard set the ideal of a subjective thought directed by *passion* and exclusively concerned with subjective human existence and its spiritual needs. In his book *Concluding Unscientific Postscript*, Kierkegaard wrote: "Passion is the culmination of existence for an existing individual—and we are all of us existing individuals. . . . All essential knowledge relates to existence, or only such knowledge as has an essential relationship to existence is essential knowledge."[14] According to Kierkegaard, only ethicoreligious knowledge has an essential relationship to the existence of the knower.

Kierkegaard applied his passional existential subjectivism to the objects of his strongest passions: God and Christianity. "It is subjectivity," he wrote, "that Christianity is concerned with, and it is only in subjectivity that its truth exists, if it exists at all; objectively, Christianity has absolutely no existence."[15]

As for the existence of God, Kierkegaard said that there is and always will be "objective uncertainty." It is "in all eternity impossible to bring God to light objectively." With Kant, he admitted that God was only "a postulate," that is, a supposition, assumed without any objective proof and yet demanded and upheld for extratheoretical reasons. For Kant, these extratheoretical reasons were moral; for Kierkegaard, they were purely existential, passional, and he described himself as "driven by the infinite passion of his *need* of God." This postulate *has* to be true, he exclaimed, because without it I cannot live. And when people objected that his belief in God was purely subjective, without any objective proof, he retorted: "Truth *is* subjectivity,"[16] at least for the existing individual. "Only in subjectivity is there decisiveness; to seek objectivity is to be in error." Thus, for Kierkegaard,

14 Kierkegaard, *op. cit.*, p. 176.
15 *Ibid.*, p. 116.
16 *Ibid.*, p. 169 ff.

God consisted only in man's inward relationship to God. And in a famous example, approvingly quoted by Unamuno in *Del sentimiento trágico de la vida*, Kierkegaard wrote:

> If one who lives in the midst of Christendom goes up to the house of God, the house of the true God, with the true conception of God in his knowledge, and prays, but prays in a false spirit; and one who lives in an idolatrous community prays with the entire passion of the infinite, although his eyes rest upon the image of an idol: where is there most truth? The one prays in truth to God though he worships an idol; the other prays falsely to the true God, and hence worships in fact an idol.[17]

Here we see that subjective sincerity becomes in a way a criterion of truth—an idea also upheld by later existentialists, such as Unamuno, Heidegger, and Sartre.

If equating truth with subjectivity and using sincerity to measure validity involve the risk of worshiping a void nonentity, Kierkegaard replies: "Without risk, there is no faith." And he defines faith by writing: "Faith is precisely the contradiction between the infinite passion of the individual's inwardness and the objective uncertainty."[18] Thus, objective uncertainty becomes a presupposition of faith, and this seems very logical to me; for if we had objective certainty in metaphysical, theological matters, we would have *knowledge*, and would *not need* faith.

All these existentialist ideas—existentialist, because they take into account only the existing individual's spiritual needs—were extremely appealing to Unamuno, who suffered so deeply from his own religious uncertainties and his frustrated will to believe. Yet his spiritual problems were quite different from those of Kierkegaard, so that the basic ideas we find in the latter reappear in Unamuno in a completely different form. While Kierkegaard was mainly concerned with the problems of faith and sin, and the choosing of one's own self, and while his anxiety was linked to the idea that he might not be equal to the task for which God had singled him out, Unamuno was not interested in any of these problems. The Spanish thinker's philosophy resulted from his thirst for personal immortality, and his God was supposed to be the guarantor of this immortality. He had a tremendous subjec-

17 *Ibid.*, pp. 179–180.
18 *Ibid.*, p. 182.

tive existential need to believe in God and personal immortality, but since his penetrating reason recognized the impossibility of any rational objective proof of the existence of God and immortality, he was thrown into the anxiety of uncertainty. "It is thus no rational necessity, but vital anguish, which makes us believe in God," he wrote.[19] This passage confirms Statius' old saying, "Primus in orbe deos fecit timor." But since Unamuno recognized, with Kierkegaard, the rights of subjectivity and of man's existential needs, he could remain attached to what Kierkegaard had called a "desperate way out": Christianity. Unamuno himself spoke of the *ilusión vitalizadora*,[20] the vitalizing illusion offered by Christianity.

In his *Tusculan Disputations*, Cicero wrote: "Tota philosophorum vita commentatio mortis est" ("The whole life of the philosophers is a preparation for death," or, as one could also translate, "a meditation on death").[21] Cicero ascribed this saying to Cato, but it certainly goes back to Plato's *Phaidon*.[22] If this sentence ever applied to a philosopher in an almost literal sense, it was to Unamuno. As a child he was already meditating on death, and felt the prospect of nothingness so frightening that even the horrors of hell seemed preferable to him. Thus, from the outset, Unamuno's life was—in the words of Ortega y Gasset—a *meditatio mortis*.

We all know that we have to die but, as Tolstoy showed in his masterful story "The Death of Ivan Ilich," all of us try to flee from this certainty by pointing to the general character of this fact, expressed in the formula "*one* has to die." The German existentialist Martin Heidegger called this idea the "unauthentic" approach to death, because in saying "*one* has to die" everybody means "no one" ("dieses Man ist Niemand")[23] and, especially, not "I." In its tendency to individualize all basic questions, however, existentialism transforms the general problem of "death" into the individual problem "I have to die." How difficult this transformation is has been shown in Tolstoy's story of the death

---

[19] *Obras*, XVI, 311 (*TSL*, p. 184).

[20] *Ibid.*, p. 325 (*TSL*, p. 198).

[21] *M. Tulli Ciceronis Tusculanarum Disputationum* Liber I, XXX, 74.

[22] Plato, *Phaidon*, 67E: "Those who pursue philosophy truly study to die" (οἱ ὀρθῶς φιλοσοφοῦντες ἀποθνήσκειν μετελῶσι . . .).

[23] Heidegger, *op. cit.*, pp. 252, 259.

of Ivan Ilich. But Unamuno's approach to death was, from the outset, an authentic one. To him it was the problem "I have to die, but I want to live eternally." I consider Unamuno to have been an existentialist by temperament.

Unamuno found a kind of justification of his ardent longing for immortality in Spinoza's principle: "Unaquaeque res, quantum in se est, in suo esse perseverare conatur" ("Everything, in so far as it is in itself, endeavors to persist in its own being").[24] Unamuno felt that if consciousness were nothing but a flash of lightning between two eternities of darkness, there would not be anything more cruel than human existence.

But how can man know whether or not he is immortal? His will and his feelings answer "yes," but his reason answers "no." And the tragic, insoluble problem of philosophy is to reconcile the necessities of reason with those of the heart. Here we see a tragic consequence of Unamuno's existentialist principle, mentioned earlier, that man should not philosophize with his reason alone, but also with his will, his feelings, and even with his body; for, necessarily, each of these entities must come to different conclusions, incompatible with one another. Because we cannot overcome these contradictions, Unamuno realized that life is tragedy, the tragedy of a perpetual struggle without victory, and even without the hope of victory.

Herein lies also the deeper meaning of the word "agony," which Unamuno used in the title of his book *La agonía del cristianismo*, written during his Parisian exile in 1924. There he took up again the problems he had dealt with twelve years earlier in his *Del sentimiento trágico de la vida*: those resulting from the struggle between the requirements of life, that is, the requirements of human existence, on the one hand, and those of reason on the other. Here Unamuno restored the word "agony" to its original, etymological meaning, because the Greek ἀγωνία means "struggle." There is a perpetual struggle between life and truth, he says, truth killing our hopes for immortality and life maintaining us in this self-deceit.[25]

But even this hopeless situation brought Unamuno to an inter-

---

[24] Benedictus de Spinoza, *Ethica ordine geometrico demonstrata*, Pars tertia, Propositio VI.
[25] *Obras*, XVI, 463 (*AGC*, pp. 6–7).

esting theoretical insight, namely, to a new interpretation of the history of philosophy as a permanent struggle between reason and life: reason endeavoring to rationalize life and to force it to submit to the inevitable, to mortality, and life trying to vitalize reason, so that it might serve as a support for its own vital existential desires. From this follows, according to Unamuno, a rhythmic movement in the history of philosophy, an alternation of periods in which life imposes itself, giving birth to spiritualistic systems, with periods in which reason imposes itself, giving birth to materalistic systems, whatever the names these two kinds of systems may adopt. But neither reason nor life will ever acknowledge defeat. It would be extremely interesting to try to write a history of philosophy, based on this principle.

As far as this perpetual struggle, this true agony between life and reason, between the will and the intellect, between the heart and the head, took place in Unamuno's own tortured soul, we have to ask ourselves: Was he not a Catholic and does not this creed give assurance of immortality? Well, Unamuno was a Catholic with his heart but not with his reason, and he was unable to sacrifice his reason, like Pascal, or to submit it to the iron discipline of his Basque compatriot, Ignatius de Loyola. In his essay *Mi religión*, Unamuno wrote:

> I frankly confess that the supposed rational proofs . . . of the existence of God, prove to me nothing; that all the reasons adduced to show that God exists appear to me based on sophistry and begging of the question. In this I am with Kant. . . . Nobody has succeeded in convincing me rationally of the existence of God, nor yet of his nonexistence. . . . If I believe in God . . . it is, first of all, because I wish that God may exist, and then, because He is revealed to me through the channel of the heart.[26]

This latter affirmation is very similar to Pascal's: "C'est le coeur qui sent Dieu, et non la raison" ("It is the heart that feels God and not reason").[27] But Neo-Thomism, which, since the encyclical *Aeterni Patris* of Pope Leo XIII, has been the only authorized, official philosophy of the Catholic church, insists that

---

[26] *Ibid.*, p. 120 (*ESS*, pp. 157–158; *PEP*, p. 4).
[27] Blaise Pascal, *Pensées*, ed. L. Brunschvicg (Paris: Hachette, 1904), Vol. II, Sec. IV, no. 277, p. 201.

the existence of God has been rationally demonstrated by St. Thomas' famous "five ways"; and that position is what Unamuno could not take. He believed in God, but he added: "I am not convinced of it as I am of the fact that two and two make four."[28] With his great intellectual honesty and courage, he refused to interpret his subjective, psychological, existential needs as objective logical and ontological necessities.

Unamuno's will to believe was not pragmatic, like William James's, but purely subjective, existential, in Kierkegaard's sense. "Creer en Dios es anhelar que le haya y es además conducirse como si le hubiera" ("To believe in God is to desire strongly that He may exist and, besides, to act as if He existed"), he wrote.[29] This is pure religious subjectivism and, as the formula *como si* or "as if" shows, it is almost fictionalism in the sense of Kant's, Nietzsche's, and Vaihinger's *als ob*: God as a fictitious construct, created for existential purposes. Unamuno admits himself that "creer en Dios es, en cierto modo, crearle,"[30] a pun not translatable but meaning that to believe in God is in a way to create Him. We have to create God in order to save the universe from nothingness.

Unamuno summarized his attitude toward the Catholic solution in the following passage:

> The Catholic solution of our problem, of our one vital problem, the problem of immortality and eternal salvation of the individual soul, satisfies the will and, with this, life; but the attempt to rationalize it by means of dogmatic theology fails to satisfy reason. And reason has its exigencies as imperious as those of life. It is useless trying to force ourselves to consider as super-rational what clearly appears to us to be contra-rational.[31]

The statement "reason has its exigencies as imperious as those of life" shows how wrong it is to classify Unamuno—as is usually done—as an irrationalist. Had he been an irrationalist, he would have accepted Tertullian's *credo* without being disturbed by the *quia absurdum est*. Only because he took reason so seriously did

---

[28] *Obras*, XVI, 120 (*ESS*, p. 158; *PEP*, p. 4).
[29] *Ibid.*, p. 312 (*TSL*, pp. 184–185).
[30] *Ibid.*, p. 282 (*TSL*, p. 154).
[31] *Ibid.*, p. 205 (*TSL*, p. 78).

Unamuno suffer so deeply from its incompatibility with life. "It must remain established," he wrote, "that human reason, within its limits, not only does not prove rationally that the soul is immortal . . . , but rather proves . . . that individual consciousness cannot persist after the death of the bodily organism on which it depends."[32] And Unamuno defended reason against the attempts of so-called rational theology to violate it by trying to force it to sustain life's irrational religious hopes and desires. Thus, rational theology almost "pulverized" reason.

Unamuno admitted God and immortality only as *vital, existential* necessities, but he refused to recognize them as rational necessities; therefore, the Catholic church which, since the days of St. Thomas, has tried to use reason as a means to bolster faith, considers Unamuno almost a heretic. In criticizing him, the Spanish Father Oromí wrote: "It is understanding and reason that must believe."[33] But Unamuno always defended reason courageously against such coercion. "It is no longer enough to believe in the existence of God," he wrote, "but the sentence of anathema falls on him who although believing in it, does not believe that His existence can be demonstrated by rational arguments or who believes that, up to now, nobody has ever demonstrated it irrefutably by such arguments."[34]

It surprises me that even so competent a scholar as Jesús-Antonio Collado fell into the error of considering Unamuno an irrationalist, and even a greater one than his Danish counterpart. "Kierkegaard," says Collado, ". . . is not so irrationalistic as Unamuno, who affirms that all that which is rational is antivital."[35] But with this affirmation Unamuno only asserted a fact that he had rationally demonstrated: the logical incompatibility between the requirements of life, in the sense of human existence, and reason. He *would* have been an irrationalist if he had *denied* the validity of the point of view of reason; but he fully recognized it,

[32] *Ibid.*, pp. 231–232 (*TSL*, pp. 103–104).

[33] Miguel Oromí, "Cuestión personal con Unamuno," *Ateneo: las Ideas, el Arte y las Letras* (Madrid), no. 42 (Sept. 15, 1953). See also Miguel Oromí, *Unamuno y su siglo: agonías intelectuales* (Madrid: Pylsa, 1957).

[34] *Obras*, XVI, 203 (*TSL*, pp. 76–77).

[35] Collado, *op. cit.*, p. 26.

adding, however, that we must also recognize the requirements of life, of human existence, with its emotional needs.

But since reason does not succeed in converting truth into consolation and feeling does not succeed in converting consolation into truth, Unamuno continued struggling. Recognizing the antagonistic exigencies of both reason and life, he suffered all the tragic consequences of their perpetual clashes in his consciousness, but he allowed neither of them to dominate or violate the other. Therefore, Unamuno stands out as an example of intellectual honesty and courage.

"Es mi razón que se burla de mi fe y la desprecia" ("My reason laughs at my faith and despises it"), Unamuno wrote.[36] With this confession he expressed the tragic conflict that torments many modern men. And he openly admitted that his religiosity and his hopes for immortality had their roots only in his *passion*.[37] Of course, if, as a true existentialist, a person philosophizes not only with his reason but with his whole personality, then he must also satisfy the philosophical demands of passion. This is, however, very difficult, for being based on the demands of reason, philosophy can hardly ever satisfy those of passion. But like Kierkegaard, Unamuno was a passional thinker, and therefore philosophy was to him at the same time intellectual delight and passional torment. He saw the struggle between reason and passion symbolized in Don Quixote's soul, dominated by the conflict between what the world is as reason shows it to be and what we wish it to be with our passions, our dreams, our religious faith. To Unamuno, Don Quixote appeared as the representative of a faith that reason could not sustain, but also could not shake.

I think that, in contrast with Unamuno, Kierkegaard was truly an irrationalistic thinker. In the middle of the nineteenth century, the naturalistic philosopher Ludwig Feuerbach wrote that Christianity had become an obsession, a fossil, in open contradiction with modern science and civilization. As the philosopher of the "either-or," unable to accept half measures, Kierkegaard declared

[36] *Obras*, XVI, 425 (*TSL*, p. 302).
[37] *Ibid.*, p. 415 (*TSL*, p. 292).

that he would rather keep Christianity and let modern science and civilization go. According to the dogma, Christ is the union of two incompatibles, God and man; therefore, Kierkegaard considered Christ as the "absolute paradox," to be appropriated by faith, which crucifies reason. And he demanded that man crucify reason. This is *true* irrationalism, but Unamuno's recognition of the rights of both reason and passion is not.

If Unamuno has been so often classified as an irrationalist, it is perhaps partly owing to the fact that he often wrote as he spoke. He must have been a very powerful speaker, and he preferred speaking to writing, considering speech a more perfect medium of communication because of its being less material. This habit of writing as he spoke had its great advantages, for it gave Unamuno's style a strong oratorical power. But it had also its disadvantage: a lack of self-control. One often says things that one would not write, for writing gives time for reflection. With the spoken word we have always the possibility of attenuating, interpreting, and even withdrawing it, when we are confronted with the reactions of the listeners. There is much wisdom in the way Socrates explains to Phaidros the advantages of the spoken word over the written word. But the spoken word should not be written down such as it is. Our sometimes violent oral utterances usually become respectable when we have to write them down. Horace's statement "verbum semel emissum volat irrevocabile" ("the word once uttered flies irrevocably") holds especially for the written word. If we merely transcribe our spoken words, we are likely to get into trouble. I guess that is what happened to Unamuno, especially in his book *Vida de don Quijote y Sancho*, which is full of verbal invectives against reason, science, technology, and scholarship, and which attacks logic—*la cochina lógica* ("swinish logic")—as worthless.[38] But, as Unamuno's later books, especially *Del sentimiento trágico de la vida* and *La agonía del cristianismo*, show, he did not truly despise logic and reason, for otherwise he would not have suffered so deeply from their incompatibility with life, will, feeling, and would not have insisted so strongly on their legitimate rights. His rejection of "intellectual-

[38] *Ibid.*, IV, 71.

ity" in favor of "spirituality" should have freed him from all these problems, but it did not, because, in spite of himself, Unamuno remained an intellectual.

Since I spoke of some of the basic differences between Unamuno and his existentialist predecessor Kierkegaard, I wish also to mention a difference in their approach to politics. Kierkegaard was an outspoken reactionary. When, in 1848, revolutions flared up all over Europe in order to break the centuries-old absolutism of the monarchs, Kierkegaard sided with the princes against their peoples. The one answer of authority to revolt, he said, must be the imperious "thou shalt," backed by force. He felt that kings were appointed by God to rule, and should therefore rule absolutely. The unique equality that mattered, he said, was Christian equality, which did not seek to alter earthly conditions but created a spirit in which they were seen not to be worth altering. This Christian equality of all men before God was so precious to him that political equality did not seem worth fighting for.

On the contrary, Unamuno fought monarchy and dictatorship with all his passion. To be sure, Ferrater Mora insists that Unamuno did not fight monarchism in general, but a specific monarchy, the Spanish one, and a specific king, Alfonso XIII.[39] We may add that he also fought only a specific dictator, General Primo de Rivera, and was less outspoken in his attitude toward Franco. This specifically directed antagonism was, however, in complete agreement with Unamuno's existentialist hostility toward abstract generalities and his unique concern with the concrete, the individual. It did not prevent Unamuno from fighting King Alfonso XIII and dictator Primo de Rivera so courageously that he was arrested and deported to Fuerteventura, one of the Canary Islands. He continued his fight there and, later, after his adventurous flight from the island, in France, during years of exile. He willingly paid this high price for his right to speak out against tyranny, in spite of his excruciating nostalgia. His homesickness became so overwhelming that he finally left Paris and

[39] José Ferrater Mora, *Unamuno: Bosquejo de una filosofía* (Buenos Aires: Losada, 1944), p. 29; see also the English translation of this book by Philip Silver, *Unamuno: A Philosophy of Tragedy* (Berkeley and Los Angeles: University of California Press, 1962), p. 16.

settled in the small town of Hendaye in southern France, so close
to the Spanish border that he could look over it from his windows
into his beloved Spain and caress with his eyes the green moun-
tains of his native Basque land.

No political party was ever able to claim Unamuno's loyalty.
"No soy un partido, soy un entero,"[40] he said in another untranslatable pun, playing on two meanings of *un partido*, "a party"
and "one who is parted or divided," as contrasted with *un entero*
("one who is entire, whole"). Yet he must have felt himself close
to Liberalism, for in 1912 he wrote these bitter words: "The true
sin . . . is the sin of heresy, that of thinking for oneself. The
saying has been heard here, in our Spain, that to be a liberal—
that is, a heretic—is worse than being an assassin, a robber or
an adulterer."[41] Unfortunately, the attitude that Unamuno sati-
rized is still very much alive today, half a century later, and not
only in Spain.

We must, however, not overlook the many illiberal attitudes of
Unamuno, some of which I find shocking: for instance, his praise
of war as a cleansing of hate and a sanctification of homicide, as
a school of fraternity and love, and as a revelation of God; furthermore, his praise of slavery which allowed Plato to philosophize. Unamuno even rejected Christian democracy and Christian
socialism. The true Christian should seek eternal life outside
history, and the problems of democracy, civil liberty, dictatorship, tyranny, social justice, and economic security—all these
have nothing to do with Christianity, Unamuno affirmed bluntly
in his *Agonía del cristianismo*. "Eso de la democracia cristiana es
algo como química azul,"[42] he declared ironically, which means
that Christian democracy is just as contradictory an idea as blue
chemistry. To be sure, this extreme position is only one of the
many antitheses in the "agony of Christianity," but Unamuno
defends it apparently with deep conviction.

In his early essay *La vida es sueño* ("Life Is a Dream"), written after Spain had lost the remaining vestiges of her American
colonial empire, Unamuno implored the world to allow the

---

[40] Cf. Ferrater Mora, *Unamuno: Bosquejo*, p. 29.
[41] *Obras*, XVI, 198–199 (*TSL*, pp. 71–72).
[42] *Ibid.*, p. 511 (*AGC*, p. 81).

humble Spaniard to muse away the slow, monotonous dream of a simple routine life, without any historical mission, and not to "be sacrificed to progress." "¡Que no le sacrifiquen al progreso, por Dios, que no le sacrifiquen al progreso!" our thinker exclaimed pathetically.[43]

Later on, in his book *Del sentimiento trágico de la vida*, Unamuno tried to give a new project to his nation: that of being the tragicomic Don Quixote among the nations, a living expression of a people's refusal to submit to logic and science, that is, to the modern world and its truth. The ultimate aim of this project, he said, was "to save the Middle Ages from the Renaissance, in order not to lose the treasure of its infancy."[44] In my book *Philosophy of History and the Problem of Values*, I expressed my doubt that such a project could gain the adherence of a nation. The past cannot be brought to life again. Likewise, I rejected Unamuno's thesis that even a restoration of the past would be tantamount to the creation of a future. Historically speaking, such a restoration would be sterile, for a collective project that does not create new values, values not yet realized in history, has no historical reason for being.[45]

There was in Unamuno a strange mixture of a national and religious traditionalist and a revolutionary. We have to accept these contradictions as an expression of the tremendous richness of his dynamic personality and the extraordinary fertility of his mind. Once, in a humorous mood, Unamuno said: "Si un hombre nunca se contradice, será porque nunca dice nada" ("If a man never contradicts himself, it may be because he never says anything").[46] However, *he* always said many things and *had* to say them, things that still make us think. In a more serious mood, Unamuno said that a man who never contradicts himself does

[43] *Ibid.*, III, 411.

[44] *Ibid.*, XVI, 444 (*TSL*, p. 323).

[45] Alfred Stern, *Philosophy of History and the Problem of Values* (The Hague: Mouton, 1962), pp. 202–244; see also the Spanish version of this book, *La filosofía de la historia y el problema de los valores* (Buenos Aires: Eudeba, 1964).

[46] This remark was repeated to me by the internationally known physicist and Nobel Prize winner Erwin Schrödinger, who heard it from Unamuno during the summer of 1934 at the International University of Santander.

not truly live, because life is contradiction and war,[47] and he designated himself as an *hombre de contradicción*, a man of contradiction. His mind was a microcosm that reflected the many incompatible aspects of the macrocosm in which we live. What he called *agonía* is the perpetual struggle among these incompatibilities.

· Summing up the teachings of Plato and Cicero, Michel de Montaigne wrote: "Philosopher, c'est apprendre à mourir" ("To philosophize is to learn how to die").[48] Unamuno would not have been a true philosopher had he not, finally, solved his most tormenting lifelong problem by learning how to die. To a philosopher, this does not mean to learn how to undergo the physiological process of disintegration which, unfortunately, takes place by itself, whether we have learned it or not. To the philosopher, to learn how to die means to overcome by thought the paradox of an existence that, after many struggles and sufferings and a few satisfactions and achievements, is condemned to disappear in the void of nothingness.

In this difficult learning process, Unamuno gained inspiration from the French writer Sénancour, who in 1804 had published a kind of philosophical journal in the form of letters and poems. Its title is *Obermann*. In reading it, Unamuno was struck by the following: "L'homme est périssable. Il se peut, mais périssons en résistant, et si le néant nous est réservé, ne faisons pas que ce soit une justice" ("Man is perishable. That may be; but let us perish resisting, and if it is nothingness that awaits us, do not let us so act that it be a just fate").[49] Unamuno changed the last sentence by saying: "Let us so act that nothingness shall be an unjust fate." And his final categorical imperative reads: "Act so that in your own judgment and in the judgment of others you may merit eternity, that you may become irreplaceable, that you may not deserve death."[50] On this noble imperative one can build an ethics of altruism and creativity, an ethics that invites us to leave on all things the imperishable impress of our signature, to

---

[47] *Obras*, VIII, 994.
[48] Michel de Montaigne, *Essais*, Bk. 1, chap. xx.
[49] E. P. de Sénancour, *Obermann*, Lettre XC.
[50] *Obras*, XVI, 387 (*TSL*, p. 263).

immortalize ourselves in our works. The fact that today, a century after Unamuno's birth, we are assembled here, in a country thousands of miles away from his native Spain, trying to rethink his thoughts—this fact shows that he really immortalized himself in his work.

4

"AUTHENTICITY" AND THE IMAGE
Carlos Blanco-Aguinaga

It seems quite clear that though existence is grounded in solitude, full self-consciousness demands that the individual be not alone in the awareness of his being. Being for others is, indeed, "not an ontological structure of the For-itself,"[1] but it "is a constant fact of my [i.e., any] human reality."[2] As Sartre indicates in his analysis of Hegel's *Phenomenology*, "The appearance of the Other is indispensable not to the constitution of the world and of my empirical 'Ego' but to the very existence of my consciousness as self-consciousness."[3]

Even the hermit when he seems to have repudiated all otherness hopes to rest at least, or at last, in the presence of God. Only thus is apparent isolation bearable (or even desirable). Indeed, though every man is an island, no man can ever be alone on an island, as Pincher Martin discovers once and for all by the radical masterstroke of his creator William Golding, who, quite simply, takes away from him the possibility of the copresence on his rock of any Man Friday. Since there is also no God for Chris Martin, it is no surprise—though it may be a shock—when we find out at the end of the novel that he has been dead from the beginning of his difficult life on the island.

No one can seriously doubt his own existence, but we are in a world of others against whose presence is projected the historical dimension of our being, that is to say, our image, which, though it transforms us from *subjects* into *objects*, is nevertheless (or therefore) the objective proof of our existence and thus a

[1] Jean-Paul Sartre, *Being and Nothingness*, trans. Hazel E. Barnes (New York: Philosophical Library, 1956), p. 282.
[2] *Ibid.*, p. 280.
[3] *Ibid.*, p. 235.

48

necessary dimension of our self-consciousness. It might even be said, to put it radically, that "the road of interiority passes through the Other."[4]

It may, of course, seem to us that this statement stresses too much the importance of "the other" and, therefore, of "the image." Not many words in our society today carry more unpleasant connotations than the word "image," not only because, in all sorts of vague ways, we tend to believe that "truth is subjectivity," but also because, ever since Madison Avenue has become part of our daily living (and since we have even seen the White House seeking ways of changing whatever image this nation is thought to have abroad), image has come to mean "the inauthentic." It is only proper, of course, that it should be so, for the image, like the *persona*, or mask, may serve for the projection or representation of a true character, and yet this character is not the man playing it, but only a representation carried out by the man playing the role, who is an actor, that is to say, a *hypocrite*.

And yet, within the view of life that sustains itself in the metaphor "world as stage," it is strictly necessary to conceive of the image as corresponding to authentic being. I am referring to that old and basic way whose most systematic and complex presentation is perhaps to be found in the theater of Calderón. We may reduce it to this formula: Act properly the role you have been assigned and you will cease being a hypocrite to become the man you were meant to be.

As for the question, "Are we ever *any more* than our image?" there is also an answer in an old Spanish proverb: A man is the son of his deeds. The works, or deeds, being a man's alienation from himself, the reduction of his self to publicity, are the history of his being, and history is all we have. Thus Ortega y Gasset's radical statement: "Man has no nature; what he has is . . . history." Much before Ortega, of course, and, interestingly enough, in reference to the proverb I have just quoted as Spanish, the idea is to be found in Hegel when he concludes that the inner is the outer and that consciousness is history.[5]

---

[4] *Ibid.*, p. 236.

[5] Indeed, as Walter T. Stace indicates (*The Philosophy of Hegel* [New York: Dover, 1955], p. 209), this is a favorite, if not *the* favorite, theme of Hegel. In this respect, Hegel has been curiously misunderstood.

But most of us, of course, have no knowledge of the role we may have been assigned to play, and then, to make matters worse, we are hopelessly dualistic so that we feel sure that there must be more to our true being than what is reflected by our deeds; that there is, or should be, a person inside our *persona* who is not what he appears to others (in perhaps a multiplicity of images), but a self known only, perhaps, to God—or, let us say, to the psychiatrist. After all, as against the proverb quoted, there is Wordsworth's statement that "the child is father of the man," and it may seem quite obvious to us that as we proceed *through* our acts, which are, indeed, always matters of choice and commitment and, therefore, very much ourselves, we leave behind an incalculable number of works undone that, had we done them, would have been ourselves. Because we are not only what we do but what we project to do, we think those deeds still possible as long as we are alive and we tend to see in their possibility (i.e., in their lack of historical dimension) aspects of our true selves no less "authentic" because unknown to others. Very often, of course, these possibilities are felt to be anchored in our childhood, that which we were, and, surely, must still be somehow. Thus "merely passing in review the film of our own lives," writes Ortega y Gasset, "reveals our individual destinies to be the result of the selection made by actual circumstances among our personal possibilities. The individual we grow to be in the course of our lives is only one of the many we might have been but had to leave behind—lamentable casualties of our inner army."[6]

Before Ortega, and much before the elusive concepts of "project," "freedom," and "commitment" became associated in existential doctrine, Unamuno had come to understand "authenticity" as historical representation, the for-itself as dependent on the other for self-consciousness, *but regretfully*, as the most concrete and common instance of the human "agony." Before Ortega, and quoting Wordsworth always, he often spoke, with great sorrow, about the "ex-future" selves every man leaves behind as he devotes his apparent freedom to the creation of a self that always turns out to be an image; for Unamuno was,

[6] José Ortega y Gasset, *Toward a Philosophy of History*, trans. Helene Weyl (New York: Norton, 1941), p. 19.

fundamentally, a dualist obsessed with the problem of the relationship between what he called the intrahistorical (or eternal)
mode of life and the historical (or temporal). Yet, the internal
necessities of the development of his thought, the relation of his
works to his readers, and, in general, the pressures of historical
circumstances made him an existentialist, but with what appears
today as an advantage over the much firmer men who were to
follow: He never let go of the questions that make it so difficult
to accept what is, at best, a lamentable conclusion. After him, the
exact equivalent of the word "existence" is still "agony," in the
many different contexts in which he employed it and as it reappears, for instance, in this statement of Jean-Paul Sartre: "Conflict is the original meaning of being-for-others."[7]

In the text that follows, I shall try to outline the way in which
the question of "authenticity" and "the image" grows in importance in Unamuno's works and how it culminates, like most
everything else, in a return to the basic concept of "agony." My
approach is fundamentally biographical and, therefore, narrative,
not only because, as Ortega puts it, "to comprehend anything
human . . . one must tell its history,"[8] but because, like most
everything else in Unamuno, this question has in his work a biographical origin. Not only should this biographical approach help
us to understand the problem and its development, but, as I hope,
it may help us to realize, once more, why it is that so-called
existentialist writers have managed to bring into philosophic
thought questions (and difficulties) inconceivable before them.
With Unamuno, as with Kierkegaard, biography enters the realm
of thought and makes itself into, as he put it, the object and
supreme subject of all philosophizing.

1864–1897

We must begin with the most commonly known fact of Unamuno's life: His was a perfectly Catholic and peaceful childhood
which was often to appear to him in recollection as an indestructible world harmony, a kind of Limbo in which, as he was

[7] Sartre, *op. cit.*, p. 364.
[8] Ortega y Gasset, *op. cit.*, p. 214.

to express it later, the child could breathe "the perfume of the flower (of life) without having to taste the fruit."[9] If we remember that Unamuno once defined original sin as the condemnation of the Idea to Time, it is clear that the reference points to an existence lived without self-consciousness. He made it quite unambiguous when he wrote in 1934 that the child has no consciousness, for he receives with his mother's language the idea of life that language contains.[10] As for his Catholicism, the core of that "idea of life," he was to declare, in a little-known and very important letter, that with him, as with most Catholics, it had been "inherited and imposed."[11] Indeed, throughout his childhood and early adolescence, Miguel de Unamuno is the one he is told he is, and he allows himself to live in the beliefs of others, in perfect harmony with the world around him.

But, as is well known, the unity was broken between the ages of sixteen and eighteen, during his university days in Madrid, when Unamuno ceased to attend Mass regularly. It is all part of the process by which, as he declared, he was trying, as a student of philosophy, to "rationalize" his faith. Yet, the departure from orthodoxy—and, therefore, from his childhood—took place without turmoil. The passage from the *Spiritual Exercises* of Bilbao's Congregación de San Luis Gonzaga to the study of Hegel's *Logic* (which Unamuno was translating in his sophomore year) is perhaps the most important step in Unamuno's life, and it should have provoked some confusion; but, if we read from the first paragraph of the *Logic*, it becomes conceivable that the change as it was then taking place should not have appeared sufficiently radical to demand a total confrontation with himself (a *toma de conciencia*) for the young man who wanted to "rationalize" his faith. Hegel writes in that first paragraph: "The objects of philosophy . . . are upon the whole the same as those of religion. In both the object is Truth, in that supreme sense in which God and God only is the Truth."[12] For the young man who had gone

[9] *Obras*, I, 315.
[10] *Obras*, VII, 1085.
[11] Federico Urales, *La evolución de la filosofía en España* (Barcelona: Revista Blanca, 1934), II, 205.
[12] *The Logic of Hegel*, trans. by William Wallace from *The Encyclopaedia of the Philosophical Sciences* (2d ed., rev. and aug.; Oxford: Clarendon Press, 1892), p. 3.

to Madrid to pursue the study of the philosophical questions that had attracted his attention in secondary school, it must have been quite easy to slip from one world into the other—and, then, on to Spencer, from the study of whose work Unamuno emerges as an enthusiast of progress, of reason, and of the scientific method, quite unaware of the fact that the one he had been as a child was becoming, or had already become, another.

At this level of apparent unconsciousness, common to the majority of men, several more years elapsed, and although one critic has spoken of Unamuno's probable reinsertion into Christianity in the year 1884,[13] as far as I am concerned there are no proofs of such a "return," nor of any crisis; and back in his home town (Bilbao), Unamuno managed to pass for a perfectly normal citizen who gave private lessons in Latin and French and wrote "costumbristic" articles for the local press, with occasional excursions into the praises of rationalism and the attitudes that, at that time, went with rationalism. Since the socialistic articles that he also wrote were published, as of the middle eighties, under a pseudonym, he was, for all practical purposes, still living as the "others" wished him to.

Unamuno was not, of course, the first man to live through a period of gestation in that neutral and ambiguous world in which ideas are not yet what Ortega calls "functioning beliefs"; but when in 1891 he obtained the chair of Greek at the University of Salamanca, things changed in one important sense: He began to publish for a national audience. His major theme was the "regeneration" of Spain, and he appeared to his readers not only as a very learned defender of reason and of progress but, also, as a very polemic one and, paradoxically, as an enemy of tradition who, nevertheless, injects a religious tone into his writings. By 1897 he had published many essays, a book on the "Spanish problem" (*En torno al casticismo*), and a novel, and he was well on his way to becoming the most important figure of a new generation of writers who wished to change Spain radically, to modernize it, to—as they used to say—"Europeanize" it, when suddenly, on a night in March, 1897, he had a terrifying revelation of death as nothingness. The accompanying anguish ended the

[13] Antonio Sánchez Barbudo, *Estudios sobre Unamuno y Machado* (Madrid: Guadarrama, 1959), pp. 15–29.

long period of gestation, and Unamuno was forced, at the age of thirty-three, to consider a new beginning.

SIGNIFICANCE OF THE CRISIS OF 1897

This revelation is the so-called "religious crisis" about which so much has been written. We already know all that it is necessary to know about it; yet, in order to understand its significance in terms of the question that occupies us here, we must remember that the word "crisis," a much-abused word, quite properly used in this instance, derives from the Greek *krinein* meaning, first of all, "separation." Indeed, if Unamuno's departure from Bilbao to Madrid, his absence from Mass and, let us say, the writing of socialist articles—all acts of separation—were not sufficient to exile him from those in whose image he had been raised (i.e., to alienate him from others and to throw him upon himself in an act of self-appraisal), then the March night of 1897 signifies a radical moment of alienation at all levels and meanings of the word, for Unamuno's encounter with nothingness was the radical experience by which, unexpectedly, he found himself deprived of his being (*despojado de su ser*), naked, without past or future, while, in terror, he tried to keep hold of what, as of that moment, will forever after be the self's fall through absolute emptiness, being escaping from itself in its very center. Abstracting even further from this unique (i.e., strictly concrete) experience, we may say that in it the for-itself was all of a sudden faced by the fact that he was for death, for the absolute otherness that invades all reality and seems to empty it of any meaning. Yet, since at this very point anguish reveals the existence of a consciousness whose only characteristic seems to be the will (or the necessity) to negate the revealed nothingness, the for-itself will try to lift itself up, without support, as it were, by its bootstraps, in order to affirm against *any* negation what is now, forever, the core of his being, the simple and primitive will to exist (not to capitulate); for, as Unamuno would express it later, "Consciousness cannot conceive of itself as not existing."[14]

And thus Unamuno was ready to enter into time and its dia-

14 *Obras*, XVI, 165 (*TSL*, p. 38).

lectical processes (of which the first had already taken place). But in order to get beyond the mere awareness of one's being as a negation of what would negate *it*, an affirmation is necessary that can be founded only on the apprehension of the being one recognizes as one's own. Hence, a *naming* (or definition) of the self from *outside* the very moment of crisis is required; and this *posterior* naming of one's self in the face of the recollection of nothingness perforce demands—short of madness—an appeal to an *anterior* self which will be given by the authority of memory. But the difficulty for Unamuno resided in the fact that the one he had acted as being in the years immediately preceding the crisis, the rationalist and "progressive" man, was precisely the one whose being had been emptied of meaning. Every one of his ideas, his words, his gestures appeared to be founded on a vacuum when what he needed to affirm was an existence, a belief, as absolute as the negation that opposed the very conception of existence. Had Unamuno read Kierkegaard in 1897, he might have come across an answer to this difficulty in which is ironically summed up what the Dane called, from the point of view of the ethical, the paralysis of the intellect: "I perceive perfectly that there are two possibilities, one can either do this or that. My sincere opinion and my friendly counsel is as follows: Do it, or don't do it—you will regret both."[15]

Fortunately for Unamuno, the authority needed to avoid either a radical choice or a paralysis was close at hand, for at the moment of crisis he was in the company of his wife, who soon came to symbolize the native land, his childhood, and the Catholic faith; and in the consolation offered by her, he found the answer and a way out of immobility: he tried to be again the one he was before Madrid, the one *she* knew then, the *other* Unamuno, the one whose faith should have served as a firm bulwark against rationalism and the consequent thoughts of dissolution. Thus, as strictly required by the crisis, he tried to become *another*, but he tried to become the one that others (his wife, his confessor) wanted him to be; in short, he had to be for others (and, as is clear from his still unpublished diary, he had to be

---

[15] *A Kierkegaard Anthology*, ed. Robert Bretall (Princeton: Princeton University Press, 1947), p. 98.

against others also, against those who admired his writings of the years immediately preceding the crisis).

Thus, from the very moment in which Unamuno tried to take what appeared then as the necessary step of giving a religious content to his crisis, he initiated a struggle to affirm a self that, at all levels, would take the form of being for others. From here on, as the effort to recover his being became a will to immortality and this—the only question, as he called it—became the major theme of his work, the presence of others (of all otherness) was at the center of his life, his philosophy, and his art.

1897–1905

I have tried to show in a recent study[16] how Unamuno's efforts in the project for the recovery of his being led him at first, but for a short period, to the paradoxical Christian attitude of humility (not to be in order to be; or, to be as others indicate), and how, very soon after 1898, between 1899 and 1905, actually, we can trace in his work a progressive abandonment of this solution culminating in its very opposite, a will to re-create himself *against* all others. This final and characteristically Unamunian posture signifies the acceptance of the responsibility for his own being, by which responsibility, to put it in Sartrian terms, he lays claim to the being that he is, from which derives the project of the recovery of his self as "fundamentally a project of the absorbing of the Other."[17]

This effort, from which originate both Unamuno's major works and his "legend" as the great egotist, has, of course, a variety of causes, but we may perhaps reduce them to three: (1) the impossibility of recapturing the faith of his childhood (even after his seclusion in a monastery); (2) the need, therefore, to keep

[16] Carlos Blanco-Aguinaga, "De Nicodemo a Don Quijote," in Germán Bleiberg and E. Inman Fox, eds., *Spanish Thought and Letters in the Twentieth Century: An International Symposium Held at Vanderbilt University to Commemorate the Centenary of the Birth of Miguel de Unamuno—1864–1964* (Nashville: Vanderbilt University Press, 1966), pp. 75–100.

[17] Chapter 1 of François Meyer's excellent book *L'Ontologie de Miguel de Unamuno* (Paris: Presses Universitaires de France, 1955) can be interpreted as an analysis of this situation.

the original "anguish" of the crisis alive as the only proof of existence (since the crisis was a result of the encounter with otherness, he systematically opposed all otherness, *contra esto y
aquello*); (3) a very common practical necessity of opposing
two sets of "others": those who admired his early works, and
those who wanted him to return to his "original" self. Thus, at
all levels, "otherness" was from that time on present in every
form of Unamuno's affirmation of existence as centered in self-
consciousness.

We cannot go into the details here and it should be sufficient
to indicate that the crucial work in this development is the essay
¡Adentro! (1900) written, precisely, in the form of a letter, that
is to say, addressed to a "you" whom Unamuno, ironically
enough, advises to reject all advice from others and even to
attack any such advice if he is to be himself. Unamuno gives himself as an example; and, after exclaiming *¡mi centro está en mí!*
and declaring that his talent (his only *talent*), the one he must
exchange, is that of the writer (and not that of the monk), he
sets the golden rule: "Do not allow your past to become the
tyrant of your future." Life is the development of one's symbol;
one discovers oneself as one acts; the future is the reign of liberty;
and one can only have faith in the future, in freedom. Although it
is true that man is a being-for-death, we must see to it that death
is a *coronation* in the sense that one's being is not complete until
then.[18] And although Unamuno rejects the idea that one must
plan one's future ("You are not a building," he reminds his
reader), he nevertheless expresses the conviction that life is a
project of self-creation. The only requisite for any man (and,
most surely, for the writer) is that he must be sincere in the daily
act of, as he puts it, "coming out of oneself," of "revealing" oneself to oneself and to others.

One might easily be carried away here—and perhaps one
should be—to indicate that in *¡Adentro!* Unamuno anticipates
both Ortega's and Sartre's simple and fundamental idea that

---

[18] If we consider that Unamuno had been reading *Don Quixote* and
writing on it since the 1890's, it may not be too far-fetched to see in
this idea a reflection of Ginés de Pasamonte's answer to Don Quixote
when the *pícaro* states that the autobiography he has written is not finished since his life is not over yet (*Quixote*, I, chap. xxii).

"man is no more than what he makes himself be" and that he has come to this conclusion from a personal experience (from a situation), which corresponds exactly to Sartre's idea that "man . . . is not definable precisely because at the beginning he is nothing. He will be afterward, and he will be exactly as he makes himself."[19]

Rather than pursue that parallel, it will be more fruitful for our purpose to perceive in ¡Adentro! the germs of future difficulties as they appear at two different levels: First, it seems clear that, by stressing the importance of liberty (of the future), Unamuno is trying to arrive at a concept of continuous self-creation; but he seems to conceive of the freely created (and always future) self as the revelation or exteriorization of what one *already is*. The obvious dualism, left over from Hegel as against existential anticipations, is also evident in the double advice given in the essay: One must go inside oneself (¡Adentro!) to discover oneself and *then* bring out that inner self sincerely or authentically. I believe this is more than a didactically necessary separation of the "inner" and the "outer"[20] and that it betrays Unamuno's inability to break away from a dualistic view of life, in which view there is always implicit the possibility of conflict between authenticity and the image. Second, we should notice that even if we should grant that one's life, as crowned by death, can be understood only when all is said and done (i.e., when there is no more future), it is nevertheless true that at any one moment we are not only what we project to do but what we already have and have not done. The fact is we are constantly being checked against our deeds (hence, the importance, not only of freedom, but of responsibility); and, in this sense, there is always a past acting as tyrant of the future. This past is, of course, the "image" that interferes with whatever liberties we wish to take in the expression of what we may at any moment conceive of as our authentic selves.

[19] Jean-Paul Sartre, *L'Existentialisme est un Humanisme* (Paris: Nagel, 1946), pp. 21–22. And Ortega writes (*op. cit.*, p. 116): "Life means to [man] at once and primarily the effort to bring into existence what does not exist offhand, to wit: himself."

[20] For a study of this conflict in terms of the opposition between the "inner" and the "outer," cf. my article "Interioridad y exterioridad en Unamuno," *Nueva Revista de Filología Hispánica*, VII (1953), 686–707.

But Unamuno was quite unaware of these and other difficulties in 1900, for, after all, *¡Adentro!* signifies his beginning, the moment at which, indeed, all was future. And thus, for the next five years he proceeds enthusiastically to discover himself and to reveal himself; to create himself publicly: as president of the University of Salamanca, as political figure, and, above all, as essayist, poet, and novelist whose major themes are the exaltation of consciousness, of sentiment against reason, of the existential "I" against death, and of himself against his readers.

This first period of self-creation culminates in 1905 with his book *The Life of Don Quixote and Sancho* in which, through an apparently paradoxical, yet purely dialectical, process, he affirms himself by an act of identification with Don Quixote in whom he finds (quite properly) the perfect secular example of self-creation through imitation and alienation. If we are to understand both Don Quixote and Unamuno's relation to him, it is crucial not to lose sight of the obvious fact that, when the *Quixote* opens, a man whose name is improperly remembered—it may have been, we are told, Quijada, or Quesada, or Quejana—has gone mad because of his tendency to alienate himself in the reading of romances of chivalry, the adventures of whose knights he desires to imitate. Thus, we are told of a loss of being through a surrender to otherness which is immediately followed by an act of self-creation when the hero of the story gives himself a name (Don Quixote) and then sets himself a project for living in which he is to fulfill his existence through the imitation of Amadis.

Like no other reader of the *Quixote* before him, Unamuno was prepared to see the implications of this, and he saw them with perfect clarity: "We know nothing of the birth of Don Quixote," he writes on the opening page. "All memory of his lineage, birth, childhood, and youth has been lost; we have it neither in oral tradition nor in written testimony. . . . In respect to his lineage, he once declared to Sancho . . . that although he was a hidalgo . . . he was not a descendant of kings, but that in spite of it, the wise man who would some day write his story would surely be able to discover that he had been the fifth or sixth grandson of a king. For, as a matter of fact," adds Unamuno, "in the long run everyone is a descendant of kings. . . . But he, Don Quixote, was of those lineages that are and were not. *His lineage begins with him.*" Unamuno continues, "It is amazing, nonetheless, that the diligent scholars who have so searched into the life and miracles of our Knight should not yet have arrived at discovering any traces of his ancestry. . . . That Cervantes should not have bothered with it is no surprise for, after all, he believed that everyone is the son of his deeds and that every man creates himself as he lives and acts."[21] To which, a few pages later, in a mild show of scholarship, Unamuno adds a passage from Dr. Juan Huarte, a contemporary of Cervantes who wrote thus on the meaning of the word "hidalgo":

> The Spaniard who invented this name, *hijodalgo*, made it clear
> . . . that men have two kinds of births. The one is natural, in
> which they are all equal, and the other spiritual. When a man
> accomplishes a heroic act or some strange deed, then he is born
> anew and he gains new and better parents, and he loses the being
> [*el ser*] he had before. Yesterday his name was son of Pedro and
> grandson of Sancho; now he is called the son of his works. From
> which originates the Castilian saying: Every man is the son
> of his deeds.

To which Unamuno adds: "And so Don Quixote: a descendant of himself, a man who was born in spirit when he decided to go out in search of adventures, and when he gave himself a new name in view of the great deeds that he intended to accomplish."[22]

The interpretation not only corresponds exactly to what is written at the opening of the *Quixote*, but it must also serve as the best way of beginning to understand why what happens in the opening pages of the *Quixote* is fundamental to the birth of a new literary genre, for the novel (i.e., one of the things that distinguish the *Quixote* from earlier prose narrations) is action in time, during which (in which) characters create themselves before us as they act, and of them we know nothing beyond what they do and say in the book.

But at this point some of the difficulties we found in *¡Adentro!* should become even more evident, since it is clear in the *Quixote* that even this most authentic act of self-creation, because it has been carried out in imitation of another's life (that of Amadis), relies totally on the recognition granted to the individual by

---

[21] *Obras*, IV, 84–85 (*LDQ*, pp. 3–4).
[22] *Ibid.*, pp. 91–92 (*LDQ*, pp. 11–12).

other men. We cannot forget that, from the very beginning, it is Don Quixote's declared intention to gain "fame" and, indeed, the whole novel is about Don Quixote's relationship to his "image," a relationship that in a sense culminates in that magnificent third chapter of the second part in which the Knight discusses the merits and the authenticity of the story of his adventures, as written in that first part which, by then, was being widely read. Don Quixote's act of self-creation is, thus, in its very nature, the commitment to an image, to a historical dimension of his being of which he will eventually become the prisoner and from which he will liberate himself only with death. And yet, it is this will to fame, this commitment to the image, this desire for immortality in history, which Unamuno—afraid as he always was that there might not be any other kind of immortality—applauds enthusiastically in *The Life of Don Quixote and Sancho*.[23]

The religious form of imitation and alienation leads to man's discovery of his authentic being independent of any world image precisely because it is alienation from the world in imitation of Christ. Thus, for the saint, alienation (*enajenamiento*) means—in the mystic paradox—interiorization (*ensimismamiento*) to the point that only one image of his remains: that which is true for God. But because Don Quixote imitates not Christ but Amadis, he falls madly into the trap tended by history (and through fiction, at that!) where reality is, at once, itself and its contrary in never-ending dialectical struggle or, as Unamuno preferred to say it, in "agony."

The difficulty implicit in Unamuno's approval of the radical act of alienation (*enajenamiento*) is further made clear when Cervantes' conviction that man is the son of his deeds is seriously considered in relation to the fact that the first deed of the nameless hero is an act of self-creation based on a project for the future considered as open and free. Since from this act result a series of irreversible deeds whose relationship to the future is one of tyranny, we must conclude that Don Quixote is not only what he wills to be, as Unamuno claimed time and again, but, at every

[23] Unamuno does not for a minute doubt that "el ansia de gloria y renombre es el espíritu íntimo del quijotismo" (quoted by E. K. Paucker in her edition of Miguel de Unamuno, *Cuentos* [Madrid: Ediciones Minotauro, 1961], I, 13).

step, what he has already done or not done, what he has been. We must agree with Ortega when he writes that "man is not . . . an eternal Adam."[24] Short of ever-renewed irresponsible falls into madness, there is no freedom from oneself. From this truth derives, I must insist, the importance of understanding freedom of choice as inseparable from responsibility in commitment. Whether he likes it or not, Don Quixote is committed to his image, and if "Alonso Quijano," at the end of the novel, can disclaim any responsibility for the deeds of Don Quixote, it is, quite simply, because Don Quixote was mad; because throughout his madness, he whose name *was* Alonso Quijano was *not* himself.

Historical action (or, simply, action) cannot, in fact, be anything but alienation, in which from one reality emerges its dialectical contrary, as Unamuno later realized in the peculiar, existential return to Hegel implied in his concept of "agony." And although he did not see it at this time, it was precisely his *quijotismo*, his willful identification with Don Quixote, that finally forced him to become aware of the antagonism between his intentions to express himself authentically (or sincerely) and the resulting image; because when, after 1905, his image continued to grow in the Spanish scene, it grew precisely in terms of his "quixotic" doings and sayings. "Este donquijotesco / don Miguel de Unamuno," Antonio Machado wrote of him in 1906; and as we read Machado's poem, we must remember that he was a poet who insisted on using only adjectives that, as he explained it, defined the noun essentially, or absolutely. And, indeed, no other adjective like *quijotesco* has since been more often and more properly used to *simplify* Unamuno, for most of his enterprises between 1900 and, let us say, 1930 were, or seemed to be at the time, of a quixotic nature.

AFTER 1905: GROWTH OF THE IMAGE

In his opposition to science and progress, his rejection of reason as existentially negative (but, therefore, necessary); his inversion of Descartes's first conclusion; his concept of solitude and of man as a being-for-death; his religious tone; his analysis of

24 Ortega y Gasset, *op. cit.*, p. 220.

the agony of Christianity; his pragmatic approach to the question of the validity of beliefs; his desperate encounter with hope in despair; his very early discovery of Kierkegaard (when only those who could read Danish, as Unamuno could, knew of his work); his rejection of Hegel, from whom nevertheless he kept the central concept of consciousness as struggle; his systematic destruction of the forms of the nineteenth-century novel, and his utilization of fiction as a way of knowledge in which the experience of the presence of others is relived through the imagination; his defense of poetry; and, above all, his insistence on speaking mostly about himself (for there is no abstract "I," but only the concrete man of flesh and bones)—in all these and related matters Unamuno was for a long time in Europe, if not totally (i.e., "quixotically") alone, in very select company as against the dominant trends of his time, the leftovers from idealism and positivism.

Even more "quixotic" (perhaps absurd and even, as he said, ridiculous) was his claim that it was meant for Spain, and for him in particular among Spaniards, to show the way to Europe, to "illuminate [Europe's] mind against the darkness of Logic,"[25] to, as he expressed it, conquer Europe and "Hispanize" it.

That eventually, twenty or thirty years later—and after two wars—Europe, in one of the two philosophies that matter today, came around to the questions that matter, that is to say, to Unamuno's questions, is of no significance here: the enterprise *then* was indeed absurd, ridiculous, and "quixotic." And it was the kind of enterprise from which legends are made, especially when the man behind the legend was in his own country opposed to (and opposed by) those who, like him before them, were now trying to make Spain more "European." And very especially when this man not only wrote in daily papers and monthly journals, but lectured at universities and in public squares and concerned himself with political questions in a liberal, progressive, and even radical manner,[26] while he taught Greek at the University of Salamanca and was its president for eleven years, during which time he tried so many basic reforms that he ended up

[25] *Obras*, IV, 378 (*LDQ*, p. 322).
[26] Cf. Unamuno's letter to Ortega of November 21, 1912, now published in *Revista de Occidente*, Año II, 2ª época, no. 19 (Oct., 1964), pp. 19–22.

by antagonizing not only his colleagues but the Minister of Education, who finally deposed him from this presidency, which act, in turn, provoked a widespread protest by Spanish intellectuals during which the legend continued to grow.

"There will be silence in Spain for a long time to come,"[27] wrote Ortega after Unamuno's death, for, indeed, there was no silence from Unamuno during the long years of self-creation in which he developed the habit of autoanalysis which led him to write such things as ". . . the myth drowns the mortal personage, and even acts upon him, forcing him to do this or that";[28] or, "I am a myth that I go on creating day after day as, with back turned to what is to come, I am borne toward the morrow, toward the abyss. My job is to create my myth, to create myself as myth";[29] or, "I am only a fancy of the hero of my story."[30]

1924: THE FINAL CRISIS

But the definitive experience of the problem does not begin for Unamuno until 1924 when, as might be expected, a purely historical event finally throws him into the most anguishing complexities of the antagonism inner-outer, eternity-time, authenticity-appearance (image). The experience begins, as we all know, when he is exiled by the then dictator of Spain, Primo de Rivera, to the island of Fuerteventura, and Unamuno asks himself whether he is not perhaps playing now the role of the exile, putting a mask on his authentic self in order to leave a name in history. "I now play the role of the exile," he writes. "Even my present sloppy appearance [el descuidado desaliño de mi persona] . . . depends on the role I am playing. . . . Am I acting out a melodrama even for my relatives?"[31]

But how was Unamuno to avoid playing the role of the exile if, according to the best of traditions, he had been put by the

[27] José Ortega y Gasset, Obras completas (Madrid: Revista de Occidente, 1961), V, 266.

[28] Obras, III, 384 n. 2.

[29] Quoted by Manuel García Blanco in Miguel de Unamuno y sus poesías, Acta Salmanticensia: Filosofía y Letras, t. VIII (Salamanca: Universidad de Salamanca, 1954), p. 178.

[30] Obras, II, 779.

[31] Ibid., X, 884.

dictator in that role? He had been taken off one stage and placed on another, precisely on an island, the scenery conventionally given to public figures whom governments wish to, literally, *isolate*. I find an almost unbelievably perfect poetic justice in the fact that this man who had meditated so much on Robinson Crusoe and the concept of isolation, this man who had so needed others, should now begin his most ambiguous and difficult role on an island. But, had he not been brought up in the Calderonian idea that it is man's function to play his given role properly? And had not Augusto Pérez, the character of his novel *Niebla*, almost managed to escape the world of fiction by accepting a role and playing it to the hilt?[32] The temptation to emulate the likes of Victor Hugo was too great and Unamuno fell, or, perhaps one should say, accepted its consequences. The island, after all, was the perfect place from which to defy others, the King and the Dictator, and to transform, once and for all, the for-itself into a for-others by making his absence present and unavoidable on the Spanish scene. And thus, in Fuerteventura, Unamuno wrote violent political poems, letters, and pamphlets which he published outside Spain. Yet when a Madrid newspaper offered him the opportunity to continue writing in the Peninsula, he accepted immediately; but since, obviously, he could not write there against the Dictator, what he wrote for "Los Lunes de *El Imparcial*" is a series of articles on style! These articles have generally been overlooked by students of Unamuno,[33] and yet they are most important because they are the strongest expression to that date of his surrender, or his commitment, to the idea that man is his historical image.

This conclusion is based on the most common of notions about style: style reveals, and therefore is, a man's personality.[34] There is no style without personality, and no personality where one does not represent a historical role.[35] The secret—and here the echoes of Calderón are clear—is in discovering what role one has been

[32] Cf. my article "Unamuno's *Niebla*: Existence and the Game of Fiction," *Modern Language Notes*, LXXIX (1964), 188–205.

[33] In his *Unamuno en su "nivola"* (Madrid: Taurus, 1960), p. 343 and *passim*, Armando F. Zubizarreta does refer to these articles.

[34] *Obras*, XI, 795.

[35] *Ibid.*, p. 796.

assigned; when that is done, one finds oneself and one's style.[36] And then, one becomes historical.[37] Furthermore, this historicity is arrived at, of course, through the relationship with others: "No one can know himself through himself alone [*nadie se conoce sino en los demás*]," Unamuno wrote.[38] "Even though the image of ours which is projected in the . . . eyes of others may be very small, it is the seed of the knowledge we have of ourselves."[39]

It is quite true that the "works of a writer that do not seem to be his, that lack style, that seem to belong to another, are nobody's, they are not works. The 'another' is nobody."[40] But, he insisted: "One finds oneself through the others."[41] "And when one finds oneself it is because he has found his work [*obra*]; it is because his work has made *him*."[42] And thus: "Of the truly immortal person, of the one who will be a word, a phrase, a strophe of God's poem . . . don't ever say, 'He died,' when he has died; but say rather, 'He lived,' when he is dead. For he who lived, lives, and will live."[43] "Will live," that is, *in history*, I may add, for Unamuno, like Hegel, believed at this point that history was the development of God's Idea. That this is what Unamuno meant may be confirmed by rereading from a page written a little more than a year before (in April, 1923), when at the height of his fame before the exile he commented on Schopenhauer's idea that the phrase "what one represents" means "how the others represent us as being." Unamuno wrote: ". . . what one is, is only a representation: one is what others imagine one to be. . . . To be is to be for oneself [*para sí*], and to be for oneself is to be for others. He who is not for others, he who lacks representation, is not. . . . And when he looks at himself in the mirror, he does not see himself. The animal that one is simply is; the person that one is [*se es*], is for others. And this person is the historical man, he who acts his role on the stage."[44]

[36] *Ibid.*, p. 797.
[37] *Ibid.*, p. 799.
[38] *Ibid.*, p. 800.
[39] *Ibid.*
[40] *Ibid.*, p. 836.
[41] *Ibid.*, p. 839.
[42] *Ibid.*
[43] *Ibid.*, p. 841.
[44] *Ibid.*, V, 1191–1192.

We might, at this point, remember the parallel between these
conclusions and Sartre's basic statements on the subject; and,
of course, we should be aware of their common source, to be
found, for instance, in these words of Hegel: "Self-consciousness is real only in so far as it recognizes its echo (and its reflection) in another,"[45] an idea related to the distinction Hegel
makes between the animal and human forms of being, exactly
Unamuno's distinction.[46]

But, we are still far from Unamuno's definitive stand on the
question, since at this point (1924) his "historicity" was playing
against that other way of being of his which he called his "contemplative self,"[47] expressed even now in beautiful pantheistic
poems in which a world harmony similar to that of his childhood
is found again. And, also, because there must be limits to a
man's histrionic exercises if he is to continue keeping some hold
on himself as something more than an "object" for others. And
so, when the owners of a French magazine hired a yacht to
"rescue" Unamuno from Fuerteventura and Unamuno accepted
their offer to escape to France, he became truly suspicious of his
role as exile, for the well-publicized, melodramatic "escape" con-
verted him, for French audiences (and for the semicultured
European readers in general), into the symbol of Spain's political tragedy. He had often pretended to be a new Quixote; and,
as a result of his escape, he came to be rhetorically called a
modern "Quichotte" fighting for his nation's freedom. He had
often claimed to represent Spain; after the escape, he was made
to represent it (in opposition to the official representatives). In
spite of the fact that his friends and readers knew, or should
have known, of his other preoccupations (of his contemplative
self, for instance),[48] his image is flattened out and he is made to
pass for what he hated most: a man of only one piece (*un hombre
de una sola pieza*). From the moment he arrived in Paris—a

[45] As quoted by Sartre from Hegel's *Propedeutic* in *Being and Nothingness*, p. 237.
[46] Cf. *The Logic of Hegel*, sec. 24, in particular pp. 47–48.
[47] Cf. my *El Unamuno contemplativo* (Mexico: El Colegio de México,
1959).
[48] Although, of course, the idea the French reading public had of Unamuno at the time was very limited and simple.

city loaded with history, as he was to complain—his image inevitably grew in only one direction and he found himself returning to the questions that we might think he had solved in
the essays of April, 1923, and later, in the essays on style, when
it seemed so traditionally easy to be "isolated." "Am I not," he
exclaimed in Paris, "about to sacrifice my intimate self, the one
I am in God, the one I must be, to the other one, to the historical
self, to the one that moves about in its history and with its history?"[49]

But although the pages of *Cómo se hace una novela* ("How a
Novel Is Made" or "How To Write a Novel"), the book written
in Paris in an effort to objectivize his conflict, abound in such
questions and in tortured paradoxes that pretend to answer the
questions but only echo the agony of the writer, finally the turmoil of history—banquets, interviews, political meetings, pam-
phleteering—forced Unamuno to a categorical answer: "Am I
a hypocrite?" he asked. "No! My role is my truth and I must
live my truth, which is my life."[50] And if anyone should think,
as he did, that this idea of historical action is propitious for the
creation of legends, Unamuno will answer that "there is a legend
of reality that is the substance, the inner reality of reality itself."[51]
And then: ". . . if I do not create my legend I will die altogether,"[52] because the "essence of a man like that of a nation is
his history." It is quite true, he continues, that "this legend, this
history, devours me," but it is also rigorously true that "when it
is over I shall be over with it."[53]

Unamuno was growing old, and there was for him less and less
future, less liberty left as he discovered that he was what he had
done. Nicodemus' question to Christ which he had so beautifully
glossed in 1898, "How can a man cease to be himself and become another," how can he be born anew,[54] could not even be
asked any more: there was no time left for a new act of re-cre-
ation. And thus, already speaking of himself in the third person,

[49] *Obras*, X, 882.
[50] *Ibid.*, p. 884.
[51] *Ibid.*, p. 863.
[52] *Ibid.*, p. 882.
[53] *Ibid.*, pp. 863–864.
[54] *Ibid.*, III, 130–132.

he wrote: "The Unamuno of my legend, of my novel . . . this Unamuno gives me life and death, this Unamuno creates me and destroys me, he sustains me and he drowns me. He is my agony."[55]

The conclusion has been reached, but by force, and hence the paradoxical expressions, the effort at fusing all contraries, but no harmonious synthesis; hence the precision with which Unamuno writes the crucial word of all his works: "agony." Agony, as we know, is the struggle of contraries, in which struggle between the for-itself and *all* otherness, especially, of course, death, man encounters his awareness of existence. And so the original question, "Am I as I believe myself to be or am I as the others believe me to be?" loses all meaning in the face of the inevitable fact that when our legend is no more, we disappear with it. "Any man who is really a man, is the son of a legend, written or oral. And no more than a legend, that is to say, a novel."[56]

And so we understand that Jugo de la Raza, the would-be character of *Cómo se hace una novela* should never be able to force the creation of a novel out of the would-be novelist for, as Unamuno explains, Jugo de la Raza is not really a man "because he lives only in himself, in the insignificant 'I' below history, in the sad self that has not become a novel. And that is precisely why he likes to read novels."[57] In the reading of novels Jugo de la Raza can alienate himself and live in another's historical dimension, from which passive act he expects perhaps to become like Don Quixote, mad enough to go out into the world in order to gain, like Don Quixote, the fame that only in true existence can be had. And so when Jugo de la Raza finds one day in Paris a novel that absorbs him, he surrenders to it so completely that there comes a moment in which "he could no longer live without the book . . . ; his life, his intimate existence, his reality had become finally and irrevocably united to that of the character in the novel."[58]

[55] *Ibid.*, X, 865.
[56] *Ibid.*, p. 916.
[57] *Ibid.*, p. 866.
[58] *Ibid.*, p. 868.

Yet, the would-be novelist tries to imagine a way by which Jugo de la Raza might still try to escape from the truth. "My Jugo," he writes, "would give up the book. . . . in order to escape from the fatal reading he would go back to his homeland, . . . and there he would find his very childhood, his eternal childhood, the age at which he still could not read, in which he was not yet a man of books. And there he would find his inner man."[59] But, obviously, it cannot be done and the would-be novelist, obsessed with *his* own self, is incapable of creating such a reality for Jugo de la Raza: both are committed to external history and, like Unamuno, Jugo de la Raza cannot escape from the otherness that absorbs him and gives him life as he returns, again and again, to the book, to the fiction by which he lives, for "the inner man, the intra man . . . , when he becomes a reader, becomes thereby an author, that is to say, an actor."[60]

And so the question of authenticity and the image is resolved radically: ". . . a historical man? A real man? An actor of the drama of life? A fictional character? He shows his entrails in his face. Or, to put it in another way, his entrails [*intranea*], his insides, are his 'ex-trails' [*extranea*], his outsides: his form is his content."[61] And again: "What seems to be an extrascenic reality is a comedy of the comedy, a novel of the novel . . . and Kant's noumenon is the most phenomenal thing there can be, and substance the most formal. The bottom of a thing is its surface."[62] All of which is, after so many years, a return to a basic Hegelian idea, further explored in the 1928 preface to *The Life of Don Quixote and Sancho* where Unamuno distinguishes between *ser* ("to be") and *existir* ("to exist"), a verb meaning originally (and Hegel also used the argument) "to exsist," "to be out of oneself."[63] History is alienation, in which

[59] *Ibid.*, p. 906.
[60] *Ibid.*, p. 911.
[61] *Ibid.*, p. 917.
[62] *Ibid.*, pp. 895–896.
[63] "*Ex-sistere* means 'to be' (*sistere*) 'out of oneself' (*ex*). And one exists only for the others" (*Obras*, IX, 829). And it must be emphasized that the association between "to exist" and "to be mad" ("alienated; out of oneself") is *also* made by Unamuno, in relation, precisely, to Don Quixote, in the preface to *Cómo se hace una novela* (*Obras*, X, 850).

concept is implied, of course, a never-ending struggle. The unity of the inner and the outer forms of being is, therefore, an *agonic* unity, to be recognized as such. We must not think when Unamuno writes in 1934 that "what I once called intrahistory is history proper, its entrails,"[64] he has reached Ortega's conclusion on the same subject, for the difference is a vital one: the abyss that there is between tranquil, and even joyful, acceptance of a fact in Ortega[65] and an anguishing personal discovery of it, an anguish deepened by the suspicion that a man's historicity, his image, is, indeed, no more than a novelistic fiction.

Afterward it was said that existence precedes essence and that man has no nature but history; Ortega also wrote that a man's life is the novel he writes of himself; and recently we have even had in Sartre's *Les mots* an autobiography turned beautifully, inevitably, into a novel. Unamuno would have approved (as he would have approved of Sartre's even more recent contribution to his legend, the rejection of the Nobel Prize), but regretfully; for throughout his life he tried to either separate or harmonize the intrahistorical and the historical, the eternal and the temporal, the inner and the outer, the true being and the image; the authenticity of his self in God and his desire to, as he put it, "be looked at, and be admired and to leave a name!"[66] Yet his efforts always resolved themselves in living proofs of the fact that existence is a never-ending struggle of contraries, for "this is the art of living in history,"[67] where "alas, there is no peace without war!"[68]

---

[64] Quoted by Antonio Sánchez Barbudo in "El misterio de la personalidad de Unamuno," *Revista de la Universidad de Buenos Aires*, 4ª época, t. VII, vol. 1 (July–Sept., 1950), pp. 214–215.

[65] Writes Ortega: "Let us renounce valiantly, joyously, this convenient presumption that the real is logical and recognize that thought alone is logical" (*Toward a Philosophy of History*, p. 196).

[66] Also quoted by Sánchez Barbudo, "El misterio de la personalidad de Unamuno," pp. 249–250.

[67] *Obras*, X, 919.

[68] *Ibid.*, p. 922.

5

MORAL PSYCHOLOGY IN UNAMUNO
Paul Ilie

By moral psychology I mean the relationship between the psychological motivation of an individual and the formation of his value judgments. This definition takes into account the structure of personality and its reflective mechanisms, insofar as they influence the ethical position of the conscious mind. To think of Unamuno as a moral psychologist is to include him among such philosophers as La Rochefoucauld, Pascal, and Nietzsche, and to associate his method of valuation with the technique—not the ideas—of *The Genealogy of Morals*, the classical work of this genre. The purpose of my discussion is to determine the kind of moral psychology that operates in Unamuno's writings. I will begin with an analysis of *desdoblamiento* ("separation from self"), and then go on to the appearance of *el otro* ("the other"), examining after this the concept of the *satánico yo* ("satanic ego"), and ending with a survey of Unamuno's ethics of ambiguity.

The highest psychological value for Unamuno is self-knowledge. This is achieved by means of self-consciousness developed during the state of *ensimismamiento* ("self-absorption"). The individual begins to contemplate himself as if he were another person, thus initiating the process of *desdoblamiento*. His self-awareness consists of the fact that one part of him withdraws in order to watch the behavior of another part of him, with the result that he finds himself observing an ego fragment removed from him as an objectified, exterior, social self. The structure of this condition involves the process of rational dissociation. What happens is the following: The individual has a basic, integrated

72

self that exists in the world even before he becomes aware that it is there. This undifferentiated self is a prereflective phenomenon called the *precogito*. When the precogito undergoes *desdoblamiento*, the result is a differentiation into a self-in-the-world and a consciousness of that self. This reflective awareness of the self-in-the-world is called the *cogito*. When the cogito emerges, it comes to understand that it is able to know everything about the self except its own nature. As a consciousness, it cannot reflect upon itself. This is a terrible realization for the individual, for it weakens his confidence in whatever knowledge he has of himself. If the cogito cannot know itself, how reliable is its information about other parts of the self? And if the cogito remains unknown, who can say what tendencies, for good or for evil, are potentially within its capacity?

The result of this uncertainty is that the cogito can develop into a divisive agent, turning the fragments of the self against one another. For example, once the individual is aware that only part of him is a social self and that another part of him is watching this entity perform, he begins to question the legitimacy of each fragment in turn. He examines one self from the point of view of the other, and vacillates between them. The cogito is always the center of activity for these doubts, and it is this faculty that executes the role of the disrupter of ego harmony. At this point Unamuno begins to refer to the presence of a *satánico yo*. The cogito instigates the man against the components of his self, undermining the security that each element had enjoyed prior to being subjected to self-conscious analysis. This impulse to doubt has its source in an overactive self-awareness, but the *satánico yo* makes its appearance after the cogito has taken sides. That is, when the cogito adopts a given perspective and decides that the other alienated fragments are not part of the individual's real self, the repudiation is said to be made by the *satánico yo*. The cogito, in other words, is really a psychological field rather than a "self," and it confers legitimacy on the *satánico yo* by articulating the latter's feelings. Once the mechanism of self-awareness is localized to the viewpoint of a specific fragment, the cogito can say "I am," thus identifying itself as a faculty residing in a particular "self." This localization is possible for the perspectives of many selves, but only in the instance of the *satánico yo* is a self-consciousness so exacerbated that the entire ego structure is imperiled.

The actual process of subversion by the *satánico yo* is direct and simple. The reflective faculty has the ability to say "I," but knows when doing so it destroys the authenticity of the other parts of the self. These other fragments cannot say "I" at the same time that they are being objectified, and, having lost their capacity for self-identification, are contemplated as disconnected objects instead of as components of an integrated self. Since the *satánico yo* acts as an interstitial corrosive in this ego disintegration, it must be considered as an evil force: "It is said that the enemies of the soul are three: the world, the devil, and the flesh; but it is necessary to add a fourth and worse enemy: the soul itself—unless this enemy, which others call the satanic ego, is already included within the devil. The satanic ego is dangerous while we keep it enclosed, contemplating itself, and re-creating itself in this contemplation."[1]

Unamuno calls this influence "satanic" because it questions the individual's motivation in every respect. As soon as an action or feeling becomes objectified, its sincerity is placed in doubt and an adverse moral judgment is attached to it. This is true for any social act in which the individual watches his own performance, and especially when he is aware of being virtuous. In this light, one can say that even a saint is acting out a part, and, indeed, Unamuno writes that "saintliness does not transcend the stage setting." The saint exalts his role as if it were truly his personality, and he suppresses any awareness of the fact that he is acting: "The suffocation of the satanic ego (why satanic?) is the supreme affirmation of personality."[2] The thought that he is only a performer comes as an ugly intrusion upon his feeling of virtue, and so he terms this disturbing thought diabolical.

But is it? asks Unamuno. Upon reflection, his answer is to admit that the *satánico yo* is indeed a harmful and divisive agent, but that it cannot be judged to be evil. Instead, claims Unamuno, the fact is that all ethical values arising from the process of *des-*

[1] *Obras*, III, 818.
[2] *Ibid.*, V, 1193–1194.

doblamiento are suspect. Whether they represent the "good" side of an individual or his so-called evil inclination, the very occurrence of these values in a psychologically splintered state of mind is sufficient reason to doubt the authenticity of one over another; and in any event, the psychological process that produces them is much more fundamental to the individual's nature than are the values themselves. Man, by definition, is made of contradictions; hence the supreme importance of personality structure. On the other hand, moral judgments are useful only to the degree to which they are not subjected to the faculty of self-awareness. They are genetically dependent upon psychology, and so are second in importance to it. To examine values during "internal struggles with the evil enemy" is to invert them. By casting doubt on an attitude and on the self that embraces it, the *yo enemigo* ("ego-enemy") not only overthrows a set of values, but appears to establish itself as an immoral agent, the adversary of conventional ethical positions. Furthermore, it suppresses the hope that reliable standards of behavior can be found and adhered to; and, most of all, it betrays the individual as an actor, an impostor, a hypocrite.

The result of this state of mind is that the individual begins to feel alienated from himself, and he is anguished over what amounts to a partial loss of self. In contrast, the man who is most fully himself is the one who lacks a reflective mechanism, for this inability to reflect permits him to be unaware of himself and of others. His absorption within himself is so complete that there is no way for him to draw apart for self-contemplation: "The man of absorbing individuality hardly . . . notices himself." This unawareness characterizes the state of plenitude, in which the individual is so filled with self that there is no room for an "other" entity to enter and displace part of it: ". . . it is to the fact that each one is filled with himself that you have to attribute the little or no interest that the rest receive from us."[3]

This fullness-of-self is not a contemplative condition, however, and so there is no subject-object structuring within it. But as soon as consciousness begins to operate reflexively, the loss of self is immediate. This is true because alienation consists of

[3] *Ibid.*, pp. 379–380.

objectifying part of the self, thus estranging it from the rest of
the ego: and also, because this objectified fragment, now called
el otro, has turned into a *possession* of the self. It has lost its
subjective relationship and is now an object.

Similarly, when the individual attempts to act in the exterior
world, he is removed from possessing himself, and if he "has to
make use of his body or of other bodies, he remains bound to
their rigid laws; he is a slave." He is bound to the conditions and
qualities of these objects, so that even when they are his posses-
sions they are never fully his, in the sense of being integrated into
his plenitude of self. (" 'My acts,' he thinks, 'are never exclusively mine: if I speak, I have to make use of air that isn't mine
to produce my voice; and, as a matter of fact, not even my vocal
cords are mine. . . .' And he adds: 'I myself, am I mine?' "[4]) In
other words, the subject-object relationship, by definition, consists of the object's independence, even though the subject may
possess it; but the contemplating self is unable to admit that the
self under observation can achieve an objectified state and still
be genuinely part of the individual ("Am I mine?"). The fact is
that the alienated self still does belong to him, but not in the old
subjective way. It has lost its identity with the subject, and therefore cannot be accepted as anything but a spurious ego fragment.
The individual is capable of consciousness by virtue of his subjective self, not the alienated, contemplated self. In short, the
alienated self cannot be identified with the self's subjectivity, and
since selfness means subjectiveness, this other self must indeed
be an *otro*.

Thus *el otro* emerges from the initial fact that "each one is no
more than his own first neighbor",[5] but the effect upon the individual is to make him feel depersonalized. Part of his identity
has been transformed into something that is perceived by his
consciousness but no longer partakes of it. Both his private
efforts to know himself and his activities in the world lead to a
surrender of the part of his ego which is thus objectified. Unamuno sees the situation in terms of a "tragic struggle" between
him and the external world, he trying to personalize it and to

[4] *Ibid.*, III, 705 (*ESS*, p. 175).
[5] *Ibid.*, p. 195.

avoid being depersonalized by it in turn. Within the context of personality, he is attempting to preserve the unity of his consciousness while acting in the world, and at the same time not acquiring the objective qualities of that world. This, of course, is impossible unless one is willing to completely avoid all action and awareness. What happens, therefore, is that "whatever I say, write, and do, I have to say, write, and do by means of the world; and so immediately the world depersonalizes it and makes it its own, and I appear to be another than I am."[6]

Consequently, *el otro* is both a psychological product of alienation and the social alter ego that the individual uses in order to participate in the world. But since activity is an external form, *el otro* loses its identity with the originally integral self. And since Unamuno cannot be conscious from within this objective self, it must perforce appear to him as an "other." Unamuno feared this depersonalization because it meant ceasing to be what he had been in order to become someone else. This loss of self would be an ontological loss, since his being would be nullified and supplanted by another being. In other words, the change is tantamount to losing one's being altogether, because one ceases to be what he has always been: ". . . for me, to make myself another, breaking the unity and the continuity of my life, is to cease being the one I am; that is to say, it is simply to cease being. And this I can not do."[7]

The problem is expressed dramatically in Joaquín Monegro's strange psychic fragmentation. In him are found all the ramifications of the alienation theme, including the fact that it is a condition of involuntary differentiation. That is, *el otro* is the ego fragment that, free of volitional stricture, is the least likely to be viewed as originating in the self. It appears in the last phase of depersonalization, where an intimate segment of the ego is lost through the inability or the unwillingness of the individual to recognize that he himself is its source. *El otro* represents an alternative personality, either a different self for which the individual strives, or the result of an ego transformation during

---

[6] *Ibid.*, p. 706 (*ESS*, p. 176).
[7] *Ibid.*, XVI, 137 (*TSL*, p. 11). The same idea is also expressed in *Abel Sánchez* (*Obras*, II, 1090; *ABS*, pp. 103–104).

desdoblamiento. Joaquín refers to both types in a conversation with his daughter: " 'It makes you happy to hear me say that I will be another?' 'Yes, Papa, it makes me happy!' 'You mean to say that the other, that the other, the one that I am, displeases you?' "[8] The "other" person, the "one that I am," is Joaquín the hater, a man whom Joaquín does not recognize as himself because his moral (i.e., conscious) self resists the idea. His plan to be someone else ("I will be another") is not a conversion to a new state as nonhater, but a reversion to the original, nonhating Joaquín.

Joaquín compounds the significance of *el otro* with extrapersonal associations. The companion to his anguish is "the constant presence of the other, of Abel, in his spirit," a presence inseparable from "the sad, ailing conscience that presented itself to him."[9] The interdependence of Abel "el otro" and Joaquín's awareness of him turns into an ambiguous identity of the two. *El otro* becomes an irrational replacement for the anguished, conscious self: ". . . in his solitude, he never succeeded in being alone; the other was always there. The other! He reached the point of catching himself in dialogue with him, contriving what the other was saying to him . . . in these solitary dialogues, in these dialogic monologues."[10] With this ambiguity comes a confusion in the perception of *el otro*: Does Joaquín hold a mental dialogue with another person or a mono-dialogue with himself? The question is futile, since Joaquín appropriates Abel into his own awareness, fusing Abel "el otro" with the self as "otro." In fact, the use of the Cain-Abel myth reinforces the ambiguity, because in Unamuno's own mind the brothers' roles are reversible, and in each individual the characteristics of both men are found in equal proportion.

Thus moral and psychological principles become analogs in the analysis of human behavior. The fruit of introspection is an alienated self that, through the technique of transference, enables the subject to engage itself ethically with its neighbor. *El otro* is the objective self which the individual comes to know and, one

[8] *Obras*, II, 1095 (*ABS*, p. 109).
[9] *Ibid.*, p. 1068 (*ABS*, pp. 76–77).
[10] *Ibid.*, pp. 1068–1069 (*ABS*, pp. 77–78).

would hope, to love, and which becomes identified with the neighbor as *el otro* by virtue of common moral traits. Thus, while alienation may be a final psychic state, it is also a means for achieving ethical goals: "Become absorbed in yourself in order to become alienated from yourself." In other words, "becoming absorbed in yourself, you go inside of yourself and move forward through the shadowy, intimate galleries of your soul; and you don't know when you have left your own spiritual substratum to enter your neighbor's."[11]

This is why Unamuno was so fond of such biblical myths as the Cain-Abel and Jacob-Esau rivalries. He found that in all men the most fundamental human emotions are distributed equally ("spiritual substratum"), as are the basic psychological mechanisms. It is thus an easy transition from one's own *otro* to that of another person by means of the "shadowy, intimate galleries." The deeper into the subliminal areas one penetrates, the closer to identity the two *otros* approach. Passions such as envy, hate, and love are too primitive to be differentiated by personality, and for this reason Unamuno uses them as emotions to illustrate the emergence of *el otro*, "the other."

This much being said for psychology, we may now take up the matter of moral judgments. To begin with, Unamuno's overall value system falls safely within the Judaeo-Christian ethic. There is no doubt that he would have repudiated Nietzsche's transvaluation if he had been confronted with a choice between it and this tradition. Nevertheless, there are a considerable number of instances where Unamuno makes some dangerous suggestions about value judgments, and these are what I propose to study here, in the light of what has already been said.

Unamuno's fundamental attitude toward ethics is irrational. Rationalism in moral philosophy is for him futile, and if attempted, becomes absurd. It imposes a rigorous pattern of behavior which conditions the spontaneity of human nature. Its worst form, moral theology, forces action into a harness of consistency, with the result that man betrays himself by exchanging sincerity for consistent appearance. Above all, ethical

11 *Ibid.*, IX, 842.

intellectualism is a category external to the structure of man's conduct, and "to be consistent usually means to be hypocritical; and this hypocrisy finally poisons the very springs of intimate moral life."[12]

Despite the subjectivity of this axiology, its context is always social. Moral behavior is opposed to the selfish interests of solitude, and indeed makes "an immense paradox—or rather, a great, tragic countersense—[out of] the whole morality consisting totally of submission and quietism."[13] For Unamuno, the self must be judged by its interaction with other selves. It is absurd to speak of morality or consistency in isolation; but how do interacting selves adhere each to its "intimate moral life" without causing anarchy? By refusing to consider Christian ethics to be a slave morality that prevents freedom of action ("anarchism") and by embracing instead "panarchism," "not that concept of neither God nor master, but rather gods and masters all, struggling to become divine, to become immortal, and, to this end, dominating the rest."[14] Thus, even within a Christian framework, absolute or rational value judgments are untenable because they are unrelated to the individual needs of human nature.

This attitude toward valuation leads to a methodology that dispenses with logic in favor of antithesis. By ignoring the conventional search for an unequivocal idea or answer to an issue, Unamuno allows himself to entertain antithetical or even paradoxical statements in which both elements are recognized as true. For example, if he constructs a polarity between Tolstoy's morality of renunciation and Nietzsche's of striving, he sees no necessity to resolve or synthesize the opposites. He simply sets them side by side with the explanation that life itself "is bound with antitheses and antinomies." Thus "one can profess and even practice the two moralities (Two? Is there more than one?) at the same time; and one can struggle while resigning himself, and can become resigned while struggling."[15]

Unamuno uses a similar technique to form a moral judgment,

12 *Ibid.*, III, 1047.
13 *Ibid.*, XVI, 409 (*TSL*, p. 286).
14 *Ibid.*, p. 407 (*TSL*, 283–284).
15 *Ibid.*, XI, 169.

and he views a situation as a composite of opposing positions. Here, an entity is knowable only by its antithesis, or at least by the cause that precedes it. An act, for example, is said to be a sin because a law exists prohibiting it. The act in itself is neutral; what makes it sinful is the prohibition: "He never recognized the sin except for the law; he would not have known liberalism if the law hadn't said to him: liberalism is a sin. The sin, through the existence of a commandment, renewed the rebelliousness of Pérez' blood; because without the law the sin was dead. Juan Pérez lived without law for some time, but when the commandment came, the sin came to life again."[16] A sin, therefore, even a political sin, is not a quality of the act but an independent judgment about it whose existence can be determined only by that which forbids it to exist. This prohibitional entity, while not exactly an opposing quality, is closely enough identified with it to be considered antithetical as far as method is concerned.

This same technique produces some disturbing results when Unamuno, by thinking of the antithesis of a statement, undermines the entire validity of the position conveyed therein. Take, for example, the situation in *Abel Sánchez*, where Joaquín's maid receives his violent blasphemy with gentleness and humility. He judges her refusal to react not as virtue but as arrogance, and when she denies this, he shouts, "You see? It is hypocritical pride not to recognize it. She is practicing on me, at my expense, exercises of humility and patience; she uses my accesses of bad humor like a hair shirt to do exercises in the virtue of patience." In this instance there is ostensibly a single and absolute term: the act of humility, the moral judgment of which is "virtue." But such virtue is recognizable if it stands in contrast to some opposite value. If Joaquín were not present to exemplify arrogance, it would be impossible to judge the servant as virtuous. Joaquín thus converts a self-sufficient entity into one term of the antithesis humility-arrogance, or virtue-sin. But if this humility can exist only as a function of its opposite, what is its ethical merit? None, says Joaquín, who protests that he is being used as an "instrument to make merits for heaven, [which is] hypocrisy!"[17] In fact, the

16 *Ibid.*, II, 676–677.
17 *Ibid.*, p. 1063 (*ABS*, p. 71).

implication is that to ignore the true nature of humility is itself the worst kind of arrogance, for it is self-deceptive.

Unamuno clearly understood the role of revaluator played by Joaquín, and years later proclaimed how vastly superior morally Joaquín was to all Abels.[18] Unamuno was arguing for a new ethical perspective that would see behind every gain someone else's loss, and behind every evil a compensating good dependent upon it. "Good" men were really evil because they caused "evil" men to suffer, and "those who believe that they are just are usually the arrogant ones who are going to humiliate others with the ostentation of their justice. Someone has already said that there are no greater scoundrels than honorable people." This reversal of Christian valuations was made, however, with an ulterior Christian motive. It was wrong in Unamuno's eyes for any mortal to cause his fellowman pain. Thus he reasoned that "the Abels have invented hell for the Cains because, if not, their glory would result in insipidity. Their bliss is in seeing others suffer when they themselves are free from suffering."[19]

The final aspect of this antithetical method is to inquire into the means by which goodness is achieved. Here too the answer is that the temple of virtue is supported by pillars of vice. From this standpoint it is clear that one man may use his neighbor as a stairway to paradise, cultivating another man's weaknesses in order to increase thereby his own supposed merits. Unamuno wonders "if this isn't perhaps an abominable doctrine: the tacit belief that it is necessary to have bad people so that the good ones can act, offenses to make pardon possible, poor people for charity, and iniquity to promote meekness."[20] If this is truly an ethic of instrumentalism, then its worth would collapse with the removal of the instruments; but since it is impossible to make the latter disappear, it must be conceded that the so-called un-virtuous also possess virtue, not just negatively but in a direct structural relationship to the realization of "goodness."

Unamuno's revisionist attitude toward ethics constituted a deeper radicalism in method than in value. Nevertheless, his

18 *Ibid.*, p. 1006.
19 *Ibid.*, p. 1042 (*ABS*, pp. 46–47).
20 *Ibid.*, IX, 148.

particular conception of what the Christian ethic entails often led him to a transvaluation that obscured his Christian intent. For example, the traditional interpretations of the roles of Cain and Abel become reversed as soon as the effect of remorse on the killer is seen as a suffering equivalent to the victim's death. The slain victim is borne by conscience and memory within the slayer's mind and continues each day an implacable, deadly assault. Abel is therefore the evil one because of his psychological murder of Cain: ". . . Abel is killing me. Abel, what are you doing to your brother? He who becomes a victim is as evil as the one who becomes a murderer. To make oneself a victim is a diabolical revenge."[21]

Thus, to Unamuno, it is not morally perverse to consider the slayer as a victim of the slain, since the latter has in fact executed a kind of punishment on him. Indeed, there is no difference between the brothers: they are both victims and victors. True Christian judgment, based on compassion, dissolves the conventional moral distinction between the two: "The murderer believes himself the victim; he carries inside him the cadaver of the victim, and this is his pain. . . . I love Cain as much as Abel . . . and I love Abel as a possible Cain, as a Cain in desire. . . . How honor weighs on the shoulders of the honorable! Just as vice does on the shoulders of the vicious."[22] Good and evil thus become reversible functions, each one, like "faces of a single figure," forming with its counterpart a complete entity.

At the same time, these individual examples are not the only ones in which reversibility appears as a genetic principle that permits one value to be seen as originating from its opposite. There is another factor involved, the contrast between individual and collective moralities. Unamuno often finds that what people are prohibited from doing as individuals is sanctioned for the group. When Unamuno must choose, therefore, in the light of social justice, between criminal individuals and our own "pharisaic societies," he declares that "we feel inclined to pardon and even to like bandits like Roque Guinart, because there is no duplicity or falsity in them, and their bands appear to be precisely what

21 *Ibid.*, XIII, 828.
22 *Ibid.*, XII, 859–860.

they are."[23] Going further, he says: "Thus it can be said of every manner of human justice that it issued from injustice, from the necessity of the latter to be sustained and perpetuated. Justice and order were born in the world to maintain violence and disorder."[24]

Unamuno's heterodoxy in the analytical form of his valuations, consequently, consists of his turning traditionally "immoral" results into sources of morality, while converting traditionally "moral" precepts into the consequences of immoral sources. But he goes even further, and judges a moral act in terms of the agent's motivations, sometimes doubting the latter's good intentions. For example, when Don Quixote is caged by the priest and the barber, Unamuno attributes the deed to "envy disguised as charity, the envy of prudent men who can't bear heroic madness, the envy that has established common sense as a tyrannic leveler."[25] He tries to determine whether the virtue in question is being practiced in a virtuous way, and he seeks psychological explanations, rather than evidences of good work. The point is that a man might adopt a virtue not for its own sake, but because he is too weak to do otherwise. In such an instance, why should any positive value be attached to his act? Under such circumstances, a virtue like humility might be interpreted as the external form of the inability to be arrogant. Thus, when one asks a hypothetical moral question—such as "Why should a man be less than God in displaying his glory?"—Unamuno imagines how a virtuous man would answer: " 'Satanic pride!' shout the impotent ones . . . all those grave gentlemen infested with common sense."[26] These moralists should judge not their fellowmen but the morality of their own disguised weaknesses. If they do not, it is because they lack the strength to contemplate their real impulses. ("Cowardice is each one's not integrating with his own nature, not hearing the voice of his conscience.")[27]

So much, then, for positive acts of virtue. But what of immoral

[23] *Ibid.*, IV, 323 (*LDQ*, p. 262).
[24] *Ibid.*, p. 322 (*LDQ*, p. 262).
[25] *Ibid.*, p. 211 (*LDQ*, p. 138).
[26] *Ibid.*, III, 696.
[27] *Ibid.*, XII, 228.

deeds? Here Unamuno pushes his ethical limits beyond the simple idea that evil acts can provide a catharsis for the individual. He conceives of instances in which an injurious act may not be considered evil at all, because it was not the individual's purpose to do harm. This "purity of intention" is, in its highest degree, innocence; but innocence is understood to mean complete naturalness, a state of animality. There is no malice in the attacks of a wild animal and therefore the consequence of its acts cannot be considered morally evil. So too is saintliness the purest form of spiritual innocence, and those who achieve this state have reached an animal purity that sets them beyond moral reproach. Even if "one of those saints bit, clawed, or devoured someone . . . it was with as much purity of intention . . . as the viper bites and the tiger claws or devours. Through grace, they had been returned to pure nature."[28]

This very Nietzschean view is related to the problem of consciousness. He who acts without being aware of himself has so fully integrated a personality that there is not the slightest element of self-contemplation to detract from the completeness of his act. Hence there is no room for the kind of moral judgment that occurs during *desdoblamiento,* when the *satánico yo* and other warring selves condemn one another. Instead, action is so complete and unreflexive that it is carried out with animal innocence. Evil enters only when some extraneous contemplative factor destroys this purity by making room for the analytical self-awareness that divides the personality.

Here, then, is a psychological genealogy of morals. From consciousness man derives his conscience. If he is oblivious to the latter's voice, it is because he has not adopted a critical awareness of himself and cannot perceive any discrepancy between his thinking and his acting selves. "He who is not conscious of doing evil, does no evil," says one of Unamuno's alter egos to another, "because the intention . . . " And then the other alter ego interrupts, "The intention! Do we know our own intentions? Do we know if we are good or not?"[29] But the very nature of the Unamunian mono-dialogue is itself a negative answer. We do not

28 *Ibid.,* III, 831–832.
29 *Ibid.,* II, 756.

know if we are good because we do not know who our real self is. Thus we are capable of conflicting intentions, for "every good man carries inside him the seven cardinal virtues and their seven opposing vices; and with them he is capable of creating all kinds of agony sufferers."[30]

But Unamuno does not mean by this that there is a clear alignment of virtues and vices pitted against each other, or that there are unequivocal good and evil selves. The ethical dilemma is the product of motivational disengagement on the part of the valuator. If there is an emotional or intellectual gulf between the judge of an action and the latter's purpose, then the judge's valuation of the act will be adverse. Guilt, therefore, is not determined by the external deed, but by how aware the agent is of being disaffected from it—hence, the criterion of the harmony of intentions. One is guilty only to the extent that he feels himself guilty. "When someone commits a pernicious act, believing in good faith that his action is virtuous, we cannot judge him morally guilty; and when another believes that an indifferent, or perhaps a beneficial, action is wrong, and he carries it out, he is guilty. The act passes, the intention remains; and the bad thing about an evil act is that it corrupts the intention, that knowingly doing wrong predisposes one to continue doing it, and the conscience grows dark. And doing wrong is not the same as being evil. Evil darkens the conscience—not the moral conscience, but the entire consciousness, the psyche."[31]

With the foregoing statements before us, the question arises as to whether anyone knows what the true moral perspective is. Unamuno's doubt that this is possible originates with the idea of the ambiguity of the self, and ends with the fear of wrongly judging his fellowman. He was skeptical of any system based on a single ethical perspective, but he was just as emphatic in using charity to determine his ethical orientation. What counted for him was less the moral consequences of an act than the individual's psychological state: character, self-awareness, motivation. Thus he arrived at a relativist position from which all perspectives are admissible provided they are guided by charity.

[30] *Ibid.*, IX, 422 (*TEN*, p. 30).
[31] *Ibid.*, XVI, 414 (*TSL*, p. 291).

The external formulations of morality are useless because they are inadequate measurements of the human spirit. Since these formulations were created by the spirit, they cannot have, consequently, a dimension great enough to measure spirit. This is why love, which is not a product but a faculty of spirit, is the only suitable standard. And this is also why Unamuno considers psychology the only legitimate basis of morals. The sources of thought and action are internal, and no valuation that derives from the latter is profound enough to judge those sources.

Unamuno's point of departure in analyzing motivation is, as in Nietzsche, the idea that man spontaneously seeks to exalt or immortalize himself, and that this impulse is the deepest root of traditional sin. But the sinfulness of such a life does not diminish either its holy or its heroic quality. In both saint and hero, ambition and boldness of desire are profoundly human, yet their heroism stems from the effort to transcend human limits. Consequently, "the superhuman quality of perfection touches on the inhuman and becomes submerged in it."[32]

If traditional moralists condemn the individual morality of quixotic and satanic rebelliousness, Unamuno tries to find out the motivation for such a judgment. He discovers their valuations to be just as much the product of inner needs as the values they have damned. As unheroic and unoriginal men, they hate those who possess the imagination they themselves lack. What they call "dangerous, daring, impious ideas are only the ones that do not occur to the poor men with routine minds." Herein lies the source of all orthodoxy: envy and resentment of the superior qualities of the few. "Coarse, vulgar spirits do not succeed in distinguishing themselves, and as they cannot stand for others to be distinguished, they want to impose upon them the uniformity of dogma, which is like a soldier's uniform, so that they cannot become distinguished."[33] Unamuno argues, therefore, that there should be no illusion concerning prevailing ethical standards. Indeed, if merit must be sought, let it be recognized in the superior quality of the motivations revealed by the select minority: the Cains, Don Quixotes, and Roque Guinarts. These figures do

---

[32] *Ibid.*, IV, 95 (*LDQ*, p. 16).
[33] *Ibid.*, II, 1057–1058 (*ABS*, pp. 64–65).

not conceal their purpose, absent in them is hypocrisy, and they affirm their self-assurance, thus earning the epithet of "arrogant" from those incapable of such confidence.

In all of this Unamuno reveals a Nietzschean suspiciousness when approaching moral judgments. He scrutinizes them for traces of secret attitudes that may be the opposite of what the judgments actually declare. He cannot accept, for instance, the praise men bestow upon him because he feels that "when they praise me for certain things it is only to condemn me tacitly for others," and so too in general, "when you hear someone being eulogized, you ought to ask, 'Against whom is this eulogy directed?' "[34] Similarly, he states that those who cloister themselves from the world are really carrying worldly thoughts with them in their hearts.[35] In all of this motivational guesswork, there is the insinuation that ethical postures are the fruits of duplicity. The moralist fights against the very evil that he harbors within him. Unamuno's most frequent illustration of this is his critique of ascetic ideas. Pointing to the sin of pride, he notes that its repression in the ascetic man has always been accomplished by means of a deeper pride hidden within the man himself. For proof we have only to observe "the preventions that those who profess humility have always taken so that their humility will not become pride."[36] He notes "with what frequency the masters of spiritual life, on commenting on the blessedness of the meek, warn us that to be humble with this in mind, in order to be blessed for having been humble, is the most refined form of pride."[37] Since these moralists are professional definers of good and evil, they are overly aware of their personal feelings in relation to ethical values; and this excessive self-consciousness destroys their sincerity. Moreover, if they are successfully meek, the recognition of this virtue being fulfilled within them may awaken a sense of pride that would counteract the original virtue. On the other hand, if they are trying to extirpate their pride, the mere affirmation of humility as a moral value will become nothing more than an

34 *Ibid.*, IX, 707.
35 *Ibid.*, III, 809.
36 *Ibid.*, p. 807.
37 *Ibid.*

ethical abstraction of what should properly be resolved in the heart. Instead of externalizing and ridding themselves of pride, they keep it dormant within them. And in the meantime, the concept of humility serves only as an intellectual reminder of the contrast between the moral state as it should be and as it is.

In conclusion, it must be said that Unamuno found external human behavior for the most part equivocal. It could be a force for good or ill, but it was never symbolic of the agent's moral nature. To the latter Unamuno ascribed all criteria for ethical orientation. He knew that this viewpoint would "scandalize the timid reader," but he was more concerned with the personal sources of action than with the exteriorized deeds. It was important to first maintain the moral soundness of one's character, and Unamuno was convinced that "committing a sinful act often purifies us of the terrible desire to do so which was gnawing away at our hearts." To repress evil thoughts is infinitely worse than to act them out. If man releases this evil, he will revert to his original characterological goodness, and in addition he may discover the virtues of repentance, pity, and love.[38]

Unamuno's concept of evil is, in fact, realistic and clinical: "The action frees us from the evil feeling, and it is the evil feeling that poisons the soul."[39] The feeling of rancor is not a quality of man's spirit but a toxic accumulation that must be discharged before spiritual health can be restored. The liberating act in itself is beyond valuation, for it is purely instrumental; any judgment that considered it evil would be correct but shallow, in that the agent's moral traits would be ignored. Morality is not a behavioral science. The norms of good and evil are found in the psychological and affective realms—character, spirit, soul—and not in any field of action. For Unamuno, a mode of conduct is an extension of personality, but not always an expression of it. An outward act might have adverse social consequences without reflecting evil in the heart of the man who committed it. This idea, of course, is unacceptable to the tradition-minded moralist, for it dissociates the agent from his responsibility. And yet this was precisely the difference that Unamuno was fond of speculating

[38] *Ibid.*, p. 810.
[39] *Ibid.*, II, 1077 (*ABS*, p. 87).

about: the question of conduct as a social phenomenon as opposed to the basic psychological and moral qualities of the individual.

This basic dilemma formed the core of Unamuno's existential psychology. The fragmentation of his personality led to the ambiguity of value formation. When he spoke of the alternatives "devour or be devoured," he added a third possibility, "to devour oneself." By this he meant also "to make fun of oneself," because the self-eating process was a matter of ironic self-consciousness. Thus, he slyly suggested, "Devour yourself, and as the pleasure of devouring yourself will become confused with and neutralized by the pain of being devoured, you will arrive at perfect equanimity of spirit, at ataraxy; you shall be no more than a mere spectacle for yourself."[40] From this point of view, it would be impossible to commit oneself to a specific set of values, and as the ironic perspective shifted, a new moral criterion would be in operation.

What happened to Unamuno was precisely this. He had always said: "I carry inside two contradictory principles that fight and destroy each other."[41] But at the same time that his writings proclaimed his many contradictions and paradoxes, he cultivated his secret irony. If the terms "good" and "bad" faith were used, we would have to say that Unamuno acted in bad faith, because he took seriously, in turn or alternately, his contradictory selves. That is, he found nothing serious within himself except his irony. This is why he was so skeptical of metaphysics and moral philosophy. In them he saw the failure of reason to function as anything except rationalization: man's instrument for justifying himself by affirming a priori the rightness of his behavior regardless of fact. As a result, he felt it was only "natural that the conquered cultivate the philosophy of defeat, and the conqueror, the philosophy of victory. And it is a form of cruelty to seek the conquered's acceptance of the philosophy of the conqueror, or the conqueror's acceptance of the philosophy of the conquered."[42]

In this respect Unamuno and Nietzsche meet at the crossroads

[40] Ibid., pp. 968–969 (MST, p. 283).
[41] Ibid., p. 715.
[42] Ibid., III, 961.

of modern irrationalism, but Unamuno never went further than his search for the motives and prejudices behind a philosopher's rational thought. He was unwilling to take the final step beyond good and evil. Nevertheless, he would have agreed with Nietzsche's words that "every philosophy also *conceals* a philosophy; every opinion is also a *lurking-place*, every word is also a *mask*."[43] And yet Unamuno's particular anguish consisted of the wish that these conditions might not be so. He could never give up the desire to possess a single self and the sentiments that went with it. It did not matter which self, as long as he sincerely believed in it at the time that he was writing about his feelings and ideas; hence, his determination to safeguard the right to contradict himself. And so Unamuno fought to overcome his divisions; yet he always discovered new ideological abysses and deeper caverns of personality, while hoping that one of these would turn out to be the real and permanent self.

[43] *Beyond Good and Evil* in *The Complete Works of Friedrich Nietzsche*, ed. Oscar Levy (New York: Macmillan, 1924), XII, par. 289, pp. 257–258.

THE NOVEL AS SELF-CREATION
Leon Livingstone

In one of his essays[1] Ortega y Gasset dwells on that dramatic moment in which the writer, poised on the brink of his creation, finally prepares to begin his narration. It is a moment of solemnity in which all the long and arduous preparation that has preceded is at stake. The author cannot but feel a tremendous sense of responsibility in his choice of the opening phrase, for it will set the basic tone of the entire work, establishing indelibly the impression that the reader will constantly carry with him.

The temptation to imagine Unamuno at this crucial juncture is difficult to resist as we visualize him readying the opening paragraph of *Niebla*. It is a moment obviously fraught with significance, for Unamuno conceives of himself as being at the threshold of a new literary era. What he proposes is not simply to write one more novel but to create a new vehicle that will refute all the outmoded and falsely conventional productions that pass for novels, and in so doing to express his whole philosophy of existence. His self-imposed task is, in short, nothing less than to offer a compendium of his thought in a form that will revolutionize the art of the novel. What ponderous reflections are to herald this new age? What dynamic, resolute character will be their prophetic spokesman? Let us listen to the opening paragraph that ushers in this new millennium:

> When Augusto appeared in the doorway of his house he held out his right arm, palm open and downward, and looking up at

[1] José Ortega y Gasset, *Invertebrate Spain*, trans. with foreword by Mildred Adams (New York: Norton, 1937), p. 19. The example discussed is that of the historian Theodor Mommsen beginning his narration of Roman history.

92

the sky remained a moment stationary in this statuary and august attitude. It was not that he was taking possession of the external world, but that he was observing whether it was raining. And as he received on the back of his hand the freshness of the slow drizzle, he frowned. It was not the sprinkle that bothered him, but having to open his umbrella. It was so elegant, so slim, folded in its case! A closed umbrella is as elegant as an open umbrella is ugly.[2]

The patent triviality of this introduction is heightened by the indecisiveness, nay, by the sheer aimlessness, of the character, a mere stroller through life,[3] as his author calls him:

Having spoken, he bent down to hitch up his trousers. He finally opened the umbrella and remained a moment suspended in thought. "And now, where do I go? Shall I head right or left? . . . I'll wait for a dog to go by"—he said to himself—"and follow the initial direction he takes."

At this moment there went by down the street not a dog but a handsome lass, and after her eyes, went . . . Augusto.[4]

The mixture of the serious and the humorous, of philosophy and banter, which marks the style of *Niebla* from the very outset—it is a "tragic jest or jesting tragedy,"[5] says the author in his prologue—recalls the oft-expressed opinion (an opinion paradoxically not shared by Unamuno)[6] that the ability to combine weightiness of thought with lightness of tone constitutes perhaps the finest quality of the Spanish genius.

We are, of course, not deceived by the frivolity of the presentation—the punning about the "august" attitude of Augusto, the malicious combination of the sublime and the ridiculous, the mock sententiousness of the reflections on a closed umbrella. Even before we encounter the serious element of the novel, the quality of message in the playful presentation is clearly underscored by contrast and heightened by a repetitious use of nega-

---

[2] *Niebla*, in *Obras*, II, 804 (*MST*, p. 21).

[3] *Ibid.*, p. 805 (*MST*, p. 22). The allusion to Rousseau's *promeneur solitaire* is obvious.

[4] *Ibid.*

[5] *Ibid.*, p. 787 (*MST*, p. 9). See later discussion on the technique of jumbling opposites.

[6] *Ibid.*, p. 786 (*MST*, p. 8).

tive inversion, a technique of ironic inference strongly reminiscent of Cervantes.

The message contained in *Niebla* and Unamuno's other novels, as in his essays, is one that is completely and irrevocably ambivalent, for it applies equally and indiscriminately to the biological and the artistic, and not alternatively or consecutively but simultaneously and reciprocally, in a particular symbiosis that equates life and literature. In the all-embracing scope of this view of existence, art is the expression of the vital, and life itself, a form of fiction. The synonymity of life and art is achieved when both attain their authentic level of creativity. The clue to this genuine existence is the independence of man and literary character alike, their freedom to create their own destiny, unhampered by a materialistic subservience to things or by imprisonment in a physical and logical causality. In Unamuno's view, the fallacy of all positivistic and deterministic philosophies, especially as they extend to the prevailing concept of literature in general and of the novel in particular, becomes readily apparent when one accepts a criterion of free creativity. The realistic novel, especially in its aggravated form in the naturalistic phase, establishes the material environment as the index of human life and portrays the latter as a formula of logical equation between cause and effect. In the light of Unamuno's antimaterialism and antideterminism, the initial reflections of Augusto, as he debates opening his umbrella, assume a special significance; and the reader, originally titillated by the seeming ridiculousness of the character, suffers what will be the first of a number of assaults on his complacent acceptance of the substantiality of the physical world:

"It is a misfortune to have to make use of things, to have to utilize them," thought Augusto. "Use spoils and even destroys all beauty. The noblest function of objects is to be contemplated. How beautiful is an orange before being eaten! This will change in heaven when our whole function is reduced, or expanded, to contemplating God and all things in Him. Here, in this poor life, we worry only about using God; we try to open Him, like an umbrella, so that He can protect us from all sorts of evils."[7]

[7] *Ibid.*, p. 804 (*MST*, pp. 21–22).

When utilitarianism is rejected, the dominant role of objects is overcome and the path is left clear to chart the course of our lives without hindrance. Instead of being the victim of events, one becomes their originator. The niggardliness of the concept that reduces life to a rigorous relationship of cause and effect yields to the generosity of the concept of creative will in which events develop freely through chance association, as with the fortuitous appearance of Eugenia, the girl with the beautiful eyes:

"A fortuitous appearance?" (Augusto asks himself as he lights up his cigar). "And what appearance isn't? What is the logic of appearances? That of the succession of these figures formed by the smoke from my cigar. Chance! Chance is the intimate rhythm of the world, chance is the soul of poetry. Oh, my chanceful Eugenia!"[8]

It is chance (*el azar*) that governs, or rather frees, human actions and makes life an uncharted course in which human will actually *creates* reality, and thus man becomes the novelist of his own existence. Things, in short, happen to us because we will them to happen, not as the mechanical product of physical laws, but as an exercising of the human spirit:

"Who is Eugenia?" (Augusto asks himself). "Ah, I realize that I had been looking for her for some time. And while I was looking for her, she came out to meet me. Is this perhaps not encountering something? When one discovers someone or something that he was seeking, is it not that someone or something, feeling sorry for his search, comes out to meet him? Didn't America come looking for Columbus?"[9]

How inspiring, and at the same time how terrifying, is the thought that life is of our own making, that it is neither pre-formed nor predestined, apparently subject to no external restraints! And now we realize that what appeared to be the aimlessness of Augusto is not a matter of indecisiveness, but of undecidedness. He lacks direction because he is not directed, and he is intentionally not directed so that he can freely create his own life. This freedom, however, makes of life a constant problem—whether the problem is to open or close one's umbrella,

[8] *Ibid.*, p. 810 (*MST*, p. 31).
[9] *Ibid.*, pp. 810–811 (*MST*, p. 31).

or to head left or right, or to decide one's destiny—and the combination of freedom and responsibility, of the discovery of strength in oneself and the feeling of terrifying abandonment, of loneliness in the universe, produces "the saddest and sweetest of anguishes: that of living."[10]

Now we realize, as we are forced to reconsider what we had initially looked on as the ridiculous antics of a weakling, that we are actually in the presence of a new type of literary personality and with him in a revolutionary novelistic situation: both character and plot are as yet uncreated. The character does not spring full-fledged into the predetermined action of the novel but is given that compulsory independence to create his own life which is characteristic of human existence. As he creates himself through the exercising of his will, that is to say, as he comes into being, the novel also begins to assume definite form and to come into being. The novel, in other words, creates itself as the character creates himself. And as the character creates himself, so do author and reader create themselves. In inventing a character the author is actually revealing himself to himself and, in this way, realizing himself. The purpose of art, says Unamuno, is "to discover oneself, so as to live in oneself, to be oneself."[11] And this also is true for the reader of novels, who is similarly subjected to the living experience of self-creation. In *Cómo se hace una novela* ("How a Novel Is Made"), we read: "Why or for what is a novel made? For the novelist to make himself. And what does the novelist make himself for? To make the reader, to make himself one with the reader."[12] As the author reveals himself to himself by projecting himself novelistically, so the character discovers himself by creating of his life a novel-within-the-novel. Examples of this type of character self-creation are Víctor Goti, who is writing fundamentally the same novel as Unamuno in *Niebla*, and the tortured Joaquín Monegro in *Abel Sánchez*, who also becomes an author, the author of his own existence, as he pens his "Confessions." Since life is a creative activity in which man is forced to novelize his existence, this novelizing of exis-

10 *Ibid.*, p. 837 (*MST*, p. 74).
11 *Ibid.*, X, 866.
12 *Ibid.*, p. 922.

tence by author and character becomes the pivotal element of action in the novel, its basic "plot." The reader is similarly drawn into the orbit of self-creation, of rebirth, because he is forced to make himself over entirely as the author obliges him to question his most cherished convictions, his true identity, the authenticity of his very existence, by sowing in him the seeds of disquieting doubt. "The most liberating feature of art," says Augusto, "is that it makes one doubt that one exists."[13]

For both author and reader, then, the novel becomes an active ingredient in the formation of their life, a vital experience of formative value. Neither Unamuno nor the reader of *Niebla* is the same person when he concludes the novel; both have achieved new dimensions of personality. The novel is a living experience in the fullest and most literal sense of the word, not to be confused with passive literature, the "nonsense of art for art's sake,"[14] especially if its exclusive object is to distract, to "kill time," as the saying goes. Those who seek to kill time are merely killing themselves, says Unamuno on more than one occasion. True art is creation, that is to say, "poetry."

The paradox of the frivolous opening of *Niebla* is now clarified for us. It is a reverse statement of what is profoundly important. The immediate reason for this comic understatement is the desire to disassociate the style of the novel from the pontifical pomposity of the nineteenth-century literary variety. That novel was convinced in its earnestness that it was presenting life in all of its massive reality, but actually succeeded only in offering a superficial, anecdotal form of entertainment in the course of which it perverted the authentically real. Plot now is no longer a decisive, nor even a legitimate, ingredient in the novel. In the revision of the novel which *Niebla* represents, the impatient reader who is accustomed to turning first to the conclusion to find out how the plot is solved is entirely frustrated. What holds one in suspense is not idle curiosity about what happens to a "fictitious" being— whether he gets the girl or loses her—but what will be his own destiny, for the character's struggle with life and death is also that of the reader. This is the true meaning of "recreation." "One

[13] *Ibid.*, II, 972 (*MST*, p. 289).
[14] *Ibid.*, XVI, 179 (*TSL*, p. 51).

enjoys a work of art because one creates it in oneself, re-creates it, and recreates oneself in so doing," says the author in the prologue to his *Three Exemplary Novels*.[15] The anecdotal type of narration does not conform to the expression of this self-creation, for the graphic summary of action which is plot is necessarily the recounting of what has already happened. But the novel, like life, must create itself as it proceeds, and that is why Unamuno titles his essay on the creation of the novel *Cómo se hace una novela*, "how a novel is made," he insists, "not how a novel is told."[16] That is why the author must reject the superficial reader. "I have no reason to satisfy your frivolous, serial-story curiosity," he tells him chidingly. "Every reader who in reading a novel worries about how the characters will finish, without worrying about how *he* will finish, does not deserve to have his curiosity satisfied."[17] It is this preoccupation with the destiny one creates for himself which is the essence of true realism, a created, not a copied "realism," which is merely "literature." "Nothing is more ambiguous than what is called 'realism' in literary art," writes Unamuno on one occasion. "Because—just what is the 'reality' of such 'realism'? The truth is that 'realism' so-called—something purely external, apparential, cortical, anecdotal—relates to the art of literature and not to poetry or creation. In a poem (and good stories are poems), in a 'creation,' the reality is an intimate, creative thing—it is a thing that is willed!"[18]

The perversion perpetrated by what Unamuno refers to derogatorily as "literature" consists of the unnatural and unwarranted inversion of art and life in which, instead of literature assuming vital force, life falsely assumes "literary" proportions. This results in the realistic novel's investing itself with the theatrical type of plot—with its artifices of complication, crisis, and denouement—and in the tone of histrionism imparted to the work by the grandiose events it narrates. But life is not histrionic. It does not have a neatly contrived building toward a crisis, nor contrasting heights and depths of tragic stature. All this is novelesque, sheer literary posturing. Life is not made up of great sorrows and

---

15 *TEN*, p. 22 (*Obras*, II, 983).
16 *Obras*, X, 890.
17 *Ibid.*
18 *TEN*, p. 17 (*Obras*, IX, 415).

joys but is an interminable accumulation of routine details endlessly repeated. This basic triviality of the material of human life is what motivates the seeming frivolity noted in *Niebla* and, as a matter of fact, prompts the very title of the work. "This gentle, routine, humble life of mine," says Augusto Pérez, "is a Pindaric ode woven with the thousand trifles of daily life. Daily life! . . . Give me, oh Lord, the thousand trifles of each day. Men do not succumb to great sorrows or great joys, because those sorrows and those joys are enveloped in an immense mist of little incidents. And life is just that, *la niebla* ["mist"]."[19]

The momentous events with which the nineteenth century identified reality are, if a distinction is to be made, more appropriate to what is generally considered the particular province of history. But even this interpretation is unacceptable to Unamuno, for whom the true history of man, what he calls "intrahistory," the history of the "intra-man" and not the "superman," is not that of spectacular events—battles and changes in dynasty—but is fabricated out of the prosaic details of routine, daily existence.[20] Triviality is thus the essential characteristic of human life, and chance, its dominant form.

Unamuno's antideterministic concept of chance seems at first blush to involve a contradiction, for the relationship between the

[19] *Obras*, II, 810 (*MST*, p. 31).

[20] In one of his major essays, *En torno al casticismo*, Unamuno distinguishes between the *fondo histórico*, the historic background of momentous events, and the *fondo intrahistórico*, the endless succession of little deeds that make up the warp and woof of human life. The so-called historic background is spectacular but constitutes actually only the provisional and transitory, whereas the "intrahistoric background" is the permanent, the eternally true. The concept of the element of the prosaic details of daily life as the basic human ingredient of history and art is not exclusive to Azorín with whom, thanks to Ortega's epoch-making phrase, *primores de lo vulgar*, it is most generally associated. Pedro Laín Entralgo, in his doctrinal study of the Generation of 1898, confirms the distinction between history and historic reality on the part of many of the principal figures of the Generation—Unamuno, Ganivet, Baroja, Valle-Inclán, Antonio Machado—as well as Azorín. He notes a special parallel between the latter and Unamuno: "Azorín, esteta, reduce a materia estética la distinción de Unamuno entre historia e intrahistoria. No es preciso ser un lince para advertir que los 'grandes hechos' y los 'menudos hechos' de Azorín, son por entero equiparables a los 'sucesos' y a los 'hechos' de Unamuno" (*La generación del noventa y ocho* [Madrid: Diana, 1945], chap. vii: "Historia sine historia," pp. 261–302, esp. p. 278).

will of the individual and the events that it conjures into existence appears itself to have the aspect of causation, rather than of a free and creatively independent association. The difference, however, between the relationship of chance and the events in our lives, on the one hand, and cause and effect, on the other, is exactly that between the unpredictable variability of life and the fixity of logic. If the vital impulse of the individual creates its own fortuitous realities, this is not accomplished with a logical straightforwardness that is mathematically predictable but through the devious and disconcerting processes of life, which is essentially incompatible with logic. "All that is vital is antirational, not merely irrational," writes Unamuno in refutation of Hegel in *The Tragic Sense of Life*, "and all that is rational is antivital. And this is the basis of the tragic sense of life." Chance, then, is not a law, for laws are fixed, objective, invariable rules, whereas life is precisely the irregular, the unforeseen, the unpredictable, the as yet unformed—"a wild and dense jungle without paths," as Augusto calls it. "We make the paths for ourselves with our feet," he adds, "as we walk at random."[21]

It is the attempt to transfer the genuine reality of the living organism, of the biological, to the elaboration of the novel which prompts Unamuno's rejection of the method—largely followed in his first novelistic venture, *Paz en la guerra* ("Peace in War") —of what he calls "oviparous," as distinguished from "viviparous," creativity.[22] The oviparous method, as the term implies, involves a long process of incubation in which the writer "makes an outline, plan, or first draft, and then works on it; that is to say, he lays an egg and then hatches it." The viviparous method, on the other hand, is that of live birth. The viviparous writers seek to eliminate the intermediation of the critical (i.e., the rational) faculty and to make their creations the spontaneous expression of their own vitality. "When they conceive the desire of writing a novel," Unamuno comments, "they turn it over in their minds, asleep and awake, that is to say, they gestate. And when they feel real labor pains . . . they sit down, pick up their pens, and give birth." The necessary quality of vitality can be ensured only by the method of directness, of spontaneity, with-

21 *Obras*, II, 835 (*MST*, p. 71).
22 "A lo que salga," *Obras*, III, 789–805.

out which the work of art must inevitably degenerate into reflection. The reader will thus not find in *Niebla* the felicitous expression, the lambent phrase, for cultivated "style" is willful self-deception. "The word, this social product, was made for lying," thinks Augusto. "What is a social product is a lie."[23] The aim of uncomplicated spontaneity, however, is never of easy accomplishment, for, in the very act of transmitting emotion to the printed page, the process of devitalization has already begun. "My own thoughts," writes Unamuno on one occasion, "revolving tumultuously in the depths of my mind, when lopped from their emotive origin and set down on this paper in unchangeable forms, are already corpses of thoughts."[24]

As in the gestation of the novel so in its fabrication the guiding principle is that of spontaneous vitality. This is achieved by what Unamuno labels the "come what may" method ("A lo que salga"). It is a procedure that hinges directly on the principle of the self-creation of human destiny through chance. Its invention and the esthetic of free form to which it leads are explained in a dialogue between Augusto Pérez and his friend Víctor Goti:

> "So you have undertaken to write a novel? And what is its plot, if one may ask?" [says Augusto]
> "My novel has no plot, or rather, it will be the one that happens to develop. The plot develops by itself."
> "And how is that"?
> "Well, one fine day . . . I said to myself: I am going to write a novel, but I am going to write it the way one lives, without knowing what will happen. I sat down, took some sheets of paper and began to write the first thing that occurred to me, without knowing what would follow, without any plan at all. My characters will form themselves as they act and speak, above all as they speak; and their character will gradually take shape. And at times their character will consist of not having any."
> "Yes," [says Augusto,] "like mine."[25]
> [And Victor adds:] "In this novel I am planning to set down everything that occurs to me."
> "Well, it will finish up by not being a novel," replies Augusto, "not a *novela*."
> "No, it will be . . . it will be . . . a *nivola*."[26]

[23] *Obras*, II, 901 (*MST*, pp. 172–173).
[24] *Ibid.*, XVI, 217 (*TSL*, p. 90).
[25] *Ibid.*, II, 894–895 (*MST*, p. 163).
[26] *Ibid.*, p. 896 (*MST*, p. 165).

The *nivola,* then, is marked essentially by the element of freedom of invention, a freedom that, guided only by chance, leads into the most unexpected of situations. This is exactly what happens to Augusto himself, as he is forced in constant bewilderment into adjustment after adjustment. His subconscious desire to fall in love makes him the object of a "chance" encounter with the eyes of Eugenia. The pursuit of the girl is advanced by another fortuitous occurrence when her mother accidentally drops a canary cage which is retrieved by Augusto, who just happens to be passing by. In a world not governed by logical cause and effect, anything can and indeed does happen. Truth is stranger than fiction.

Truth is also more complicated than fiction. The apparently felicitous development indicated by the incident of the canary cage does not materialize, for the simple reason that Eugenia is not an abstraction of the mind, as in Augusto's preconception, but is a very real person, a living being, with a very definite will of her own. She is a woman. "Una mujer!, toda una mujer,"[27] Augusto is forced to admit, and being "all woman," is far removed from the artificial type of soft, yielding femininity that insipid novels and even society itself would have us believe. She is defiant of authority and more than self-sufficient; in fact, she adopts the role of protector toward the opposite sex, in her relations with the weak-willed Mauricio. She represents, indeed, all the resoluteness of character that the indecisive Augusto lacks. This inversion of the traditional roles of the sexes prevails also in the relationship between her gentle uncle, Don Fermín, and his strong-willed wife, Doña Ermelinda.[28] The explanation is to be found in the intuitive, emotional nature of woman, guided by her feelings and not by reason and therefore, in the Unamunian table of values, more in tune with the current of life than her male counterpart, who is more submissive to the appeal of the rational.[29] The dualism passion-intellect, which is the basis of the

[27] *Ibid.,* p. 842 (*MST,* p. 81).

[28] Don Fermín and Doña Ermelinda inevitably suggest the later Don Pablo and Tía Pompilia of Azorín's *Doña Inés,* who represent a similar inversion.

[29] But if women have greater individuality, they have less personality. Cf. *Niebla,* in *Obras,* II, 939 (*MST,* p. 235), and *Del sentimiento trágico de la vida,* in *Obras,* XVI, 299–300.

inherent contradiction of human existence, is thus responsible also for the paradox of the sexes.

The attempt to reduce human existence to reason Unamuno considers a fundamental error that has prevailed since Descartes. *Niebla* is essentially a rejection of the Cartesian *cogito, ergo sum* in favor of the priority of existence over the idea of existence. It is not that thought is the proof and precipitator of existence but that existence makes thought possible, so that life precedes thought or knowledge:

> "Perhaps my love has preceded its object," [argues Augusto]. "Or more than that, it is this love of mine which has originated it, which has extracted it from the mist of creation. . . . But how have I fallen in love if I cannot strictly say that I know her. Bah, knowledge will come afterward. Love precedes knowledge and the latter kills the former. . . . To know is to pardon, they say. No, to pardon is to know. First love, then knowledge."[30]

Hegelian apriorism and Cartesian intellectualism are equally mistaken. Human life is a flesh-and-blood proposition, not a schematic theory. The ultimate significance of Cartesian logic is not "I think, therefore I am," but "I think, therefore I think (I am)," which is a reduction of life to the level of idea. The trajectory of the coming into existence of Augusto is the passage from this erroneous unity of mere idea to the duality that is human life, that living contradiction between faith and reason, between life that aspires to self-perpetuation and the rational acceptance of the finality of death. Reason cannot guarantee to us even the assurance that we exist. The basic falseness of the intellectual proof of existence is the very ability of the mind to cast doubt on existence itself. Not, therefore, "I think, therefore I am," but "I love, therefore I am," and "I eat, therefore I am"—Augusto dies from a case of overeating—are the more realistic formulations because they are rooted in the biologically human, in the reality of "the man of flesh and blood, who is born, suffers and dies— above all, dies—who eats and drinks and plays and sleeps and thinks and loves."[31] The new credo must be "I am, therefore I think," or "I think because I am," or better still, "I am, therefore I doubt," or "I am, because I doubt," summaries of attitudes

[30] *Obras*, II, 817–818 (*MST*, pp. 43–44).
[31] *Ibid.*, XVI, 127 (*TSL*, p. 1).

that express the emotional intensity of actual existence. Augusto is a direct descendant of Segismundo in Calderón's *Life Is a Dream*, who almost three hundred years before had fluctuated in agonizing confusion between belief and doubt in his existence. "What is the real world," asks Augusto, "but the dream that we all dream, the common dream?"[32]

The distance from Descartes to Unamuno can be perhaps nowhere more clearly measured than in their forms of doubt. Cartesian doubt, which Unamuno labels "a comic doubt, a purely theoretic doubt,"[33] is merely an intellectual device, a sort of tactical weapon of the suspension of judgment in order to be able to apprehend conceptual truths. Unamuno's doubt is not a mental abstraction but the passionate self-questioning of agonized creatures struggling in the living contradiction of a life that is a constant approach to death, of reason that must battle reason in order that the quality of life survive. It is a creative doubt, for without it there can be no really positive belief. The sort of faith that never questions its authenticity, that is never exposed to the searing flame of doubt, as in the religion of the average man— what Unamuno derisively refers to as "the religion of the coal merchant"—can never be true belief. It is only a form of dead, meaningless routine. True religion must doubt, and the stronger the belief, the greater the doubt. The true mystic is an agnostic. This is precisely the theme of one of Unamuno's last, and most moving works, *San Manuel Bueno, mártir*, a short novel about a priest, devoted to and dearly beloved by his parish, who harbors a terrible secret. This secret is discovered and guarded by two of his parishioners, and we learn what it is only after his death: He himself could not believe.

Doubt is as indispensable an ingredient of faith, of belief, as death is of life, and as unreason is of reason. Life is not a rational formula; it is a living paradox. The paradox is the only expression adequate to the fundamental contradiction of existence, for it lies beyond reason. It destroys irremediably those neat divisions of reality into mutually exclusive categories which are the devitalized schematizations of pure reason. When rationalism is

[32] *Ibid.*, II, 865 (*MST*, p. 116).
[33] *Ibid.*, XVI, 235 (*TSL*, p. 107).

overcome, the lines of demarcation between the spheres of existence disappear and all becomes a mingling of indistinguishable elements, an undecipherable confusion, a mist. That is the principal significance of the title of *Niebla*, which itself represents an intentional jumbling of opposites: the trivial and the portentous, essay and novel, the philosophic and the erotic, fact and fiction, chance and fate, art and life. In the prologue to the novel written by one of the characters (author and character are only conflicting aspects of each other), Víctor Goti declares:

> Don Miguel has the preoccupation of the tragic jester and has told me more than once that he would not want to die without having written a tragic jest or a jesting tragedy, but not in the sense that the comic or grotesque and the tragic are mixed or juxtaposed, but fused and confused in one. And when I made the observation that that was nothing but unbridled romanticism, he answered: "I don't deny it, but by calling names you don't solve anything. In spite of my more than twenty years of teaching the classics, the classicism that is opposed to romanticism I just don't go along with. They say that the Hellenic quality consists of distinguishing, defining, separating; well, mine consists of undefining, confusing."[34]

Indefinir and *confundir*, that is to say, to fuse, to jumble, to confuse, and to confound the rationalist.

The basic error of rationalism as a method of solving the problem of existence is that it seeks to reduce life to unity, which is death. "Any monistic systems seem always materialistic to us," writes Unamuno in *The Tragic Sense of Life*. "Only dualistic systems save the immortality of the soul." And for the particular monism of rationalism he has only unyielding opposition:

> Intelligence is a terrible thing. It tends to death as does memory to stability. What is living, what is absolutely unstable, absolutely individual, is, in fact, unintelligible. Logic tends to reduce everything to entities and genres, to give each representation one and the same content in any place, time, or relationship in which it happens to us. But there is nothing that is the same in two successive moments of its being. My idea of God is different every time that I conceive it. Identity, which is death, is the aspiration of the intellect. The mind seeks what is dead, since

34 *Ibid.*, II, 787 (*MST*, p. 9).

what is alive escapes it. It tries to congeal in solid blocks the fugitive current, to fix it. To analyze a body it is necessary to cut it down or destroy it. To understand something, it is necessary to kill it, to rigidify it in the mind. Science is the cemetery of dead ideas, although it may come out of them alive. Worms also feed on corpses.[35]

The contradictory dualism that is life is contrasted with the oneness of reason, of pure intelligence, in the confrontation of Augusto and the bookish intellectual Antolín S. Paparrigópulos. For the latter, life offers no problems, no contradictions, for he is possessed of an intelligence that "was clear, above all clear, of a marvelous transparence, without nebulousness nor embolisms of any kind."[36] A disciple of erudite escapism, "he kept his mind aloof from disputes which lead to nothing useful and took refuge in the absolutely pure region of immaculate art, which is not touched by the rubbish of passions and in which man finds consoling refuge from the disappointments of life." Paparrigópulos is a caricature of the bookish specialist whose research has no bearing on his existence. It is, in fact, precisely an excuse for avoiding coming to grips with his soul. He is one of those to whom Unamuno refers in *The Tragic Sense of Life* as "professionals of thought who think only with their brains and develop into definers."[37] With the specialist's slogan, "Everything that seems to be gained in extension is lost in intensity," as his guide, he proceeds to delve into the great body of human culture with an energy no less pitiful than perverted. "For Antolín, the principal, almost the only, value of the masterworks of the human genius consists in their having given rise to a book of criticism or commentary; great artists, poets, painters, musicians, historians, philosophers, were born so that a scholar can write their biography and a critic comment on their works, and any first-hand phrase of a great writer does not have any value until a scholar repeats it, citing the work, the edition, and the page."[38] And Unamuno crushes him with the comment: "He belonged to the class of those commentators, who, if Homer himself were

---

[35] *Ibid.*, XVI, 217 (*TSL*, p. 90).
[36] *Ibid.*, II, 930 (*MST*, p. 221).
[37] *Ibid.*, XVI, 141 (*TSL*, p. 14).
[38] *Ibid.*, II, 936 (*MST*, pp. 231–232).

to come to life and enter their office, would shove him out because he was bothering their laboring on the dead texts of his works."[39] Paparrigópulos does not progress beyond the realm of dead idea. He is not a man, and therefore not a true character, for the real man, the real literary character, is one who struggles with his own inner conflict between reason and life, who "agonizes." Antolín is not an *agonista*, a sufferer, as Unamuno calls his genuine characters. He is a refugee from life. When Augusto falls in love, he exposes himself deliberately to women, but not so Paparrigópulos: ". . . this man, I mean . . . this scholar . . . devoted himself to the study of women, in books, of course, which is, where they are concerned, the least risky, and of women of past centuries, who are also much less risky for those who study them than the women of today."[40] In the last analysis, this type of pedantic scholarship is only a cover-up for insufficiency of personality. Paparrigópulos is merely "a solitary erudite who, too timid to approach women in life and in order to take revenge on them for that timidity, studies them in books."[41]

To live an authentic existence is not to flee from the problem of life but to accept the conflict of opposites as the basis of our personality. "The fact is," writes Unamuno, "every human being has within him the seven cardinal virtues and their corresponding mortal sins: he is humble and he is proud; he is sober and he is gluttonous; and he is chaste and licentious, charitable and envious, generous and stingy, diligent and lazy, long-suffering and quick to wrath. From the same inner being he derives the tyrant and the slave, the rascal and the saint, the Cain and the Abel."[42] This multiplicity of inner selves provides the source of the various characters that people the author's novels. Within the same person it is the tension of opposites that provides the dynamic life that is denied to those who reduce life to idea or objects, for if the bearer of this emotional life is not the creature of reason, neither is he the product of a purely material environment. The novel, therefore, must avoid making man subordinate to his

[39] *Ibid.*, p. 937 (*MST*, p. 232).
[40] *Ibid.*, p. 935 (*MST*, p. 230).
[41] *Ibid.*, pp. 935–936 (*MST*, p. 230).
[42] *TEN*, p. 28 (*Obras*, IX, 421).

milieu. Consequently, *Niebla* eliminates all purely external settings—decors, landscapes, clothing, furniture—and the novel is
stripped to its barest essentials to become "a sort of intimate
drama, in skeleton form, outside time and place."[43] Even the
physical description of the character is to be avoided. The material Augusto is never revealed to us. "Don't waste your time
observing the exteriors of the people about you," advises Unamuno.[44] The "apparential, rational world"[45] cannot reveal to us
our true personality.

But what, then, is our identity, especially if identity means
oneness, sameness, which for Unamuno is death? Our true personality is not only a complex of opposing tendencies, but is basically a mystery that must forever remain unfathomable to us.
The terrible truth is that one cannot "know" oneself, one can
only "be" oneself. "The end of life," declares don Miguel, "is to
live and not to understand."[46] The oracular counsel to "know
thyself" Unamuno undoubtedly would reject as a contrasense.
One cannot know oneself when knowledge does not precede
existence but is the product of it. The oracle should have said,
"Create thyself in order to know thyself," or "Become thyself."
One can only become oneself by living, but herein arises a new
dilemma: To live means to live in the world of others, and to
live in the world of others means to be constantly under pressure
to surrender one's identity, one's authentic personality. The
novelizing of one's existence is thus inseparably bound up with
the problem of personality. Who am I? Who is this person who
seeks to create his own life?

Unamuno discusses his concept of personality by taking as
his point of departure what he calls the "ingenious theory of
Oliver Wendell Holmes . . . anent the three Johns and Thom-
ases,"[47] in the third chapter of *The Autocrat of the Breakfast*

---

[43] "Prologue" to *Paz en la guerra* (*Obras*, II, 74). Azorín goes even
further in his aspiration to "la novela de lo indeterminado; una novela sin
espacio, sin tiempo, y sin personajes" (*Capricho* [Madrid: Espasa-Calpe,
1943], p. 73).

[44] *TEN*, p. 27 (*Obras*, IX, 420).

[45] *Ibid.* (*Obras*, IX, 418).

[46] *TSL*, p. 116 (*Obras*, XVI, 244).

[47] *TEN*, p. 18 (*Obras*, IX, 416).

Table. Holmes had said that when two people, say John and
Thomas, are talking together, there are actually six talkers involved: "The real John, known only to his Maker; John's ideal
of John, never the real John and often very unlike him; John as
conceived by Thomas—never the real John, nor John's John,
and something not infrequently very unlike them both." And
similarly in the case of Thomas: the real Thomas, Thomas' ideal
of Thomas, and John's ideal of Thomas. In short, the person one
is; the person one thinks one is; the person others think one is.
Unamuno accepts this version of the multiplicity of selves, which
he restates and amplifies:

> I am going to say that in addition to the person one is to God
> (if indeed one is anyone to God), and to the person one is to
> others, and to the person one thinks one is, there is the person
> one would like to be. And this last, the person one would like to
> be, is the creator within one, in one's heart, and the person that
> is truly real. Verily God will reward or punish a man by making
> him for all eternity what he has tried to be![48]

The realization that one can never know one's true self is the
insuperable point of departure for the formation of personality.
"Every man dies, when Destiny decrees his death, without having
known himself," declares one of Unamuno's characters.[49] One
is forced to view oneself always as mirrored in others, that is, to
accept that fiction of himself that he and the others invent. "We
all like to play a role," says one of the characters in *Niebla*, "and
nobody is what he is but the one that others make him."[50]

Thus we are all obliged to adopt the mask, the *persona*, which
is personality; we are "all persons, all masks, all actors," says
Augusto.[51] Not only are we subject to the interpretation of ourselves by others, but we are prone to submit meekly to the role
assigned to us, as do Eugenia and Mauricio. She loathes music
but accepts her identification as "the piano teacher" and duti-
fully gives lessons until she finally rebels; he cynically plays the
part of an emasculated Don Juan which society has ascribed to

[48] *Ibid.*, pp. 19–20 (*Obras*, IX, 416).
[49] "El ama" in "Epílogo," *El Otro* (*Misterio en tres jornadas y un epílogo*), in *Obras*, XII, 862.
[50] *Obras*, II, 918 (*MST*, p. 200).
[51] *Ibid.*, p. 901 (*MST*, p. 173).

him: "I am so weak! I was born to be supported by a woman, but with dignity, you know. If not, nothing doing."[52] The social reflection of ourselves seeks to rob us of our birthright—the symbol of Jacob and Esau is one version of the problem of personality stressed by Unamuno—and therefore we must struggle against the constant assault on the integrity of our person which is constituted by the pressure to conform to the social norm. This aspect of the problem of personality is developed in the novel *Abel Sánchez* in which Abel represents the commonplace mediocrity that society cultivates as the hero, the "common man" of the twentieth century, or the "mass-man," as Ortega calls him. In order not to succumb to this falsification of personality, one must be the fierce dissenter, the nonconformist who must slay his other self in order to survive. This is the paradox of the Cain-Abel myth. Cain slays Abel because Abel is the potential assassin of Cain. The mask of anonymity which society forces on us is symbolized in the very names of Unamuno's characters. Augusto, for example, viewed from the point of view of others, is a mere Pérez, as Abel is a Sánchez, and Alejandro (in *Nothing Less Than a Whole Man*), a Gómez. That is to say, they are all John Does. Seen in his social perspective, Augusto is a ludicrous misfit. Viewed from within, in his tortured struggle to scale the heights of authenticity to be a real person, he assumes new proportions of dignity and becomes an "august" character, an Augusto. Those who refuse to do battle with the constant challenge to their authenticity can only be unmitigated weaklings. The scorn heaped on such puppets is reflected in the unrelieved ridiculousness characterized by the very name of the pedantic Antolín S. Paparrigópulos, and it comes as no surprise to us to learn that the "S." stands for Sánchez.

If every man is a Cain to his fellowman—a relationship that makes envy the most personal, and therefore the most Spanish, of emotions—each one is also a Cain to himself, for he is reduced always to seeing himself from without; he is always the spectator of himself who sees himself as "the other," and to pursue the eternally elusive quarry of himself must lock himself in a deadly embrace with himself, Jacob wrestling with the angel. One is

[52] *Ibid.*, p. 888 (*MST*, p. 152).

never oneself but always "the other" who observes him; that is why one can never know one's true self. "It is a terrible thing," says the character called only "the Other" in the play *El Otro*, "not to be one, one, always one and the same, one."[53] And the same character had already said, "Ah, the terrible torture of being born double!"[54] It is the "terrible torture of being born double" which makes for an inevitable element of duplicity in us as we all become compulsory witnesses to our own playing of a part, all "solitary players of [our] comedy," as Augusto says, "actor and spectator at one and the same time."[55] The realization of the inextricable amalgamation of our two selves, the actor and the spectator, does much to explain the baffling enigma of the dual personality, the composite of pose and utter sincerity, which is Unamuno himself.

But if all existence is a fiction, fiction is also life, for only by creating fictions can we live with others and with ourselves. "Oh, my sweet Eugenia," declares Augusto. "Mine? Yes, I, through my thought, through my desire, make her mine. He, the other, that is to say, the only one, may come to possess her materially; but the mysterious spiritual light of those eyes is mine, mine! . . . Is there only one Eugenia, or are there two, one mine, the other her fiancé's? Well, if that's the way it is, if there are two, let him keep his and I'll keep mine."[56] The creating of others in one's imagination through one's desire is the basic reality of life and art; reality is created; it cannot be simply apprehended or copied. The error of the realistic naturalistic procedure is now ultimately clear.

"A poet does not arrive at his creatures—living creations—by the methods of so-called realism," maintains Unamuno. "The people of the realists are puppets dressed up in costumes and moving about as their strings are pulled, and with phonographs wound up somewhere in their insides to repeat remarks which their puppet-master has picked up on the sidewalks or in the cafés, and jotted down in a note-book."[57] The creative process is well

53 *Ibid.*, XII, 851.
54 *Ibid.*, p. 837.
55 *Ibid.*, p. 901 (*MST*, p. 173).
56 *Ibid.*, p. 850 (*MST*, pp. 93–94).
57 *TEN*, p. 17 (*Obras*, IX, 415).

exemplified in one of the stories in *San Manuel Bueno, mártir*, that of "The Novel of Don Sandalio, Chess Player." The writer plays chess in the casino with an uncommunicative person who seems to be harboring some personal tragedy about which, however, he volunteers no information. Far from seeking to bring to light the mystery of Don Sandalio's life, as the proverbial novelist would be expected to do, the novelist actually avoids doing so: "I have not been able to find out anything about his life, nor does it strictly matter to me. I prefer to imagine it."[58] And that is the plot of the story. And of life.

If all life is fiction, and fiction therefore life, the highest form of fiction is that which is deliberate, freed from the contingency of existence in the "real" world. It is more real than reality itself, for reality is always less than it could or would be. Herein enters the role of art. What is the author actually accomplishing when he creates his fictional beings, when he sets the characters loose upon the printed page? He is drawing from his inner self, which is "a whole population,"[59] some of the myriad persons he would like to be, persons who struggle for recognition, characters in search of an author to give them life,[60] selves of oneself. He is creating himself in them, and this is the only way he can know himself. These selves are more the true self than their creator. They are "realizations" of oneself in which one recognizes the person to whom he aspires. As real life is a constant rebirth, an unceasing self-discovery in which man repeatedly creates himself by projecting images of his ideal self, the ones he would like to be, and then seeks to become them, so, too, the author of a novel seeks to create himself by reflecting himself in his characters and then rising to the level of his creations, who are in this way responsible for his existence. The author is thus both the creator of his characters and their creation. "*To be or not to be!* . . . so said Hamlet, one of those who invented Shakespeare."[61]

Augusto Pérez is thus the invention and the inventor of Una-

[58] *Obras*, XVI, 637.
[59] *TEN*, p. 25 (*Obras*, IX, 420).
[60] Pirandello's *Six Characters in Search of an Author* was published in 1921, seven years after the appearance of *Niebla*.
[61] *Obras*, II, 972 (*MST*, p. 289).

muno, who assumes the fictional aspect of himself by becoming a character within his own novel. "Because," asks the author, "who am I, after all? Who is this chap who signs himself 'Miguel de Unamuno'? Well, he is one of my characters, one of my creatures, one of my 'agonists'!"[62] When Augusto learns that Unamuno is preparing to kill him off, he visits him in his study and angrily challenges him: "You also will die, Don Miguel; you will die and all those who think me will die!"[63] But Augusto—and Unamuno—will live on timelessly as fictional, that is, real, creations; and in this, art realizes its true, its sublimest role, that of the achievement of immortality. "Whence was art born? From the thirst for immortality," says one of Unamuno's characters.[64]

Every man is a fiction, a legend unto himself and others. "Every man, really a man," writes Miguel de Unamuno, "is the creature of a legend, written or oral. And there is nothing but legend or, in other words, novel."[65]

What it means to be a self-invented fiction, a creation of one's own legend, can be admirably exemplified by two of Unamuno's contemporaries. Notable is the example of that Ramón Valle who created in his fictional Marqués de Bradomín the extravagant figure that he himself sought to become as the living legend known as Ramón María del Valle-Inclán, "the finest walking mask that ever crossed the Calle de Alcalá," his biographer calls him.[66] And then there is the example of Azorín, who subscribes in life and art to Unamuno's version of the created creator. "You are I," says the author domineeringly to his protagonist in one of Azorín's *novelas*; to which the character demurs: "You create me and then, instead of me looking like you, you are the one who tries to look like me. . . . That is what happens to all authors who create a character, who create him with their blood, with their feelings, with their joys, with their sorrows."[67] Such is the striking personal confirmation of José Martínez Ruiz, who creates a

[62] *TEN*, p. 26 (*Obras*, IX, 420).
[63] *Obras*, II, 982 (*MST*, p. 305).
[64] Don Fulgencio in *Amor y pedagogía* (*Obras*, II, 546).
[65] *Obras*, X, 916.
[66] Ramón Gómez de la Serna, *Don Ramón María del Valle-Inclán* (2d ed.; Buenos Aires and México: Espasa-Calpe Argentina, 1948), p. 28.
[67] *El libro de Levante* (Buenos Aires: Losada, 1952), pp. 42–43.

character called Azorín and then identifies himself with him, to be forever known by the name of his creation. And finally there is the supreme example of self-creation, the legendary thirster for immortality, the dissenter and disturber of consciences, to which Unamuno constantly aspires.

Self-creation is thus inextricably bound up with the problem of dual personality, for the self-projected image of oneself is always being appropriated by others, and thus the desire for naked sincerity, for authenticity, coincides tragically with the role of the playactor which is constantly demanded of us. The tragic sense of life revolves around a tragic sense of personality. Perhaps no better example of this unavoidable duplicity can be cited than in what might well be considered Unamuno's finest hour. Generally overlooked in the outpouring of hot words that he heaped in heroic defiance on the hapless Millán Astray who had called for "Death to intelligence!" are the remarks that prefaced Unamuno's reply: "All of you are hanging on my words," he said to the audience gathered at the University of Salamanca. "You all know me and are aware that I am unable to remain silent." Transparently simple, starkly sincere words that at the same time only thinly cover the self-conscious actor. "You all know me," that is to say, "We all know what performance is expected of me, and I shall be faithful to that role." The actor is forever forced to adopt the mask that his audience imposes on him. And herein lies the essential function of self-creation. The preservation of personality demands of man that he constantly re-create himself by projecting the image of the one he would like to be, for only thus can he replenish personality with fresh vitality and keep from becoming engulfed by the image of himself that others seek to impose on him. The cycle is as continuous as life itself: from self-creation to imitation of the public image to further self-creation, in a ceaseless round. And this constant task can be accomplished only by maintaining a ceaseless state of tension between oneself and others, between author and character, between artist and public, between man and society. Unamuno's self-assigned role of disturber of consciences, of uncompromising combativeness, is actually a necessary opposition to prevent his created self from becoming absorbed by his "outer" self.

The ultimate truth of existence is that reality is created and that all creation is self-creation, whether human or divine. "The Book of Genesis," sums up Unamuno, "says that God created Man in his image and likeness, that is to say, He created him to be a mirror for Him to see Himself in him, to know Himself, to create Himself."[68]

---

[68] *Obras*, X, 862. A comparison that suggests itself as both revealing and rewarding is that of the relative positions of Unamuno and Ortega y Gasset on the question of personality. A preliminary consideration of Ortega's theme of *yo soy yo y mi circunstancia* would seem to indicate a lack of any sense of problematicity. The very use of the copulative y in the celebrated phrase supports such an interpretation. Even more conclusively corroborative are passages like the following, in which the conformation of the individual to and by his environment is categorized as taking place "naturally": "To start with, we are what our world invites us to be, and the basic features of our soul are impressed upon it by the form of its surroundings as in a mould. Naturally, for our Life is no other than our relations with the world around. The general aspect which it presents to us will form the general aspect of our own life" (José Ortega y Gasset, *The Revolt of the Masses* [New York: Norton, 1932], p. 67).

7

ON THE INTERPRETATION OF *NIEBLA*
Alexander A. Parker

So much has been written about *Niebla* ("Mist") that it is not
easy to select the important lines of interpretation,[1] but two
things seem clear: first, that, until recently, there tended to be a
cleavage between the literary critic or historian and the philosopher; and second, that all the lines of approach converge on the
famous interview between Unamuno and his fictional character,
an interview in which Unamuno intervenes as a character in his
own fiction while, at the same time, the fictional character is made
to intervene in the life of Unamuno outside the novel.

Some literary critics have been uneasy about *Niebla*, and most
have tended to emphasize the limitations of Unamuno's technique as a novelist. Eugenio de Nora, for instance, sees the Spaniard's novels as narrations that attempt to disentangle the
contradictions in preexisting philosophical statements. Augusto
Pérez, the protagonist of *Niebla*, is not a "living" character but
a phantom, because he is an intellectual creation incarnating the
concept of the unreality or precariousness of existence. He is not
placed in a real human predicament in which he could experience
real perplexity. There is, in fact, no plot and ultimately, no character as such; there is only Unamuno arbitrarily holding forth
on his own personal problems. At the end it is not the character
who rebels against the author, but Unamuno who turns on God,
and this has nothing to do with whatever plot has led up to it.
The narrative is purely capricious; there is no novelistic neces-

[1] Some of the literature on *Niebla* was not accessible to me while I
was preparing this paper. I hope I have not been guilty of injustice in
omitting to name some particular interpretation.

116

sity, no reason that what happens to Augusto should happen at all.[2]

Serrano Poncela's attempt to analyze Augusto Pérez as a literary character produces a much more positive result, but it still leaves the critic up against the incongruity of the ending. The basic problem presented in *Niebla*, as he sees it, is that even though existential reality be not admitted, a man can be frightened by the intuition of it and shun its discovery. Augusto is thus unable to live an authentic life because he is unwilling to exercise freedom; shirking responsibility, he confuses living with dreaming, and after his attempt to fill the void has brought only humiliation, his refusal to win his freedom leads inevitably to the decision to commit suicide. But the interview with Unamuno gives the ending a perverse twist. The attempt to explain existence in terms of a dream shared by men and things, itself surrounded by a wider dream, that of God dreaming himself, reduces the structure of the universe to absurdity.[3] This, I am sure, is a sentiment that very many of the ordinary readers of *Niebla* must have echoed.

The philosopher's approach can be more typically represented by Julián Marías, for whom the task of interpreting any work by Unamuno, including his novels, is strictly a philosophical problem.[4] He therefore disregards character and plot and finds the elaboration of an "ontological scheme." Throughout the novel Augusto doubts his own reality; but a literary character, an *ente de ficción*, is "real" in the sense that a person in a dream is real: he has a temporal existence like that of a human being, but he has no substantial nature and dissolves into nothing when the author's inventive dreaming comes to an end. Similarly, a real man, looked at from God's point of view, has no substantial nature because his existence depends on his Creator; therefore, he too is an *ente de ficción*, dreamed by God, but capable in his turn of dreaming other *entes de ficción*, namely the characters of

---

[2] Eugenio G. de Nora, *La novela española contemporánea* (Madrid: Editorial Gredos, 1958), I, 23–25.

[3] Segundo Serrano Poncela, *El pensamiento de Unamuno* (Mexico: Fondo de Cultura Económica, 1953), pp. 104–105, 186–187.

[4] Julián Marías, *Miguel de Unamuno* (Madrid: Espasa-Calpe, 1943), prologue, p. 7.

literature. Fiction and reality are therefore linked in a relation of subordination: the reality of a novelistic character is subordinate when seen from man's standpoint, but man is also subordinate when seen from God's.[5]

Until recently, any reader of novels, as distinct from a student of philosophy, who asked what this ontology had to do with Augusto's story, with the events that lead up to the fateful decision to take his own life, would have been hard put to it to find an answer. Interpretations, coming, as they did, from *either* literary critics *or* philosophers, had split the novel in two, as the critics emphasized the character of Augusto Pérez, and the philosophers, the ending. This division seemed unavoidable, and the reader was left with two apparently incompatible parts. We had to take the unpredictable Unamuno as we found him and be content with the loophole he had himself conveniently provided, that of the *nivola*, a form of narrative literature that could be split into incompatible parts without detriment to itself. However, the appearance of Carlos Blanco-Aguinaga's masterly and epoch-making book, *El Unamuno contemplativo*, transformed the whole study of Unamuno's novels by disclosing a series of persistent symbols through which the almost forgotten contemplative Unamuno, submerged by the more strident Unamuno *agónico*, gave expression to a deep-lying desire to escape from reason, doubt, and struggle into a peace of the unconscious in which contraries are resolved and history fuses with eternity. In expounding the symbol of the mother and its corollary, the *niño-hombre* ("child-man"), Dr. Blanco-Aguinaga pointed out, for the first time, how the presence of Augusto's mother is diffused throughout the whole of *Niebla*, and how Augusto himself is therefore associated with the concept of *desnacer*, the sleep of the unconscious in the symbolical return to the womb.[6]

If there has been in the study of Unamuno a gulf between the literary critic and the philosopher, this work should close it. After thus fitting *Niebla* into a new interpretation of Unamuno, Dr. Blanco-Aguinaga proceeded to give us, only a few months

[5] *Ibid.*, pp. 101–102.
[6] Carlos Blanco-Aguinaga, *El Unamuno contemplativo* (Mexico: El Colegio de México, 1959), pp. 129–135.

ago, his interpretation of the novel itself.[7] His argument is so tightly knit that it is impossible to summarize; I hope I do not distort it too seriously by selecting and simplifying. A brief but excellent analysis of the character of Augusto Pérez leads Dr. Blanco-Aguinaga to the conclusion that his decision to commit suicide is intended, logically, as a positive gesture that will turn the tables on Fate; but discovering that he is only a character of fiction, Augusto finds that he cannot kill himself. The greater part of Dr. Blanco-Aguinaga's paper then deals with the famous interview, which he considers the only possible climax of the story. The important thing about the interview is that a new character, Miguel de Unamuno, enters the novel; far from playing, as he intended, the role of an omnipotent creator, he lays himself open to his character's charge of not being God and not being immortal: he is, in fact, "simply another player acting out the role of author." Unamuno's intervention results from his constant endeavor to demonstrate the injustice of death by affirming his own presence. But since the realm of fiction is the one in which the author is most in danger of disappearing, Unamuno must create a type of novel in which the author apparently creates free subjects in whom the reader can immerse himself while being aware that he (the reader) is giving them a life they do not have, and so being aware of the presence of an author who never really vanishes from his work. Unamuno thus affirms his presence in both Augusto's world and our world—but only until "our novel" ends. The purpose of this "game of fiction" is to reveal "the precariousness of existence."[8]

This is the most subtle of all the interpretations of *Niebla*. It seeks to provide, as no other does, a link between the character of Augusto Pérez and the ending of the novel. If we are to

[7] Carlos Blanco-Aguinaga, "Unamuno's *Niebla*: Existence and the Game of Fiction," *Modern Language Notes*, LXXIX (1964), 188–205.

[8] The interplay of fiction and reality in *Niebla* and the complicated perspective of its structure (a prologue by one who is a character in the novel, the interpolated stories, etc.) are attributed by Dr. Blanco-Aguinaga to the influence of Cervantes. I am more convinced by another very recent study which attributes it to the influence of Kierkegaard: Ruth House Webber, "Kierkegaard and the Elaboration of Unamuno's *Niebla*," *Hispanic Review*, XXXII (1964), 118–134.

pass from his humiliating existence as a joke for others to his attempt to assert his power over destiny by suicide, and on still further to the precariousness of existence in general, then it is a fitting climax for Unamuno to intrude, asserting his power over the destiny of his characters only to find that he has made himself a character subject to destiny. Nonetheless, we may perhaps feel that the link between the two parts of the novel is rather a weak one: Augusto's discovery that he cannot commit suicide because he is only a character in fiction is difficult to take seriously as part of the exploration of the paradoxes and ambiguities of existence.

All these interpretations of *Niebla* (and, I suspect, every interpretation) follow from a preoccupation with the interview between the character and the author. I propose a different approach, a look at the way in which the novel is presented, at the frame in which the picture is set. This "frame" consists of two prologues and an epilogue. The first prologue is attributed to Víctor Goti, a character in the novel, while the second is by Unamuno himself. As a character in the novel, Víctor Goti has a double role: he is a man with a personal story, and he is a man writing a novel. In this latter capacity, he doubles Unamuno to some extent in that it is he who first tells Augusto that he is an *ente de ficción*, and who invents the term *nivola* and expounds it.[9] Unamuno's doubling of himself in this way has been convincingly attributed to the influence of Kierkegaard;[10] Kierkegaard's influence may explain how Unamuno came to think of two different prologue writers, but it does not tell us why he needed to have two prologues. The reason is odd enough: apparently he required to put forward two different interpretations of the novel's final episode. Víctor, in one prologue, maintains that Augusto committed suicide; the author, in the other, denies this and affirms that Augusto died because he, the author, willed it. Thus, at the novel's beginning, we are presented with an "unofficial" and an "official" version of its ending. While the "author" gives us the official version, Unamuno (and I think it legitimate to make this distinction) clearly wants us to know that there is

9 *Niebla*, chaps. x, xvii.
10 Webber, *op. cit.*, p. 120.

another version and to let it remain in our minds as a possibility.[11] We do in fact find that the ending is actually presented ambiguously. This ambiguity has, I think, been overlooked, and it is one of the points I wish to examine.

The epilogue, like the double prologue, is not straightforward, for it is a funeral oration delivered by Augusto's dog, Orfeo. Dr. Blanco-Aguinaga sees this canine function as part of the general Cervantine influence behind *Niebla*. Cervantes had made two dogs, Cipión and Berganza, discuss men; Unamuno makes a dog discuss man also.[12] Although the respective dogs are very different, this influence may well exist; but it does not tell us anything about a possible function of the dog in *Niebla* which merits his being chosen to write its epilogue. On at least two occasions, Orfeo has been called the only positive, or the most human, character in the novel;[13] but only one critic, as far as I know, has seen a possible significance in him, suggesting that Unamuno might have intended to symbolize in the dog the state of natural innocence.[14] I think this supposition is correct.

A neglected feature of the first prologue raises an additional question in the interpretation of this novel. Víctor Goti anticipates that some readers may object to parts of it as being pornographic—"passages that are coarse, or, if you please, obscene"[15]—and goes on to say that Unamuno repudiates any such intention and claims that such crudities as may exist are there only as the starting point for the consideration of other matters. This prologue then proceeds to attack pornographic literature, to

[11] For Unamuno himself the second prologue was final, and that is why I call it "official." In "Una entrevista con Augusto Pérez," which he wrote for *La Nación* of Buenos Aires, November 2, 1915 (*Obras*, X, 333–343), death by decree is reaffirmed, and in the "Historia de *Niebla*," which he wrote for the 1935 edition, the question of suicide is never raised. I am concerned with the situation that prevailed when the novel was being written.

[12] Blanco-Aguinaga, "Unamuno's *Niebla*: Existence and the Game of Fiction," p. 199.

[13] Robert Kirsner, "The Novel of Unamuno: A Study in Creative Determinism," *Modern Language Journal*, XXXVII (1953), 129; and de Nora, *op. cit.*, p. 25.

[14] José Emilio González, "Reflexiones sobre 'Niebla' de Unamuno," *Asomante*, XVII (1961), 68. This suggestion is not elaborated.

[15] *MST*, p. 13 (*Obras*, II, 789).

contrast the erotic with the bellicose, and to associate the former, disparagingly, with metaphysics, and the latter, approvingly, with religion. These ideas, typically Unamunian in themselves, seem rather irrelevant in the context of our novel. The idea that any passages in *Niebla* could, even in 1914, be considered porno-graphic is absurd; perhaps that explains why these remarks have not attracted attention. Yet the fact that Unamuno so insistently defended himself against a charge that no one has ever made should make us pause: there may be a pointer here to something that troubled him and that might be relevant to the interpretation of his novel.

Three questions, therefore, are posed by the form in which *Niebla* is presented. Why should there be any doubt about the manner of the protagonist's death? Why should Unamuno go out of his way to anticipate a charge, clearly unfounded, of writ-ing pornography? Does Augusto's dog Orfeo, who speaks the epilogue, have any special significance in the novel? These are the questions I try to answer in this essay. They are, in fact, in-terconnected.

It is difficult not to be sentimental about dogs. Unamuno, in 1906, wrote a poem, *Elegía en la muerte de un perro* ("Elegy on the Death of a Dog"),[16] in which he came perilously near to sentimentality. At first sight, the end of *Niebla* with the dog's dying of grief at his master's death is near it too. It is so obvious a touch that perhaps Orfeo has been dismissed as obvious also. Further, it will be remembered that in the course of the novel, Víctor, in defending the legitimacy of a *nivola*, says that it con-sists of a great deal of dialogue and very little action. What happens then, asks Augusto, if a character is left alone? "Then— a monologue. And in order that it shall have some of the appear-ance of a dialogue, I bring in a dog, to whom the character addresses himself."[17] Perhaps Orfeo's being presented as a con-venient excuse for monologues has been another reason for ne-glecting him; but, in fact, after Orfeo makes his entry into the plot, not all Augusto's monologues are addressed to him. Augusto talks to himself on some occasions and to Orfeo on others, and the

16 *Obras*, XIII, 348–352.
17 *MST*, p. 166 (*Obras*, II, 896).

basic difference between these "occasions" results in a basic difference between the two types of monologue. I cannot prove, within the scope of this essay, that the difference exists, for to analyze all Augusto's monologues would mean summarizing a large part of the novel; however, there are fewer monologues addressed to Orfeo, making it possible to analyze them in sequence. If these monologues are placed first in the context of Orfeo's discovery, I think a certain distinctive pattern can be seen to emerge from within them. Any reader who thinks it worthwhile can check whether I am right in believing that this pattern is, in general, absent from Augusto's monologues to himself.

A clue to the significance of Orfeo is provided by another poem written in the same year as the *Elegía en la muerte de un perro*. This is the one entitled *En una ciudad extranjera* ("In a Foreign City"). A stranger in a foreign city, Unamuno watches the humanity from which he feels isolated. A dog approaches and lets him stroke it, thereby making him realize what it is that unites men in brotherhood. It is something that comes not from within their hearts but from things outside them—from plants, the trees, the domestic animals, on all of which man has left his mark. Dogs, tamed and trained by men, are the link of brotherhood between them.

> Come, friendly dog,
> creator of brotherhood among men,
> for you unite us
> more than we unite ourselves
> of our own impulse.[18]

If, continues the poem, love could one day well up from the human heart so that "man with a longing for man" should look for a brother, the earth would disappear, for Paradise would have come.

Niebla is a novel in which love, or what passes in the world for love, is very far from being "brotherhood among men." In all the principal characters around Augusto, as well as in all the subsidiary stories and anecdotes, the relation between the sexes

[18] *Obras*, XIII, 361–368, ll. 199–203.

is cynically calculating, selfish, socially deceitful, and tragic (or marred in some other way), and is redeemed, when it is redeemed, only by becoming creative in the procreation of children. In this loveless world, Orfeo is the symbol of "brotherhood among men": he holds out the promise for Augusto of a reality beyond the mist of isolation. For reality to be established through human intercommunication, love must be faithful and true; and because he is a dog, Orfeo's love for his master is of this kind. Because he is a dog, his love is also natural: it is just there, a part of him, not cerebral, not a subject for introspective analysis. Because he is a dog, his love for his master is also innocent—not just because it is guileless, but because it is without passion, without unease, without taste of forbidden fruit. And because Orfeo is a dog, Augusto's love for him can be faithful, natural, and innocent. Their love is the pattern for that which ought to exist between men and men, and between men and women.

Up to the time that Augusto feels the need to find reality by finding himself, he has been lapped in a sort of dream, lapped in the all-embracing care of a mother's love; and love between a son and his mother is a love that is faithful, natural, and innocent. But now his mother is dead, and he must wake from his dream of innocence and build a bridge from himself to others. The "other" becomes, by accident, embodied in Eugenia. Instead of a mother figure to envelop him protectively, she turns out to be inaccessible because she already has a boyfriend. How difficult it all is, thinks Augusto in chapter v, and he lets his memory re-create his mother's presence and their relation to each other. If only she were still alive, he says to himself, *she* would find the solution to this problem of Eugenia and her boyfriend. At that very moment he hears faint yelps and sees an abandoned newborn puppy. He takes it home and brings it up on a baby's bottle. "Thenceforth Orfeo was the confidant of his soliloquies and the recipient of the secret of his love for Eugenia."[19] Augusto's finding Orfeo is thus associated with his mother, and this association is maintained. Later, in the crisis when Eugenia angrily rejects Augusto's gift of her redeemed mortgage, indig-

[19] *MST*, p. 60 (*Obras*, II, 829).

nantly accusing him of the attempt to bribe her, he goes into a church and, shutting his eyes, sees his mother again before him:[20]

> And he relived again all of his life as a son, when he formed a part of his mother and dwelt under her protection; and then he thought of the death of the poor lady, of that gentle, composed, and unhurried death, without pain, when she departed like a bird of passage quietly setting out upon its flight. Then he remembered, or dreamed again, his finding of Orfeo.[21]

We have, then, on the one hand, Eugenia, and, on the other, his mother and Orfeo.

As soon as Orfeo is christened and given his bottle, Augusto utters the first of the monologues to the dog:

> "Listen, Orfeo . . . we have to fight. What do you advise me to do? If only my mother had known you—But you will understand, you'll understand, when you sleep in the lap of Eugenia with her soft and gentle hand resting upon you. And now, what are we going to do, Orfeo?"[22]

The lap of the mother is to be succeeded by the lap of Eugenia. For the moment the woman's lap is still merely an innocent resting-place for a dog—or, of course, for Augusto himself. But there is a difference between the lap of the mother and the lap of Eugenia: between them stands the tree of the knowledge of good and evil. On the one side, there is innocence, on the other, knowledge of a certain kind. The pattern of Augusto's monologues to Orfeo has now emerged: through them will be implicitly expressed the conflict between innocence and that knowledge to which Augusto's gradually awakening senses call him.

Until Augusto's finding of Orfeo, love and the possibility of marriage were mere abstractions. Even with his thoughts on Eugenia, Augusto can pass her in the street without noticing her. During a game of chess in chapter iii, Víctor tells Augusto that he is not *enamorado* ("in love") but only *enamoriscado* ("infatuated"),[23] the proof being that Augusto cannot tell him whether

---

[20] For the symbolic association of churches with the mother, see Blanco-Aguinaga, *El Unamuno contemplativo*, pp. 261–267.

[21] *MST*, p. 121 (*Obras*, II, 868).

[22] *MST*, p. 60 (*Obras*, II, 829).

[23] *MST*, p. 45 (*Obras*, II, 816).

Eugenia is dark or fair, tall or short. On his way home, musing on this conversation, Augusto admits that he has fallen in love before finding the person to love, and he wonders how he can be in love with Eugenia if he doesn't know her. "Bah!" he adds, "the knowledge will come later. Love comes before knowledge. . . . First comes love and then understanding."[24] Turning these thoughts over in his mind, he passes Eugenia again, realizing only after she has gone that the eyes he noticed might have been hers. This is indeed love without knowledge because it is love without acquaintance. When he tells his servants of his intention to marry, he finds that they, like Víctor, know Eugenia; everybody knows her except him, and yet he professes to be in love with her.

Love aspires to a knowledge other than the detached knowledge of acquaintance. Orfeo marks the stages of the inner conflict produced in Augusto by the awakening of sensuality. The second monologue to the dog takes up the whole of chapter vii. Its burden is the problem of self-knowledge, which is becoming an agonizing one, for though Augusto has not yet spoken to Eugenia, she is not now a mere abstraction but a sensation: she is the beneficent rain beginning to wash away the mist surrounding his existence, and he can now feel and touch his own soul: "Thanks to love, Orfeo, my soul is beginning to pain me in its very marrow."[25]

There follows his second visit to Eugenia's aunt and uncle. He must get to know her. "The first step," he says to the aunt, "is to see each other and get acquainted."[26] Thereupon the uncle, whose eccentricity and anarchism make him liable to express the unexpected, breaks in with this remark: "The only effective knowledge is that which comes *post nuptias*. You have heard me explain before . . . what knowing signifies in the language of the Bible. And believe me, there is no other knowledge more real and essential than that, no knowledge more . . ."[27] This is followed by Augusto's "knowing" (becoming acquainted

24 *MST*, pp. 43–44 (*Obras*, II, 818).
25 *MST*, p. 74 (*Obras*, II, 837).
26 *MST*, p. 75 (*Obras*, II, 838).
27 *MST*, p. 76 (*Obras*, II, 838).

with) Eugenia for the first time; and when he leaves her house, he steps into a world that appears illuminated with a new light:

> He was beginning to know the world. And without even guessing how he came to the idea, he set himself to reflect upon the very deep source of that common tendency to associate the sin of the flesh with the fall of our first parents, for having tasted of the fruit of the tree of knowledge of good and evil.[28]

Whereupon he enters his house and picks up Orfeo:

> "Ah, when you see her, Orfeo, when you know her!—Then you will feel the woe of being only a dog, just as I feel the woe of being only a man! And tell me, Orfeo, how do you dogs ever know anything if you don't sin—if your knowledge is not sin? Knowledge that is not sin is not what you call knowledge, it is not rational."[29]

Dogs are innocent; innocence, because it is sinless, belongs to a sphere outside that of reason. But it is out of the sphere of innocence and into that of reason that Augusto persists in stepping, wanting to know the what, the why, and the how, making his problem almost a metaphysical one. When Víctor tells him that he is not in love but only thinks he is, Augusto asks how one can know that one is really in love. Since Víctor evades an answer, Augusto goes with his question to Orfeo:

> "Let's see, Orfeo, how does being in love differ from merely thinking it? Am I or am I not in love with Eugenia? Is it true that when I see her, my heart does not thump in my breast and my blood is not on fire? Is it true that I am not like other men? I shall have to show them, Orfeo, that I am just as good as they are!"[30]

He looks for the answer to his question in the self-assertion of passion, and experiences the first stirrings of it with Rosario, after which there comes his sixth monologue to the dog: "And as he threw himself into the bed, at the foot of which Orfeo was sleeping, he said to himself, 'Ah, Orfeo, Orfeo, this sleeping alone, alone, sleeping a dream alone! The dream of one person alone is an illusion—a mere appearance; the dream of two

28 *MST*, p. 84 (*Obras*, II, 844).
29 *MST*, p. 85 (*Obras*, II, 844–845).
30 *MST*, pp. 98–99 (*Obras*, II, 853–854).

persons is truth, reality."[31] The next monologue to the dog comes after the disastrous attempt to prove his love to Eugenia by redeeming the mortgage on her house:

> "But what eyes, Orfeo, what eyes! How they flashed when she said to me, 'You want to buy me! You want to buy—not my love, for that can't be bought, but my body! Keep my house!' I buy her body—her body! My own is already too much for me, Orfeo, my own is too much. What I need is soul. Soul! Soul! And a soul of fire, like that which irradiates from those eyes of Eugenia. Her body—her body—yes, her body is splendid, magnificent, divine; but really her body is soul, pure soul; every part of it life, meaning, poetry! For myself I have more than enough body, Orfeo, and I have too much body because I am wanting in soul. Or may it not be, rather, that I am wanting in soul because I have too much body?"[32]

Through all these chapters there have been other monologues, without Orfeo. Most of these also center on the problem of his relations with Eugenia, or with women in general; but, as I have already stated, they seem to follow a rather different pattern. The difference can be illustrated by a passage from the end of chapter xvii. After hearing from Víctor about the *nivola* he is writing, Augusto starts a monologue: "This life of mine? Is it a novel? Or a *nivola*? Or what is it?" If our existing is only God dreaming, then let us keep on praying to him so that he doesn't wake up and thereby annihilate us. Then suddenly Augusto begins to think of the two women, and this is how the transition is made:

> "Ah, my Eugenia! My Eugenia! And my Rosarito . . ."
> "Hullo, Orfeo!"
> Orfeo, who had run out to meet him, was frisking about and trying to climb up his legs. He picked him up and the little animal began to lick his hand.
> "Señorito," Liduvina said to him, "here is Rosarito with the washing waiting for you."[33]

Whenever Augusto's introspection takes a concretely sensual, or sexual, form, the dog appears.

[31] *MST*, p. 116 (*Obras*, II, 865).
[32] *MST*, pp. 136–137 (*Obras*, II, 878).
[33] *MST*, pp. 166–167 (*Obras*, II, 897).

In chapter xviii Augusto kisses Rosario—a passionate, agitated kiss, his first to any woman. And he then soliloquizes on the theme that all speech is falsehood and that "the only truth in human life is that which is physiological." Whereupon the soliloquy is temporarily broken: "Feeling a tongue licking his hand, he called out: 'Ah, you here, Orfeo?' " It then continues as the seventh to the dog:

"And when night comes I shall sleep, as I sleep other nights; and she will sleep too. But will Rosarito sleep? Shall I not have disturbed the tranquillity of her spirit? And that natural manner of hers, is it innocence or is it cunning? But perhaps there is nothing more cunning than innocence; or rather, nothing more innocent than cunning."

He sees that behind Rosario's apparent innocence there was jealousy of Eugenia, and he concludes that a man and a woman are never really in love, never know that they are in love, until they experience jealousy:

"In any case there is always need of a go-between, the Celestina; and society is the great Go-Between. *El Gran Galeoto!* . . . And therefore all this business of love is only one lie more. And the physiological side of it? Bah, this physiological affair is not love or anything like it! And for this reason it is truth! But—come, Orfeo, let us go and get supper. That is certainly truth!"[34]

Eating is true, natural, and innocent because there is no possibility of lying; as this monologue had previously affirmed, "the only genuine man is the physiological man, the man who doesn't speak, hence the man who doesn't lie."[35] Physical love can be innocent and true on the same level, if it too is divorced from reason and speech, and therefore from falsehood and deceit; but this means giving up the pretense that it is love and putting it on the same level as eating. Once love is thus "devalued" to its "physiological truth," a concupiscence that does not distinguish between one woman and another is but a single, logical step away; and Augusto's problem becomes agonizingly acute when he finds himself attracted to Liduvina, his servant, and has to

[34] *MST*, pp. 172–175 (*Obras*, II, 901–902).
[35] *MST*, p. 173 (*Obras*, II, 901).

order her out of the room. "This is terrible! Really, this is terrible!" he says. And then:

"Come here, Orfeo," he continued, picking up the dog. "What do you think I ought to do? How am I going to defend myself until I make up my mind and marry? Ah, now I have it! An idea, a brilliant idea, Orfeo! Let us convert this matter of woman, which is now tormenting me, into a subject matter for study. What do you say to my devoting myself to the psychology of woman?"[36]

This question leads him to seek advice from Paparrigópulos, "who at that time was devoting himself to a study of women, though rather more of women in books than in life."[37]

Augusto's attempt to retain his innocence by avoiding the knowledge that frightens him and seeking instead a kind of abstract knowledge that will leave him with Orfeo and the memory of his mother has the contrary effect of leading him to the crisis of passion. Chapter xxiv must have been in Unamuno's mind when he made Víctor, in the first prologue, anticipate the accusation of writing pornography. The scene with Rosario, the final one, is described with restraint; nonetheless, it is clear that it ought to have culminated in Rosario's seduction as she herself expected and wanted. What is not clear is the reason for Augusto's withdrawal. Rosario seems to attribute it to ignorance or impotence.[38] Augusto later seems to imply that it was timidity.[39] Whatever the reason, the effect on both of them is humiliation at having appeared ridiculous. How ridiculous Augusto had in fact appeared to Rosario is evident later when Mauricio cynically and mockingly recalls the episode to him.

[36] *MST*, pp. 219–220 (*Obras*, II, 929).
[37] *Loc. cit.*
[38] *MST*, p. 243 (*Obras*, II, 944): "'. . . forgive me, Rosario, forgive me. I didn't know what I was doing.' She thought: 'What he doesn't know is—what he didn't do.'"
[39] *MST*, pp. 272–273 (*Obras*, II, 962): "And now too, just as he was about to be married to Eugenia, he found himself more than ever tormented by what Mauricio had said about carrying off Rosario. It made him jealous, madly jealous, to think of the opportunity he had allowed to pass and of the ridiculous picture of himself that he had left in the mind of the girl."

This scene with Rosario is followed by another visit to Víctor, where Unamuno applies a nicely ironical touch. Víctor begins to read aloud the latest addition to his novel:

> "But, man, it seems to me that this makes you out a different sort of person!" exclaimed Augusto.
> "How?"
> "Why, there are things here that border on the obscene, and at times they cross the border . . ."[40]

It is, of course, Augusto himself who has changed and the novel of his own life that is developing in this direction. Such crudities, says Víctor, are pedagogical: they are intended to help cure *solitarios* like Augusto, for whom the only remedy is marriage— it doesn't matter to whom. Augusto thereupon plucks up courage for the decisive step of proposing again to Eugenia, and this time he is accepted. For three chapters there has been no mention of Orfeo, for in these three chapters Augusto has stepped into a world where the dog does not belong. When finally, in chapter xxvii, Orfeo is mentioned again, it is to emphasize their separation, for Eugenia insists that once they are married the dog must go.[41]

Orfeo reappears in chapter xxviii, and the manner of his appearance is enlightening. Mauricio, who has come ostensibly to thank Augusto for the employment he has found him, discloses not only that Rosario is leaving with him but that the two are laughing together at the ridiculous figure Augusto had cut with the girl. Everything swims before the stricken Augusto's eyes, and he loses all sense of reality. He summons Liduvina for her to assure him that he has not been dreaming and asks her to call Domingo, her husband, for further confirmation. But she says that Orfeo would be better, and the dog walks into the room. Shattered by the revelation of Rosario's disloyalty in exposing him defenseless to the mockery of Mauricio, realizing that the one moment of passion has brought him abject humiliation, Augusto can turn for consolation only to the loyal innocence of the dog in what becomes his ninth monologue to Orfeo. But he has

[40] *MST*, p. 247 (*Obras*, II, 946–947).
[41] *MST*, p. 261 (*Obras*, II, 955).

to tell him that they must soon part because it is imperative he get married in order to awake to reality.[42]

The pattern of these monologues addressed to Orfeo seems to me consistent. When it was a question of Augusto's being torn, consciously or unconsciously, between retaining his innocence and seeking the knowledge of passion, Orfeo was there. When it was a question of theorizing in the clouds about love in general or, at the other extreme, of Augusto's actually turning his back on innocence, Orfeo was absent. Now that it is a question of revulsion against the callousness that passion has disclosed, Orfeo is back. And the tenth and last of the monologues comes when, through Eugenia's brutal desertion of Augusto, the latter is humiliated and hurt beyond measure. His efforts to find himself through the knowledge of love have led to his being kicked about as something worthless:

> Presently he felt something tugging at his trousers. It was Orfeo, who had run out to meet him and offer him consolation. At the sight of Orfeo he experienced, strange to say, great joy. He took him into his arms and said, "Congratulate yourself, little Orfeo, congratulate yourself! And let us congratulate one another! They won't drive you out of the house now; they won't take you away from me now; they won't part us now! ... You, Orfeo, you are faithful; you are the faithful one! I dare say that someday you'll be looking for your mate; but not for that will you leave the house, not for that will you abandon your master. You are faithful!"[43]

Augusto then shuts himself in his room. The images of the three who have mocked and humiliated him give way to the image of his mother. He bursts into tears: "He wept and wept and wept; and in the silent weeping his thought was gradually dissolved."[44] His thought dissolves; he ceases to think. Víctor, who visits him, sees only two alternatives before him, either to stop thinking or to "devour himself." Does that mean that he ought to kill himself, asks Augusto. Víctor replies: "I'll have nothing to do with that. Good-bye."[45] In this dialogue, ceasing to think is equated with

[42] *MST*, pp. 270–271 (*Obras*, II, 960–961).
[43] *MST*, pp. 278–279 (*Obras*, II, 966).
[44] *MST*, p. 280 (*Obras*, II, 967).
[45] *MST*, p. 290 (*Obras*, II, 973).

ceasing to exist; to abdicate thought is to give up the struggle, to slip into nothingness—in short, to commit suicide. "Devouring himself," on the other hand, is to go on living a tormented existence, accepting suffering, increasing it, even, by the agony of doubt—in short, to live the "agonizing life."

Of these two courses of action, only suicide is consistent with Augusto's character, that of a vague dreamer, groping clumsily after self-knowledge, reluctant to abandon innocence, frightened of passion. Such a man can quite naturally take his own life— at least commit a symbolic kind of suicide which will represent, in effect, the return to his mother's womb, which he was never happy at having left. It is far less easy to visualize such a man affirming his anguish as a positive element in the struggle to come to terms with existence.

Víctor Goti, the "unofficial" Unamuno (i.e., the novelist), insinuates the idea of suicide into Augusto's mind but does not decide definitely for or against it. The "official" Unamuno in Salamanca (i.e., the philosopher) on whom Augusto calls repudiates the idea of suicide, which he calls a *diabólica idea*,[46] not because he demands that Augusto should live on in struggle and suffering (since Augusto dies quickly in any event), but in order to assert the deaths of all of us, each one of his readers together with himself, thus bringing us all into Augusto's dilemma. If it is made a clear instance of suicide, then we are outside it, detached; if it is death by an order from on high, then we are all, each one of us, involved in it directly by reason of the death that we, like Augusto, shall have to face because God decrees it. Thus to make Augusto die a "natural" death is to introduce a philosophical, or rather, theological, consideration that is irrelevant to the novel *qua* novel, since it is extraneous to the action and contrary to the character. In the interview with Unamuno, Augusto asserts that an author cannot go against the logic of his characters' development. As regards himself, he argues, "I have my own character, my own manner of being, my own inwrought logic, and this logic demands that I kill myself."[47] This is incontrovertible. Furthermore, from the standpoint of an

[46] *MST*, p. 262 (*Obras*, II, 974).
[47] *MST*, p. 298 (*Obras*, II, 978).

artistic plot development, Unamuno's appearance in person in his own novel is an indefensible intrusion. This deliberate breaking of the law of artistic consistency accounts for the unease that some critics, and doubtless many readers, have felt about the work. But let us imagine it without the famous interview, with Augusto committing suicide like Apolodoro in *Amor y pedagogía* before him. Would we really prefer it thus? Surely no.

For thirty years the ending of *Niebla* has fascinated nearly everybody and has been one reason for an endless stream of essays about this novel. Yet it has been overlooked that Unamuno, enemy though he claimed to be of all logic and consistency, did seek to safeguard what, according to traditional, pre-*nivola*, conceptions, we might call his artistic integrity by incorporating in *Niebla* a careful ambiguity established not only by the device of the two prologues but by the fact that everything possible is done to keep the issue of suicide open. The description of Augusto's death can perfectly well be taken as pointing to it. He is suddenly seized with a voracious appetite and, to the alarm of his servants, stuffs himself so much with food that he cannot stand. He has to be undressed and put to bed. The doctor attributes his death to a heart attack; Domingo, to indigestion; and Liduvina, to his having made up his mind to die: ". . . someone put it into his head to die; and of course if a man is set upon dying, in the end he dies . . . that is suicide and nothing but suicide. That is what he wanted, and he had his own way!"[48] Clearly we must take overeating to be the immediate cause of his death, but what caused the voracious appetite itself? It is open to us to see it either as the instrument through which Unamuno's sentence of death is carried out or as the fulfillment of Augusto's suicide wish.

I would suggest that in this ambiguity, made so deliberate by the two conflicting prologues, we have an example of the clash between the two Unamunos, the *contemplativo* and the *agónico*, whose existence Dr. Blanco-Aguinaga has expounded in such a masterly way: on the one hand, a strong, nonrational desire to find peace by self-abandonment to the unconscious; on the other,

[48] *MST*, p. 318 (*Obras*, II, 991).

the agonized resistance to this desire by asserting, in the face of final death, the right of the individual to conscious existence as against annihilation. The death wish of Augusto is the desire for peace through the surrender of the conscious reason; but the Unamuno *agónico* cannot allow his creation to give up the struggle so readily. He therefore turns Augusto's death into the *agonía* of one decreed from above, against the injustice of which the victim rebels. Thus Augusto's death is transformed into Unamuno's own death and the death of each one of us. But in his heart of hearts, the author (the Unamuno *contemplativo* now), does not want to deprive his suffering creature of his death wish. Víctor insinuates to Augusto that one solution for his problem would be the cessation of conscious thought. The possibility of this was strongly present all the time in the *niebla* that had enveloped his existence—in the difficulty he found in assuming responsibility, his clinging to the memory of his mother, his constant evocation of her presence, his sexual innocence and timidity, his brotherhood with Orfeo. And this instinct to abdicate conscious thought is also present, I think, in the voracious appetite that actually kills him. He himself sees it as his body's attempt to defend itself against death.[49] Going back to a passage quoted earlier, we recall Augusto's assertion that truth is to be found only in "the physiological man, the man who doesn't speak, hence the man who doesn't lie." In the course of his search for "knowledge," experience had shown Augusto that love is expressed in speech and that all speech is lying deception. By stuffing himself with food, he is turning himself into "the physiological man," abdicating speech and thought, and seeking to return to his mother's womb: ". . . undress me completely, completely," he says to his servant. "Leave me as my mother brought me into the world, as I was born—if indeed I was ever born . . . lay me down now. I want you yourself to lay me on the bed, for I can't move."[50]

[49] *MST*, pp. 310–311 (*Obras*, II, 985–986). There is an interesting symbolical explanation of Augusto's killing himself by overeating in Fred Abrams, "Sartre, Unamuno and the 'Hole Theory,'" *Romance Notes*, V (1963–1964), 6–11.

[50] *MST*, p. 314 (*Obras*, II, 988).

Augusto's desire to be naked is associated with the theme of innocence, as Orfeo's epilogue reveals. The dog's epilogue is a beautiful ending to the novel which rounds off the theme I have been tracing, the theme suggested by the question of pornography raised in the first prologue. In this epilogue Unamuno plays with the irony of the word *cinismo* ("dogginess" and "shamelessness") and with the irony in such words and expressions as *perruno* ("currish") and *perra vida* ("dog's life"), which are so alien to the loyalty and devotion of dogs. Real "cynicism" is innocent—it is purely physiological; but this innocence has been corrupted into men's degradation of sex, the thousand "human atrocities which they are at pains to call cur-like or cynical."[51] The process of corruption began when man stood upright and "had a feeling of shame and felt it necessary to cover the parts that he was showing."[52] But clothes, by hiding sex, perverted the innocence of nakedness into *cinismo* in the sense of *atrocidades perrunas*. And for dogs, says Orfeo, the strangeness of men lies in their being, first, hypocrites and disloyal, and second, lustful. But dogs, on the other hand, are loyal and innocent; so Orfeo refers to his relationship with Augusto as: "In talking to me, thus talking to himself, he talked to the dog that was in him. I kept his cynicism awake."[53] He kept alive Augusto's natural loyalty and innocence, which ultimately he could retain only by dying, by departing from the world of men. Only in death can purity be preserved; and so with the double meaning of "pure" comes Orfeo's vision of the Platonic Heaven:

> "Poor dear Master! What can have become of him? Where can that part of him be which spoke and dreamed in him? Perhaps there above, in the pure world, on the high plateau of the earth, in that fine region of the earth, all of it in fine colours as Plato saw it, which men call divine. . . . There in that pure Platonic world, in that world of incarnate ideas, lives the pure dog, the dog that is in the true sense cynical. And there too dwells my master! I feel my own soul becoming purified by this contact with death, with this purification of my master. I feel it mounting upward towards the mist into which he at last was dissolved,

[51] *MST*, pp. 328–329 (*Obras*, II, 998).
[52] *MST*, p. 328 (*Obras*, II, 997).
[53] *MST*, p. 330 (*Obras*, II, 998).

the mist from which he sprang and to which he returned. Orfeo feels the dark mist coming. And he runs to his master, jumping and wagging his tail. Dear Master! Dear Master! Poor man!"[54]

This death of Orfeo, far from being sentimental, is the only fitting conclusion to the story of Augusto's endeavor to find reality through a knowledge that, beginning in acquaintance, was to end in love. The poem *En una ciudad extranjera* had asserted that if men could ever learn from the love that dogs bear them to feel brotherhood for each other, the earth would disappear, having been transformed into Paradise. Only in a realm of pure idea created by the heart and not by the rational conscious mind can one conceive the natural, faithful, and innocent love that Augusto never received from any human being after his mother died, a love that the whole novel, especially through Orfeo, implicitly contrasts with erotic sensuality which, as the first prologue states, produces, or is produced by, "a curious desire to know what does not concern us—the original sin, in short . . . the metaphysical instinct, a longing to possess the knowledge of good and evil."[55]

That Orfeo, the symbol of innocence, should close the novel on a note of Platonic speculation is appropriate. Under the influence of a revived Platonism, European literature in the sixteenth century had dreamt the nostalgic dream of a purified, spiritualized human love in which physical passion, stilled and controlled by reason, played no part. For the Neoplatonist philosophers of the Renaissance, concupiscence was part of the evil inherent in matter and a serious impediment to the contemplation of pure ideas. There is something similar in Unamuno, though perhaps rather remotely so. There was no abnormality in his own life, but there is an abnormality in the relations between men and women in his novels, revealing an underlying repulsion, or if not that, an unease, a dissatisfaction with the scheme of things. His men are generally weak, often abjectly humiliated

---

[54] *MST*, pp. 330–331 (*Obras*, II, 999). When Orfeo was christened, Unamuno wrote: ". . . thus he baptized him, no one knows why, nor did he himself know" (*MST*, p. 60; *Obras*, II, 829). Was it because Orfeo was to enter the world beyond the grave to find the person he loved?

[55] *MST*, p. 15 (*Obras*, II, 790).

by the women who alone are masterful and who, impelled by the maternal instinct, are praying mantises who devour their mates.[56] I suggest that *Niebla* belongs in this context, that its central theme is the sadness of the human condition which makes the brotherhood of men impossible on earth, since truth and innocence cannot coexist in love with sexual passion. Much of this theme is indirectly, and therefore delicately, stated through the symbols of the mother and the dog; nonetheless, Unamuno's scruples were such that he feared he had been too direct.

This interpretation of *Niebla,* if it is valid, does not, of course, undermine the existentialist interpretations, for in the first prologue Unamuno places erotic passion in the context of metaphysics and religion. My aim has been to widen the field of interpretation and thereby to suggest answers to the adverse criticism that *Niebla* has received. Perhaps with a less one-sided insistence on the *ente de ficción,* the character of Augusto can be clarified into something nearer the so-called real human being that most readers still hope to find in a novel. Further, if I am right in detecting a consistent pattern in the material I have analyzed, then more support is forthcoming for Miss Webber's contention, arrived at from an examination of the interpolated stories, that *Niebla* has "a carefully thought out plan" and is "a tightly constructed work."[57] Its structural and thematic consistency, in an author who claimed to scorn all consistency, is indeed remarkable. Whether we call *Niebla* a *novela* or a *nivola* is of little consequence; what matters more is that Unamuno wrote it with a sure artistic instinct and with a firm control of concepts and symbols.

---

[56] I take the metaphor from Serrano Poncela, who gives what I think is the best account of Unamuno's ideas on, and novelistic treatment of, "Eros y Psique" (*op. cit.,* pp. 179–180, 191–199).

[57] Webber, *op. cit.,* p. 130.

8

THE SOUL ON STAGE
Ricardo Gullón

ACTING LEADS TO FEELING

Paradoxically, the principle that acting leads to feeling could be stated this way: the more a character acts out a role, the better he affirms his reality. In the extensive introduction to his play *El hermano Juan* (*"Brother Juan"*), Unamuno specifies: "All the ideal greatness of Don Juan Tenorio, his whole universal and external—that is, historical—reality, consists of his being the most eminently theatrical, representational, historical character there is; of the fact that he is always acting, always playing himself."[1]

The Don-less Juan in Unamuno's play lives, or allows his life to be lived, in the theater, which is his world. He is both at the heart of the action and apart from it, like an airplane pilot flying perilously in the hurricane's eye to gauge its strength. He is the center because he is surrounded, hedged in, squeezed by the others, and pressed on. He feels himself to be the axis on which events turn, yet at the same time he feels impelled by them. While the others come and go, he stays where he is, awaiting them perhaps, knowing beforehand when they will come and what for.

These "others"—Inés, Elvira, Antonio, Benito, and so on—give rise to disconnected scenes in which Juan participates without committing himself. A spectator as much as an actor, he seems to watch with relative curiosity the events woven around him, but always keeps his distance. Sometimes he is not sure of anything, not even of his feelings. Seeing him move about in the vagueness of a legend that has shrunken into a trivial Don

[1] *Obras*, XII, 866.

Juanism, one could well ask him, just as a patient in the Sarriá sanatorium once asked Unamuno himself, if he was really the authentic one, "the real one, and not the one they're always writing about." And the character in the play would be quick to ask himself, as his author did, "whether the poor lunatic was not right,"[2] because he realizes that his awareness of himself is a reflection of what is written about him, or of the role he plays.

Is there any other "authentic" self? Unamuno himself replied by asserting that among the possible men one may be, only God knows which is the authentic one. We must resign ourselves to what is within our reach, to discover, or at least try to discover, reality in our playing of roles. In one of his later writings, he wrote to a certain convert who was attempting to instruct and perhaps convince him: "You strike me as an actor; a sincere and maybe ingenuous one, but an actor just the same. You are playing a role, or rather, playing yourself-as-a-convert on the stage of your own conscience as a convert. You find yourself more interesting that way."[3] The major difference between Brother Juan and Don Miguel's correspondent is that the former knows perfectly well that his life is role playing, whereas the latter is fooling himself by imagining that he is living a reality transfigured through faith.

Both the convert and the character identify life and role, but Juan could get along without an audience; the others in the cast suffice as accessories to his personal drama. He is not unprecedented. Unamuno had already created a character concerned only with his own inner life, in his first novel: *Paz en la guerra* (*"Peace in War"*), 1897. Don Joaquín, a pious old man, considered his soul a field where battles were being fought against the devil, and the civil war that was then bleeding his country dry seemed to him to be of little moment when compared with such transcendent warfare. As grave and sensational as events in the exterior world were, they seemed monotonous against "the inexhaustible variety" of a conscience in motion.

In the final analysis Juan, like Unamuno, depends on no audience other than himself: Juan the spectator watching Juan the person exhibiting himself in the performance. Brother Juan is not trying to convince an audience: he is trying to convince himself. He plays his role to fill the emptiness of his soul; and if he turns to the others, it is to look for a reflection of the legend he would like to incarnate. If they believe in him, they will literally bring him to life, just as the characters do out of whose acting he is constituted. The first thing he says when the play opens is that he simply cannot understand himself. Naturally! That is a never-ending process. What was his life like before the play began? Does he have a secret? The others believe he does, and they act on this assumption, even though all along they suspect the truth, which he neither hides nor denies. He says: "In this theater, which is the world itself, everyone is born condemned to a role, and everyone must play it for life."[4]

In *Niebla* ("Mist"), the protagonist, Augusto Pérez, had posed the same problem in one of his monologues addressed to his dog, Orfeo: "All we do is play each one our role. All of us, characters, masks, actors! No one suffers or enjoys what he says and expresses and maybe believes he is enjoying and suffering; otherwise life would be impossible. Basically, we are quite unmoved."[5] This tranquillity is disconcerting in Brother Juan, whose will to be is not strong enough to induce him to act. Like Augusto, he is conscious that his anxieties and concerns are essentially figments of his imagination.

SINGULARITIES, IRREGULARITIES

The protagonist of *Brother Juan* was condemned at birth to play the role of Don Juan, a literary being who has no real existence except on the stage and who, of course, is not a creation of Unamuno's but a preexisting character from the world in which artistic figures rub shoulders with, and are taken for, real people. Fernando Lázaro thinks that "practically the only value of the play lies in how it illustrates the seducer's psychology and his relation to women,"[6] who are won by compassion for him,

---

[4] *Obras*, XII, 889.
[5] *Obras*, II, 901 (*MST*, p. 173).
[6] Fernando Lázaro, "El teatro de Unamuno," *Cuadernos de la Cátedra Miguel de Unamuno*, No. VII (1956), p. 27.

not by love. I touch on this point again later in this essay, for it is one of the important originalities in the play.

Brother Juan was one of Unamuno's last attempts to shed light on the problem of personality, a constantly recurring preoccupation of his. Using Don Juanism as a microcosm of this problem, he summarized in this play much of what he had been saying and writing about it for thirty years. As always, Don Miguel wished to portray a portion of his own experience. Juan, who resembles his author on this score, lives on stage and does not try to hide it. He has one lone obsession, death, which he feels is always near. Far from being a seducer or a deceiver, he plays with his cards face up and tells Inés and Elvira plainly: "I can't love you . . . , I don't know how to love . . . , I don't want to love." If women pursue him, it is to make him fulfill his destiny as a Don Juan. He wants the impossible, and confines himself to that one desire. The dialogues in which he takes part are often abrupt, and sometimes incongruous; he jumps around from one observation to another, and from one attitude to its opposite, following the course his rambling takes. If his attitudes seem disconnected, they are so only apparently: they are sensible and coherent within the system of sudden oscillations through which facets of a diffuse personality are gradually revealed.

The encounter between Inés and Elvira, when they quarrel, not over the affections of Juan (who seems to be outside the question), but over Juan himself, almost degenerates into a fishwives' dispute. It is a "scene" in which the supposed maker of conquests leaves the initiative to those he is supposed to conquer. Benito, who loves Inés, calls the quarreling women play-actors, unaware that he too is one, speaking his lines, appearing and disappearing in the play at the whim of the author and with scant justification. The same capricious entrances and exits occur with the rest of the characters. The comment on Father Teófilo's inexplicable arrival at the park is that it occurred by "hocus-pocus," and Juan provides the key to such incidents when he adds: "The Supreme Creator moves us puppets of his around according to his divine whim and for his own amusement . . . , but he's a little short on stage technique."[7] With these words he

[7] *Obras*, XII, 910.

clears up the basic problem and the reason for the abrupt breaks in the drama: from the man-puppet identification we can deduce that what is called "fate" is the plot set down by the hand of the author of the play. The technical flaws result from an antirealistic conception of drama. The realist must logically explain steps that, in a predestined life context, are intrinsically justified as elements called for to corroborate predestination.

If we were to translate Supreme Creator as "playwright," we would come to the comparison of life with a play, the world with a stage, and to the well-known analogy between man and character, created free yet subject to the creator's will. Made in their author's image, they live their drama in order to know themselves and discover the limits of their freedom. By acting they learn to penetrate deep within, and far out from, themselves, the two poles between which man's being oscillates. This is true of Brother Juan, whom we feel to be exploring the seas of his soul for traces of the Don Juan archetype he attributes to himself. He thinks he has previously lived other lives, but they have left no track in his memory, and his present self is quite different from that attributed to the legendary figure.

He is different, yet not clearly defined. He lets women make up their ideas of him in hopes of finding himself in the image they propose to him; but before long, apathy and indifference win out. His role bores him. He takes interest again only when he is brushed by the call of death; and even when he is preparing to confront death, his spontaneity suddenly evaporates and he relapses into histrionics. If for a moment he endeavors to get a foothold in life, to walk on solid ground, he soon loses heart when he gets the feeling of being on a stage. What despair invades him when he gets the feeling that he is outside the real world, that the world has the consistency of a stage, and no more! If he were to follow Elvira's recommendation to look neither to the future nor to the past, the only thing left for him would be that fleeting present moment of acting.

His substance, if any, is mental; he is a bundle of problems, doubts, and worries. He does nothing and has no desire to do anything. He lives not even on memories but on shadows of memories or, rather, mirages he fancies are memories. Is he a reincarnation of Don Juan? There is no need to beat around the bush: he is an idea, born in Unamuno's brain, struggling to acquire individuality, to become something else, to *be* autonomously; he is an idea determined to live its own life. The first sentence of the prologue to *Brother Juan* provides a clue: "Is man an idea incarnated in the flesh of fiction, or is the idea 'a man' chronicled and so eternalized?"[8] What is decisive, in any event, is the relation between man and idea, their being irrevocably bound to each other. Juan and the idea of Don Juan are the same thing; it is on the idea that the character lives. Both are of the theater and both are of the world because there is no difference between world and theater.

A GHOSTLY DON JUAN

According to Unamuno, Don Juan does not know who he is, the way Don Quixote knew who he was. Rather, he knows the part he plays. He feels he is "always dreaming his own dream of himself and always provoking others to dream their dreams of him, that he is always a dream of his mistresses'. And dreaming his own dream of himself in them."[9] He thinks that in their dreams and imagination he can begin to realize himself (to feel himself existing). Perhaps his reflection in their dreams may help him to create himself because the idea will take root better in the make-believe world as it is shaped by the women, who in the drama can only ambiguously be called his mistresses.

If vanity is one of the traditional traits of Don Juan's (vanity leads him to brag about his conquests, and it is in the bragging, not in the seducing, that his satisfaction lies), Brother Juan does not fit the type. Nor do we discover in him any vestiges of "satanical" rebellion; nor is he given to boasting, nor pride. Why do women fall in love with him? Because of the prestige of the type, or rather archetype, still lingering in this avatar of an imaginative *petit bourgeois*. As we see him in the play, nothing justifies the flames he still awakens, without meaning to. Una-

[8] *Ibid.*, p. 865.
[9] *Ibid.*, p. 866.

muno thinks women fall in love with Juan out of "maternal" compassion, so as not to cause him suffering, and for the "pleasure of feeling that they have been distinguished in his preference and of distinguishing themselves in this way."[10] If this were true, he would be right in adding, "Poor Don Juan!" And poor, certainly, is Brother Juan, involved as he is with women who, if they were really in love, would be in love not with him but with the remnants of the archetype they glimpse in the depths of his elusive personality.

If women leave Brother Juan and go off with others, it is because they are unable to turn ashes into fire, availability into substance. Juan sees Inés leave, then Elvira, and he feels no regrets; rather, relief. And naturally his indifference has nothing to do with his conscience. If there was sin, it left no reverberations. A girl named Matilde is mentioned as someone who committed suicide because of him, or because of her unrequited love, but he scarcely remembers her, as if what had happened to him had dissolved in his memory and blended with events he had lived—acted out—in other Don Juan–like incarnations.

"I confess," Unamuno says in the prologue, "that the poor women on stage in *Brother Juan* are merely sketched in."[11] This could well be the cause of their failure to transform the real Juan into the desired Don Juan. How can they give him flesh and blood they themselves lack? Where can they get the food to nourish him and make him grow, and help him escape from the mind in which he lives? Elvira is determined to discover the secret of the rake that Juan once was, and the clarifications he offers end up in grotesque prattle, and in the decision, made by her, that they both should go back to Renada, the city (of Unamuno's novelistic world) which is nothing twice over (*renada*) and in which one is reborn (cf. Latin *renata*).[12]

The trip to Renada may be a symbol of the return to one's origins, to the city and home of one's birth, in order to search into the past for the lost key to the present. Being born, in Unamuno's opinion, is the only nontheatrical act of existence.

10 *Ibid.*, pp. 872–873.
11 *Ibid.*, p. 879.
12 *Ibid.*, p. 917.

And Elvira wants Juan to get close to his childhood and his yesterdays, which are real, in order to arouse him from the unreal dreaming in which she feels he is losing himself. She tries to stimulate him, to shake him up, but to no avail. When she thinks she is attracting him, thinks she *has* attracted him, distant bells summon him away from her to the dark presence that obsesses him. As he looks vacantly at Elvira and hears her words, he sees other shadowy phantoms file by: Encarnación, Milagros—they are victims of Juan's although it is hard to imagine in what way. In his dialogue with Elvira, he limits himself to disillusioning her and recommending another man, the rival who is suddenly to appear.

If the scheme fails, if Elvira with her love, with her desire—for it is, above all, a matter of will—is unable to create the Juan of her imagination, it is because it is impossible first to destroy the vague creature of indefinite yearnings that he feels palpitating deep inside. And Juan is unable to devise the plot of the work, to channel the action, because each character seeks his own interests, enters to play his scene and make a hit in it. Enter Doña Petra, the mother of the girl who committed suicide, and her excessive romantic rhetoric inundates everything; her twaddle submerges everything except Juan's conviction when, in answer to her reproaches, he tells her that he is only the way they make him. "I am their creation!" he confesses.[13]

It is no accident that Antonio, who loves Elvira, is a doctor and, moreover, a psychiatrist. He could cure her, set her back on the right track, as Juan says, making an untranslatable but transparent pun to mean that maternity will restore her to sanity.[14] The doctor sees the situation lucidly and diagnoses the case exactly: "You're both dreaming. . . . Worse still, you're acting out a nightmare." And without accusing Juan, he tells him as a simple matter of fact how with his acting he is "sowing misery, maybe deep-rooted tragedies."[15] The statement is sound: whoever truly lives his role suffers when the stage directions say to;

[13] *Ibid.*, p. 933.
[14] *Ibid.*, p. 937.
[15] *Ibid.*, p. 940.

and love, even if only the invented kind, hurts no less, or no less truly. According to pure Unamunian theory, to love is to want to love, just as to believe is to want to believe.

For the women raving around (rather than acting) in the play, to be loved is to want to be loved; their imaginations fill in the rest. Juan disillusions Inés in no uncertain terms, but she refuses to accept plain words; on her reentrance in the second act, she objects: "Talk . . . , talk . . . . What your lips said was one thing, but what your eyes said as they devoured me, was another."[16] Recalling the earlier scene, the audience wonders when the apathetic and weary man's eyes ever shone with such desire, immersed as he is in his dream as a reincarnation.

The psychiatrist's diagnosis is conclusive: Juan pretends to be something he is not, and manages to deceive the women by leading each to suppose that he has possessed the others. All of them end up thinking he has secret adventures, and his deception consists of letting them imagine what is not so. He denies his present Don Juanism so that they may fill the blank page with their inventions; in what Inés and Elvira and Rosa write, he will read the story that confirms his wishful thinking. If he disdains them, it is to take revenge for his own inability to believe in the image they offer him, as though his inability to hypnotize himself were due to decisions on their part.

Juan would like, as we know, to deceive himself. "You can't love either one of them, or anybody," Antonio tells him,[17] and this impotence of the heart is owing to his insecurity about the role he is playing. How could his *I* commit itself if he is not even sure of its existence? Acting and more acting! Letting them believe in the mask and not wearing one so that they may better imagine it, without any suggestions from the painted cardboard. Not really acting, just being on the stage in the costume of the traditional seducer and with no makeup on his face; carrying on a dialogue with himself and wondering who the character forged by all the others is; trying to discover if there is anything solid in his world or whether the most solid reality is simply the

16 *Ibid.*, p. 941.
17 *Ibid.*, p. 944.

wood of the stage and stage properties ("Sister table! Sister chair!"[18] are also phantasmal) of the story to which he clings for life. The story, where "the film of small-time heroes unwinds" (as Unamuno said in *Cómo se hace una novela*, which is neither more authentic nor less theatrical than the area where a character dreams his dream of himself: the naked conscious mind.

THE GREAT GALEOTTO

When he has been abandoned by the women at the end of Act II, Juan begins to be Don Juan, a recluse. He becomes the victim of incurable loneliness, the logical corollary of Don Juanism, of the tragic tendency to live for and within himself without giving himself to a woman and making himself one with her—an agonizing loneliness in this instance. The whole third act is a slow preparation for the final scene, his death. Having previously entered a convent, he is now "Brother Juan," a dying man trying to play this role as he should, preparing to make a good death, that is, to die with the theatricality expected of a star.

As the hour approaches, he becomes more and more sharply aware of his condition as an instrument, a toy of God's, a puppet controlled by strings from above. Act the lines dictated to you, but act them with enthusiasm, in order to be redeemed and raised through your success to the level of the impresario. Make of your acting a creation and appropriate the role for your own so that, after you, no one else will dare attribute it to himself. Father Teófilo urges him to say whether or not he believes in reincarnation, whether he thinks he has lived other lives. Juan answers him in the affirmative, pointing out that he does not think he is a blood descendant of Don Juan Tenorio's because the great seducer neither had nor could have had children, precisely because he was who he was.

In the play Juan is the mythical figure brought to life according to Unamuno's interpretation. As I have said, he is neither a seducer nor a satanic figure. What, then? He is another Galeotto, a go-between, a master procurer. He stirs love in women,

18 *Ibid.*, p. 951.

awakens them to it, and then passes them on to others. And as an extreme perversion—as had already happened with Tula, the protagonist of Unamuno's novel *La tía Tula* ("Aunt Tula") —he relishes the thought that, while others make love to them, these women will think of him, whose image in their hearts will make their pleasure more exquisite. On one hand, he knows he is "condemned to be himself forever . . . , never to be able to be someone else . . . , never to give himself to another,"[19] but at the same time he thinks: "My destiny was not to steal love, no; it was to kindle it and stir it so that others might warm themselves in its heat. . . . More than a few women, mad with their impossible love, have conceived, dreaming of me in the throbbing arms of others. That's the way they got pregnant."[20] Immediately afterward comes the identification with Cupid the archer. Don Juan represents, therefore, love, risk, catastrophe; and women's refuge from this threat is custom, upon which the continuity of life depends.

Throughout the play, the emphasis is on theatricality, carefully executed effects, rehearsals of where and how to fall, mannerisms. Since Juan knows he is a puppet, it is perfectly natural that he should enter and exit unconcerned about verisimilitude: the author's will is untrammeled, and he calls up his puppets with a mere tug on the strings. If you take a good look at it, dialogue with them is a prolongation of the monologue whose simple theme is the existential question. Juan tells the others, as he does himself, who he is, or who he thinks he is, or who he wants to be, in order to impress the image upon their minds and upon his own, hypnotizing them and himself, hoping to make himself *feel* the way he wants himself to be.

Determined to be Don Juan, the protagonist tries to establish an identity between dreaming and acting, between dreaming and living; hence, the transparent quiet despair. He can dream his dream of himself and he can act himself, but that is all. Unamuno himself once said: "The man asleep, dreaming the dream of life, must be awakened."[21] Simple souls will not lose their faith for

---

[19] *Ibid.*, pp. 961–962.
[20] *Ibid.*, p. 985.
[21] "Almas sencillas," in *Visiones y comentarios*, in *Obras*, X, 993.

having been awakened. Brother Juan clings desperately to his own, to his faith in the name and myth he considers his personal possession. When anguish is disguised, as it is here, in jokes, the audience may fail to notice it and in the end come to think it is part of the role. One must understand the suffering enacted as suffering experienced; and if Antonio smiles when Juan assures him he is suffering for the sins of his previous incarnations, he errs as a doctor and as a man: the protagonist's conscience, where the drama takes place, really does bear the burden of those earlier fates.

The last scenes of love and reconciliation are deliberately theatrical. The muttering of Benito and Inés is understandable and so is the question put to her faded hero by the woman who shortly before had been so much in love with him: "Well, actor, is the show still on?"[22] The show she is reproaching him for is not that of his deceiving her—because, after all, she jumped to the line without its even being baited—but that which is consubstantial with his very being. A strange humor, often disconcerting for its vulgar touches, weighs down the dialogue. Fernando Lázaro[23] has pointed out the misplaced slang, verbal twisting, and paradoxical antitheses that occur in Unamuno's plays. In no other work are they more annoying and obvious. They should be kept in mind, because undoubtedly they have added obscurities to the play, already so mysterious by its very nature.

MYSTERIES

Unamuno could have called this play a mystery, as he did another of his (*El Otro*, "The Other"), and with equal justification. But he tagged it a "new old play," to announce something he considered decisive: the reiteration in different form of an "old"—that is to say, eternal—theme. Unamuno is thus using the world as a stage, and the theme "Who is Don Juan?" as a pretext for posing and attempting to answer the ever timely

[22] *Obras*, XII, 975.
[23] Lázaro, *op. cit.*, pp. 13–15. Elsewhere I have indicated similar examples of this humor in Unamuno's *esperpento*-like novel, *Amor y pedagogía* ("Love and Pedagogy").

question, "Who am I?" It is a mystery perturbing to Juan, as it was to Unamuno, especially during his years of exile in Hendaye.

From 1924 to 1929, while from the French border Unamuno was inveighing against the rulers in control of the homeland and watching the film of history unwind, and as a reaction against the pressure of the circumstances forcing him to intervene, and so unequivocally, in the political struggle, he had descended into the abyss of the timeless puzzle and written the dramatic trilogy of his exile: *Sombras de sueño* ("Dream Shadows," first titled *Julio Montalbán y Julio Macedo*), *El Otro* in 1926, and *El hermano Juan o el Mundo es teatro* in 1927 or 1928. The first two had precedents in Unamuno's narrative work, in a short novel and a short story, respectively; *El hermano Juan* was entirely new. It is possible, to be sure, as Manuel García Blanco has shown, to run down, in earlier essays and articles, ideas that have passed with little or no alteration into the play; but such incorporation is common in Unamuno's creative process, and does not alter the fact that the play was composed and written from beginning to end without a break. Hence, the difficulty of the subject seems to be increased by an evident disregard for technical requirements. Introducing a character as an apparition struggling to acquire substance—this is what he was attempting at this critical moment—and reducing him to a mere nebulous scheme of a man made it necessary to create a similarly schematic setting, reduced to the essentials and as bare as those found in his *nivolas*. But in the theater the inner action must be conveyed in dramatic form and the deeper reality has to be judged by what is seen and heard. This reality is only partly revealed because the obsessed character never gets outside his obsession. The dialogues, very much in Unamuno's manner, are intersecting mono-dialogues: each sane person has his mania, and the devil take "psychology." No one bothers to adjust his role to that of the others; instead, everyone says his lines when it pleases him—or when it pleases the author—heedless of any presumable dramatic action. Perhaps this is why critics seem to have felt helpless looking at this work. What is usually called action is missing; in its place, we are offered, through Juan's mono-dialogue, an exposition of life as a creation, of life as acting's product. Scene by scene, the play unfolds the idea of Don Juanism as procuring. If we recall the traditional Don Juan, Tirso de Molina's or the romanticist Zorrilla's, this approach seems shocking, but if we stick to Unamuno's conception, Brother Juan's behavior, undeceiving in order to deceive, is coherent and clear.

The past seems ambiguous, equivocal. In Juan's past were there real seductions and affairs? Probably not; the past is a dream, and it is not presented here, as it usually is, as crystallized and definite, but as another unknown. Extending the indecisive present back toward the past and forward into the future, we will always find an identical figure on call, striving to take shape by playing his role. That at the end of the play we should find Juan in a convent as a "brother" rather than a "father" corresponds to the symbology of the character. When he rejects the total love relationship and casts his women into the arms of others, he rejects a redeeming fatherhood, something that might assure his salvation, and shuts himself off in the brotherhood that matches the figure within him. His solitude is compensated by the possibility of surviving in the myth through new incarnations in the future, in which he will go on playing the same role on the same stage. A mental stage, let me insert, for only inside the brain—or the "soul," if you prefer—is it possible to achieve the discovery of the *I* which Juan is set on making.[24]

THE SOUL ON STAGE

To let things take their course, to let women create him, is, viewed from another side, a subtle mechanism by which to dominate, and indifference is an adequate weapon for attaining the ends sought by the protagonist. *Brother Juan* is one of those rare works in which soul and idea coincide. Long before writing the play, Unamuno had said: "For each soul there is an idea that

[24] When *Brother Juan* was published, Pedro Salinas asked: "But does this mere Don Juan even believe in the eternal Don Juan? Certainly not. Unamuno's Don Juan is skeptical toward Don Juanism; he does not recognize himself" (*Literatura española. Siglo XX* [2d ed.; Mexico: Antigua Librería Robredo, 1949], p. 77).

belongs to it and is something like its formula; and souls and ideas move in search of each other."[25] In this instance they have met and fused to the point of inseparability: what impels him to be incessantly playing a role is his soul's desire to be in accordance with what the idea is. The will to identification is nothing more or less than the ardent wish to create the man according to the idea that turns into the animating project of our lives. Therefore, whoever plays a role lives, because his acting proceeds from his desire to be and to seem in accordance with project and idea. Indifference to the role playing of others has a positive and almost dynamic aspect: Juan will accept from the others what is useful for his own needs, and will ignore or look askance at the rest. In dealing with them and with the world, he will apply one inflexible criterion, that of their utility for the constitution of his *I*. This throws a new light on Juan's willingness to let women do as they wish with his image: his willingness is a subtle control mechanism, and his indifference is a weapon to help him get what he wants—himself.

Juan applies his criterion spontaneously; and as he does, he reveals the Unamunian texture, the projection of Unamuno's spirit in that of the character. Unamuno knew what he was acting out and why, as he dreamt his dream of himself. The indifferentiation of living, dreaming, and acting is straight Unamuno, as is his feeling of being on stage, his longing to be dreamt in their dreams by others and to leave behind a name—a name in which scattered longings adhere and take form; a name to make comprehensible and definable the substance, the idea that will give his soul authenticity or an eagerness for authenticity, and at the same time, fill it with anguish. He cannot have one without the other: he cannot achieve authentic being without struggle, and that struggle will cause doubting and suffering—suffering because the play or dream of life leads to an end that supposes the extinction of the dreaming actor. Death definitively ends the drama —and the man. But isn't it then childish to sustain the prolonged effort to live by playing oneself, inventing a being destined to disappear when the curtain falls on the last act? Isn't creating

25 "El secreto de la vida," in *Ensayos*, in *Obras*, III, 1037.

oneself for nothing and nothingness a mad enterprise? In the uncertainty caused by these questions, anguish burgeons; and to overcome it, there is the precarious consolation of survival in the myth.

The existential question remains unanswered or, to be more precise, open. Death, the final and irrevocable scene, is not an answer, although it does help us form an opinion, which is the most we should risk in replying to the "Who am I?" of Brother Juan, Unamuno, or our own selves. The mystery will continue to exist, because proper to it is its insolubility; if it had a "solution," it would be not a mystery but a problem and within the reach of intelligences capable of solving it.

At the end, Elvira asks Juan who he is "really"—in reality, not in fiction. There was only one possible response: "Do you think I know?" And he bursts out at her in the unmistakable style of his author: "We are nothing less than every inch a theater!"[26] Not "every inch a man," like Alejandro Gómez, the character in one of Unamuno's most famous stories,[27] but a theater, a theater in the mind, the stage of our drama where our shadow and the shadows of others pass and act in the exchange of auto-dialogues which constitutes life. Since he is a reincarnation of a theatrical figure, Juan's consistency can be only theatrical: he is really only a fiction, and in fiction he seeks truth. He discovers the devil, Satan, and discovers him to be a character playing a role. And God, can he also be a character in the play? Is that His substance? If so, the only truth is performed truth, and it lasts only as long as the performance. Appearance, as Unamuno said over and over, is the foundation, the inner core, all there is.

"A stage of ghosts" is the term Unamuno used to define both life and the theater. In a play he planned to write but never did (*Maese Pedro* was to be its title), the protagonist was to engage in a dialogue with the marionettes of his show just as Juan, or Unamuno, does with the linear figures in the present play. At the end of *La tía Tula*, the protagonist Tula murmured the confession implicit in *Brother Juan*: "Marionettes all!"[28] And in her desolate

---

26 *Obras*, XII, 980.
27 "Nada menos que todo un hombre," *Obras*, IX, 472–518.
28 *Obras*, IX, 623.

conclusion, in the depths of despair—for that "all" includes Tula as well as you, my reader, and me—I believe I detect the expression of a secret, abysmal, irrational belief; for if we are puppets or marionettes, it means that there is someone moving the strings, and that the someone, the creator of the farce and the puppets, could convoke them—and convoke us—later on for a new and lasting performance.

9

CLARÍN AND UNAMUNO: PARALLELS AND DIVERGENCIES

Franco Meregalli

It is commonly accepted that Clarín was a precursor of Spain's Generation of 1898. His influence may be observed in the high esteem in which Azorín held him, in his impact on Pérez de Ayala's work,[1] and in his personal relationship with Unamuno. The study that Manuel García Blanco wrote on " 'Clarín' y Unamuno,"[2] together with the publication by Clarín's son of Unamuno's letters to his father,[3] has apparently documented this latter relationship satisfactorily. Both authors, Clarín in his review of Unamuno's *Tres ensayos* (May 7, 1900) and Unamuno in the letter that he wrote to Clarín about the review two days later, have defined their position in respect to each other.[4] These two texts, in my opinion, are of the utmost importance if we wish to understand the two men and the two periods to which they belong.

When, however, we attempt to discover in the creative work of Unamuno the admitted influence of Clarín, our vision becomes less clear. Which of Clarín's stories are the ones that "touched

---

[1] This influence on Pérez de Ayala has not been completely explored. For instance, Alvaro Mesía in *La Regenta* undoubtedly determined Ayala's attitude toward Don Juan. Also, several short stories in *El raposín* clearly show Clarín's influence.

[2] Manuel García Blanco, " 'Clarín' y Unamuno," *Archivum* (Oviedo), II (1952), 113–139.

[3] Adolfo Alas, ed., *Menéndez y Pelayo, Unamuno, Palacio Valdés: Epistolario a Clarín* (Madrid: Ediciones Escorial, 1941), pp. 33–105.

[4] Clarín's article is reproduced by García Blanco in the above-mentioned study in *Archivum*. Unamuno's letter is included in the *Epistolario*, pp. 84–100.

156

him to the very core of his being"?[5] What remained with him of this man "who so greatly influenced [his] intellectual formation"?[6] To my knowledge, only Guillermo de Torre has even tried to base a study of Clarín's influence on Unamuno on the literary works themselves.[7] I propose to go one step further in this direction.

At the beginning of their correspondence, in 1895, Unamuno wrote: "I have followed with interest and attention your latest trend, which might, in a way, be called your mystic period. Your necrological article about Padre Ceferino,[8] as well as your short story 'Chiripa' and other works of yours, have suggested hundreds of ideas to me."[9] And again: "You are not just the first but almost the only Spanish writer who makes me think."[10] And in 1896: "*El gallo de Sócrates* suggested many things to me."[11] In his letter of May 9, 1900, Unamuno speaks of *La Regenta*, "in which I see the flower of your youthful experiences and reflections, the freshest part of you, and extracted to such an extent from a reality you have directly apprehended and felt."[12] These quotations seem to indicate that Unamuno was primarily interested in Clarín's last or "mystic" period and particularly in the short stories. The praise of *La Regenta*, although sincere, involves an argument *ad hominem*: it was principally aimed at showing that when Clarín insinuated that Unamuno's ideas in *Tres ensayos* showed excessive French influence he was committing the same injustice as the critics who had accused him of

[5] *Epistolario a Clarín*, p. 96.
[6] *Ibid.*, p. 99.
[7] "Presencia de 'Clarín,'" *Archivum* (Oviedo), II (1952), 217–226. In an earlier article of 1942 (now included in *Tríptico del sacrificio* [Buenos Aires: Losada, 1948], pp. 23–30), G. de Torre had limited himself to a commentary on Unamuno's letters to Clarín, insinuating a radical difference between the two men: "Was not Unamuno asking the impossible when he wanted a spirit as relativistic and ironic as Clarín's to vibrate in unison with his?" (p. 29).
[8] Father Ceferino Gonzáles (1831–1894), Spanish author of an extensive history of Spanish philosophy.
[9] *Epistolario*, p. 53.
[10] *Ibid.*, p. 54.
[11] *Ibid.*, p. 68.
[12] *Ibid.*, p. 98.

plagiarizing Flaubert in *La Regenta*. But, in point of fact, *La Regenta* was not based, as were other works by Clarín, on the themes that most interested Unamuno; and it is not possible to find that it had any influence on Unamuno's novels.

If, however, we use as a starting point another novel by Clarín, *Su unico hijo*, the relationship is clear. With the single exception of Azorín, critics have treated this novel quite severely.[13] One reason for such severity has been that there is no setting, that the work is therefore "rather dry and abstract."[14] Actually, the setting is simply implied: it is the usual Spanish provincial town, specifically, the Vetusta of *La Regenta*. But the fact that Clarín does not bother explicitly to create an environment around his characters gives to them a peculiar relief, as with figures painted on a monochrome surface, and to this novel, by the author who is conventionally considered the most typical Spanish naturalist,[15] a certain "dry and abstract" air, which anticipates the expressionistic atmosphere of all Unamuno's novels, with the exception of his first, *Paz en la guerra*. The protagonist, Bonifacio Reyes, is of an Unamunian stamp. This character, to my way of thinking, has been underestimated even by those few critics who have studied the work from a sympathetic point of view.

Contrary to the treatment given to the two protagonists of *La Regenta*, Clarín does not spare Bonifacio Reyes the bitter derision that the author shows toward all the characters immersed in the bourgeois-clerical atmosphere of Vetusta. Actually, he *is* this atmosphere: a handsome young man, he has married a wealthy heiress, and is living the useless and humiliating life of a prince consort, from which he is unable to escape because it is, at the same time, comfortable and allows him to drift along as a vaguely intellectual idler—in short, a type of life very common in the Spanish provinces at that time. Bonifacio plays the flute and frequents one of those nineteenth-century Spanish shops

[13] For a résumé of critical opinion regarding this work, see M. Baquero Goyanes, *Una novela de "Clarín": "Su único hijo"* (Murcia, 1952), pp. 9–14 (*Anales de la Universidad de Murcia* [1951–1952], pp. 125–130).

[14] Emilio Clocchiatti, " 'Clarín' y sus ideas sobre la novela," *Revista de la Universidad de Oviedo*, X (1949), 53.

[15] The shallowness of Clarín's naturalism has been shown by W. E. Bull, "The Naturalistic Theories of Leopoldo Alas," *PMLA*, LVII (1942), 536–551.

where sometimes they make a sale, but mostly they just gossip. His circle of friends is made up of followers of a provincial romanticism, busy with chitchat, particularly concerning the qualities and lives of opera singers, the only representatives of that world of evasion, art, and the primacy of "passion" for which they long. One of the opera companies remains longer than usual; Bonifacio becomes the lover of the soprano, a woman who, notwithstanding the sham and tinsel of her mediocrity, is not too far removed from the romantic heroine of his dreams. His wife, in turn, sighs for the tenor. Bonifacio's residence, filled with singers and friends, becomes a place of wild dissipation and illicit love affairs. The only one who feels nauseated with this life is Bonifacio, who nevertheless hears in the soprano's voice a powerful, strange call: that voice has something maternal about it which stirs in him an old unsatisfied desire for fatherhood. As if in answer, his wife has a child. Someone whispers it is the tenor's child, but Bonifacio clings to his new reality. He has a faith at last, a faith built out of doubt. The son will be what he has dreamed of being and has never been.

The work undoubtedly has its faults: Clarín's characteristic tendency toward parody and a very nineteenth-century inclination to the dramatic, which degenerates into the melodramatic. It has, however, a robust ideological structure. Bonifacio's redemption will appear impossible only to those who fail to see that from the beginning that possibility existed in him. In the appeal to his deepest instincts, he finds the foothold he needs to lift himself from the mire: spirit is creativity and can accomplish the miracle of Baron Munchausen. And like Bonifacio, so the mediocre Spain around Clarín can save itself by calling upon its deepest feelings, upon those generous impulses that may be transformed into willpower.

It is obvious that the appeal to *infrahistoria*, the redeeming desire for fatherhood, the symbolic import of the character's ups and downs, are features that anticipate Unamuno. "Have children, Apolodoro, have children," cries Don Fulgencio in *Amor y pedagogía*.[16] It is worth recalling that among the novels Clarín had in mind and did not write, one was to be entitled *Una mediania* ("A Mediocrity") and recount the failure of Bonifacio

[16] *Obras*, II, 546.

Reyes' son, in terms not unlike those used in *Amor y pedagogía*. And does not the feverish and fertile anguish of feeling himself a mediocrity, which is perceptible in Bonifacio, have an affinity with that envy of Joaquín Monegro which is the focal point of *Abel Sánchez*, perhaps Unamuno's most felicitous novel? But we have seen that Unamuno, when speaking of the influence of Clarín's work on his own, emphasized the short stories. Indeed, in them we see, even more clearly than in *Su único hijo*, motifs that will become typically Unamunian.

In what sense and up to what point Clarín may be considered a naturalist is revealed by his long-standing polemic against positivism, which anticipates Unamuno's antiscientism. In "El sombrero del cura," a short story of his last period, Clarín asserts that from the very first years of his teaching career he had been fighting the basic ideas of positivism "with all the strength of [his] convictions."[17] The parody of Lombroso-type scientism which we see in *Amor y pedagogía*[18] is also to be found in Clarín's "Las dos cajas." In this same story Clarín attacks parents who see in their children a good investment, just as Unamuno does in "La beca," one of the short stories from *El espejo de la muerte*. This is the book of Unamuno's in which Clarín's presence is most evident and manifold; and it is, at the same time, among his literarily most successful ones. Some of the stories (for example, "Cruce de caminos," "Solitaña," "Las tribulaciones de Susín," and "El semejante") have infantile, "carnal" souls in them who are quite original, and yet they bear an undeniable kinship with the childish and primitive characters Clarín sketched, not only in his better-known "¡Adiós Cordera!" and "Pipá," but in several others: "Cuervo," "Manín de Pepa José," and "El rana." Even if burdened with a certain long-windedness and lack of critical attention, typical of the nineteenth century, these stories individualize authentic characters in all their primitiveness. The literary type of the *clochard* brought to life in some of them may make us think of the French literary tradition, but in Clarín he

[17] Leopoldo Alas "Clarín," *Obras selectas* (Madrid: Biblioteca Nueva, 1947), p. 991.

[18] The same parody occurs in Pérez de Ayala's *Prometeo*, likewise clearly derived from Clarín, even down to the somewhat mechanical dog-gedness with which misfortunes and humiliations are heaped on the "pure-bred genius."

acquires a new depth. Though a bitter observer of the urban life around him, moved by it to a resentment that often prejudices the artistic result, Clarín re-created with benevolent irony, almost with tenderness, the ingenuous souls of the common people, particularly those who live in a primitive, very simple, but profoundly human loneliness of their own. It was here that he attained some of his best results as a narrator.

Unamuno expressly listed, among the short stories by Clarín which had most impressed him, "La conversión de Chiripa," which is precisely one of this type. If we reread this work, we can understand clearly the reasons for Unamuno's preference. Chiripa, like el Rana and Manín de Pepa José, loves life, free from any constraint. His consciousness of himself is so reduced that he hardly remembers his Christian name, and calls himself Chiripa, a nickname given to him by others. Like other primitive souls created by Clarín, Chiripa has a rudimentary philosophy of his own about human relationships. The fact that it can be summarized in a word does not deprive it of depth. From the upper class he does not want financial help so much as *alternancia*: that gentlemen should not disdain him, should consider him a man. Instead, everybody dismisses him and he ends up, materially and metaphorically, in the only place where he is treated like everybody else, where there is *alternancia*: the Church. In "La conversión de Chiripa" there is a sentence that is basic to an understanding of Clarín's attitude toward Catholicism: "The sputtering of the candles had something homelike about it."[19] If in his attitude toward his primitive characters his paternal spirit is revealed, in the face of his own existential anguish the recollection of his Catholic origins stirs in him a nostalgia like that which overwhelms a child who has lost his way.[20] However

[19] Leopoldo Alas "Clarín," *Cuentos* (Oviedo, 1953), p. 81.

[20] "La conversión de Chiripa" does not appear in the edition of Clarín's *Obras selectas* (Madrid: Biblioteca Nueva, 1947), nor do "Manín de Pepa José," "Cambio de luz," and "Un grabado." Clarín wrote more than a hundred short stories, published in five collections: *Pipá* (1886), *Doña Berta* (1892), *El Señor y lo demás, son cuentos* (ca. 1893), *Cuentos morales* (1896), and *El gallo de Sócrates* (1901), to which must be added the posthumous volume *Doctor sutilis* [sic] (1916). They await a thorough study as a whole. [Ed. note: There has since appeared *Los cuentos de Clarín, proyección de una vida*, by Laura de los Ríos (Madrid: Revista de Occidente, 1965).]

far, socially and psychologically, the author may be from his character, the human relationship between the two of them is clear; and the more fantasy enters into it, the more valid the result.

Clarín attained uneven results in another type of story in which psychological observation is barely veiled by more or less plausible fictional elements. Generally speaking, this group is later than those we might label as *costumbrista*, but we already have an example in "La mosca sabia," published in 1881.[21] This short story reflects an element of Clarín's psychology which is not found in Unamuno: the inferiority complex caused by his "body, emaciated and wasted by the fever of thinking and desiring."[22] The story was written before the author found the definitive equilibrium he reached in his marriage. During those years, it was not yet the religious problem that was worrying him, but rather the bitterness of his failure as a man who was full of bookish culture, but shut off in himself and insignificant to women's eyes. Many of the stories of this period deal with pedants deceived by their wives, useless men of letters, and would-be geniuses who become grotesque. In general, such stories are unsuccessful on a literary level. They abuse the *costumbrista* formula by giving us, in place of a true observation of reality, an acrid and conventional parody. Nevertheless, the motif of the frustrated genius originates in these stories and is then taken over by Unamuno, giving up, however, any autobiographical significance.

The later short stories with an autobiographical basis are generally more successful. The narrative element is sometimes reduced to a mere pretext, turning the story into a story-essay, a form that is also characteristic of Unamuno. Particularly im-

[21] The classification of Clarín's short stories may have a certain critical interest, especially if it takes account of their chronology. The general scheme adopted by M. Baquero Goyanes in *El cuento español en el siglo XIX* (Madrid: C.S.I.C., 1949), does not seem satisfactory to me. He has divided Spanish short stories of the nineteenth century into fourteen categories, based on completely heterogeneous criteria. For instance, there are rural stories, love stories, psychological and moral stories, and tragic and dramatic stories. It is obviously possible to have a story containing many or all of these elements which could be placed in any one of these categories without thereby being really characterized.

[22] *Obras selectas*, p. 937.

portant among these, as far as our study is concerned, are "Cambio de luz," "Un grabado," and "Un repatriado."

From the time of *Su único hijo*, it is no longer the romantic sense of defeat, stimulated by his physical shortcomings, which characterizes Clarín. His family and his children have relieved him of that feeling, as a son had freed Bonifacio Reyes in the novel. But children die. What is the use of creating a harmony in family life, if the family itself will be destroyed by time? Clarín feels the need of God, the traditional God, the Eternal Father, who will deliver him and his children from death. Children themselves have value only if God exists. There is no certainty that God exists, but Clarín *wants* him to exist. "Faith amidst doubt" gives to him sometimes (as it does to the protagonist of "Doña Berta," a prolix story blemished with Clarín's usual taste for parody, but important for understanding him) a "sublime and austere joy,"[23] which has something feverish about it, as is natural since it is a question of a possession concerning which we have constant doubts in spite of our efforts not to. The protagonists of "Cambio de luz" and "Un grabado" exemplify this state of mind.

"Cambio de luz" is the story of a scholar (clearly an alter ego of Clarín) who is living a happy, settled family life, contenting himself with what he has managed to attain and not looking for worldly honors, even though he must work hard to support his family. Behind this apparent serenity, however, is an anguish he cannot confess to anyone. His cultural formation leads him toward positivism, but he needs God, without whom the circle of intimate relationships he has created around him seems illusory. "If God exists, all is well; if God does not exist, everything is in a bad way."[24] But in spite of this he does not exclude the possibility that God may not exist. Overwork strains his already tired eyes, so that he is condemned to an outward inactivity. This limitation gives scope to an inclination toward daydreaming he had not previously felt. He does not know how to play the piano and cannot take lessons. Nevertheless, he derives an intimate

[23] *Ibid.*, p. 751.
[24] Leopoldo Alas (Clarín), *El Señor y lo demás, son cuentos* (Madrid, ca. 1893), p. 78.

consolation from the rudimentary chords he improvises on the keyboard. One evening, casting aside all prudence, he writes down his hallucinatory reflections and discovers at last within himself that faith in God for which he had longed. The extraordinary effort has left him blind, but he blesses it, since it has given him this inner light.

"From children to God" is again the theme of "Un grabado." A philosopher wishes to demonstrate God's existence in order to give his children a tenderer and surer protection than his own, the protection of God, the Eternal Father.

"Un repatriado" presents a theme of only slightly less importance to Clarín, one that is indissolubly bound up with that of God: the fatherland. A middle-aged scholar "has come to consider sincerity as his principal passion." Irritated by "this predominance of superficiality, of forms crystallizing over the spiritual essence of things, this servility of thought, this blind routine" which is prevalent in Spain, he decides to emigrate, though he dislikes traveling. But he returns: "I had my homeland more deeply rooted in my heart than I thought. . . . I cannot stand to live inside Spain . . . , but not outside either."[25] It may be that this work, which cannot be prior to 1898 since it refers to the Spanish-American War, was influenced by Unamuno's *En torno al casticismo* (1895). It is unquestionable, however, that it has its roots deep down in the Clarín who had lived all his life in acrimonious antagonism to the society around him. Clarín had a conception of the fatherland that was "agonistic" (in the Unamunian sense). It is not the consecrated and glorious place exalted by nineteenth-century rhetoric, but becomes in Clarín something painful and yet indispensable, like God, of whom we have need even though we may be anything but certain of his existence.

Anyone familiar with the work of Unamuno needs no quotations to demonstrate the profound affinity between his anguish and Clarín's. Although there exists the possibility of a late influence of Unamuno on the older writer, this similarity between them is better explained through the influence of Clarín on Unamuno, one of those influences, naturally, which imply a predispo-

[25] *Obras selectas*, pp. 975–978.

sition and a free and creative assimilation on the part of the individual influenced.

It would be easy to gather extensive evidence of the relationship between Clarín and Unamuno by making a more detailed study of their works, but we have already quoted sufficiently from those selected to be able to infer the character of this relationship. Our knowledge of it is, moreover, reinforced by the documents gathered by García Blanco.

To begin with, Clarín and Unamuno were congenial as men, and this was bound to be so, for rarely has the literary creation reflected the man with such immediacy as with them. The desire for immortality, the fear of death, are at the root of their humanity, of what Unamuno himself called their *egoism*. "Clarín was, as I am, an *I*. Even an egoist. We have touched our own souls."[26] They were, in this sense, individualists: they opposed materialistic progressivism as much as idealism, since both ideologies are interested in an abstract "humanity," a generalized concept of "progress," or a superindividual spiritual life, and are not concerned with the destiny of the concrete, flesh-and-blood individual. Clarín wrote, when still young and not yet obsessed by the fear of death as he was to be in his later years,[27] "The enemies of the urge to philosophize could perhaps see their desires satisfied if they could suppress the fear of death."[28] As for Unamuno, any quotation is superfluous.

The individualism of both men reveals itself in their sociopolitical attitude as well. Both started on the Left, and in both the religious preoccupation brought about an attenuation in their interest in social problems. Clarín became more and more conservative with time. Unamuno came to write in *San Manuel Bueno, mártir*:

> The social question? Never mind, that is none of our concern. They are going to bring in a new society in which there will be neither rich nor poor, in which wealth will be justly distributed,

[26] "Sobre sí mismo," *El Imparcial* (1913), quoted by García Blanco, *op. cit.*, p. 131.

[27] See especially Mariano Gómez-Santos, *Leopoldo Alas "Clarín"* (Oviedo: C.S.I.C., 1952), pp. 55–57.

[28] "Cavilaciones" (essay), *Obras selectas*, p. 1025.

in which everything will belong to everybody. So what? Don't
you think that from such general well-being will come even
greater boredom with life?[29]

In keeping with such attitudes, Unamuno undervalues technology ("Let other nations make their inventions") and asserts the
social expediency of the idle. It would be unjust, however, to
forget that the "egoism" of the two, their love of themselves as
flesh-and-blood human beings, led them to love each and every
flesh-and-blood individual, even (and particularly) the disinher-
ited, the "poor in spirit," children. This attitude, as well as being
an anticipation of Ortega y Gasset's perspectivism ("Every man
is a point of view and therefore every man is unsubstitutable"),
is an aspect of the deep paternal instinct shared by Clarín and
Unamuno.

A corollary of their love for family was their deep-rooted provincialism. Like the protagonist of "Un repatriado," they disliked traveling abroad. Clarín never left Spain; and if Unamuno
did, it was only because he was forced to do so by circumstances,
with the exception of his "rambles" in Portugal, a country he
did not consider foreign. They always lived in small cities, and
their characters are always placed in provincial towns. When
Clarín began a novel set in a big city, *Una medianía*, he left it
unfinished. The Count in *Nada menos que todo un hombre*, one
of the few characters from Madrid in Unamuno's fiction, is considered by the protagonist, as well as by the author, a well-bred
imbecile. Clarín's provincial vocation is less explicit, perhaps less
deep. Once he even had the idea of moving to Madrid in order
to take a professorship in Roman law, but he wrote to Menéndez
y Pelayo: "I have no desire to go to Madrid. Thank God, I have
done well enough for the place not to matter to me, but I would
go for my children's future."[30] He did not obtain the position,
and he did not press the matter. Perhaps he sensed that Oviedo
was his destiny, and the villa he had not far from there, in
Guimarán, became a source of physical well-being for him.
Unamuno's provincialism is tied to his "Spanishness," and the

[29] *Obras*, XVI, 613 (*ABS*, p. 200).
[30] Adolfo Alas, ed., *Marcelino Menéndez y Pelayo-Leopoldo Alas
(Clarín), Epistolario* (Madrid: Ediciones Escorial, 1943), p. 90.

union finds characteristic expression in the essay "Ciudad y campo" and in a short, but no less important, passage placed in the mouth of Angela in *San Manuel Bueno, mártir*, which reads: "I would go into the street, which was the highway, and since I knew everyone, I lived in them and forgot myself, whereas in Madrid, where I was once . . . , as I did not know a soul, I felt that I was terribly alone and being tortured by so many strangers."[31] Family and provincial life also meant, for both authors, tradition—especially, religious tradition. The absolute need for sincerity which is common to them (and which even distinguishes Clarín, for example, from Valera, a writer who was nevertheless very dear to him) forced them to repudiate Catholic dogma, but both were left with bitter regret over it. As early as 1881, Clarín wrote: "Provisional doubt is not a real kind of doubt. You can recognize it by its painlessness."[32] This is the premise of "faith amidst doubt" and therefore the presage of Unamunian "agony," the trait in Clarín which is closest to our century.

I do not wish, however, to exaggerate, for the sake of argument, the continuity between Clarín and Unamuno. Unamuno inherited some features from Clarín (as he did from others; he himself tells us that absolute originality does not exist), but he has blended them into something profoundly his own, compared with which the personality of Clarín seems archaic.

Let us pause for a moment in the realm of anecdotes, which

---

[31] *Obras*, XVI, 624 (*ABS*, p. 212).

[32] "Cavilaciones," *Obras selectas*, p. 1022. Clarín's attitude toward the Catholic religion has been studied very closely by W. E. Bull, "The Liberalism of Leopoldo Alas," *Hispanic Review*, X (1942), 329–339. Contrary to the cliché of Clarín as a freethinker, Bull asserts that he "was basically orthodox in all major points touching either the doctrine or the institution of Catholicism" (p. 333). It might be better to say that he felt Catholicism as something deeply linked to his past and to his needs as a man; he felt nostalgia for it, needed it, but he did not believe. The "continued adherence to Catholicism" which, as Bull notes, Clarín thought he found in Renan does not mean that he believed Renan a Catholic, but that, according to him, "the best of his scientific education" went back to his Catholic training. If Clarín defended Catholic education, it was not because he was a Catholic, but for reasons that anticipate those Unamuno gave in *San Manuel Bueno, mártir*.

are not so meaningless as they may appear at first sight, and note that Clarín's disinclination to travel was related to the sedentary customs of the nineteenth-century scholar, whereas Unamuno's reluctance derived from insufficient custom and a lack of taste for "social life." Far from being sedentary, he was a tireless walker and investigator of those secrets of nature and national history which can be discovered only on foot with a knapsack. One can detect something decidedly of the twentieth century in this enjoyment of sport.

Also, Clarín's intellectual position is more of the nineteenth century: he remains attached to rationalism, as he shows in his review of Unamuno's *Tres ensayos*; his attitude toward Spain is less remote from the oversimplified one of the *afrancesados*. Unamuno starts from a position close to Clarín's but then elaborates a new, extremely personal form of Hispanism and takes a stand in opposition to Europeanization. Unamuno's position is not without dangers of nationalistic involutions, but to understand it correctly it must be kept in mind that he, a provincial by conviction and a Spaniard to the core, was also a man of vast culture. In comparison, Clarín's knowledge, while extensive, reveals characteristics that are provincial in the worst sense of the word. He was acquainted with the intellectual life of other countries almost exclusively through the filter of France.[33] Unamuno's knowledge, for reasons having nothing to do with any kind of philologistic pedantry or erudite exhibitionism (things that he always hated and derided), is always drawn directly from the source. If he read in French the few French authors he found congenial (Pascal, Sénancour, and others), so did he read the English and Americans in English, the Germans in German, the Italians in Italian, the Portuguese in Portuguese (he was one of the first and one of the few Spanish writers who really knew Portuguese literature), and finally Kierkegaard and Ibsen in Dano-Norwegian. In this historicocultural sense also, Unamuno created new times in

[33] See W. E. Bull, "Clarín's Literary Internationalism," *Hispanic Review*, XVI (1948), 321–334. A certain direct knowledge may be inferred from quotations of German authors. Clarín must have known very little of the classic literatures, according to Bull. It is well known that Unamuno, on the other hand, had a thorough knowledge of classical languages.

Spain. More than anyone else, with the single exception of Ortega y Gasset, he promoted the deprovincialization of Spanish culture which took place between 1898 and 1936.

Clarín is more of the nineteenth century than Unamuno also, and especially, in the more specifically literary field. If we ask ourselves what the relationship between them was here, we must answer that it was a reflection of the affinity of the two men and their problems, rather than a direct derivative of taste. Unamuno's style, while slapdash, is free from the rhetorical luxuriances still found in Clarín. The latter, however, often frees himself from them when telling of the feverish inner life of his characters, and it is this element in his prose which most reminds us of Unamuno, not so much in his truly narrative prose as in that of his essays. The strong point of Unamuno's narrative, his dialogue, has no counterpart in Clarín, and has its source in Unamuno's underlying vocation as a conversationalist.

It would seem possible to draw certain conclusions from our study which extend beyond the particular example of Unamuno-Clarín. The concept of generation has sometimes been applied recently in such naïve and clumsy ways that it is all too easy to ridicule it; however, even when it has greater justification, even in the "Generation of 1898," which not by accident was the most characteristic example of its use insofar as Spanish literature is concerned, it is an only partially valid means of historiographic understanding, one to be used with extreme caution and many reservations. Clarín and Unamuno belong to different periods, and Unamuno's oft-quoted letter of May 9, 1900, offers proof of his awareness of the difference. Nevertheless, the points of resemblance between Clarín and Unamuno are so important that it would be a mistake to give undue importance to the difference of age. Unamuno is a stronger personality than Clarín, but the continuity between them is so apparent that it sometimes makes us think of different periods in the development of the same person, rather than of two different ones. *En torno al casticismo* is perhaps less distant from certain essays of Clarín than from others by Unamuno himself, and in one aspect *Su único hijo* resembles *Abel Sánchez* more than *La Regenta*.

Too rigorous an application of the concept of generation gives exaggerated importance to synchronic consideration, to the detriment of a diachronic view—that is, sometimes stressing the environmental anecdote over deep-seated characteristics. The more we are exalted on the scales of values and authenticity, the less important are the incidental elements and the references to the chronicled event. The great personality is undoubtedly concerned with the great problems of his time; but these problems, precisely because they are great, have a slower historical rhythm and a more universal human bearing. There are times in history when years that are quite close together turn out to belong to profoundly different epochs; but such times are not frequent, and were less so in the past. They are rarely determinative. For example, the geographical element, that is, the difference in local traditions and conditions, may sometimes be more important. And most important of all is the nature of men, who may find men who lived in different eras or in different countries more congenial than their everyday friends.

10

UNAMUNO AND CERVANTES
C. P. Otero

While planning this lecture in days past, I repeatedly wondered what anyone, short of a miracle worker, could do in an hour with so formidable a topic as mine. Not only do I have the audacity to take issue with my academic betters, but I venture beyond Unamuno's frontier into the little-known expanse of Cervantes' realm as if unaware that the difficulties have proved insurmountable to many before me. On my own behalf, I hasten to say that I do not mean to cover the entire work of Unamuno and Cervantes "in one fell swoop," nor do I mean to compare two unequally great and unrelated authors, or to suggest that they have much in common beyond their not being run-of-the-mill Hispanic creatures. I simply mean to examine briefly Unamuno's attitude toward Cervantes and toward Cervantes' work, as a means to better understand what each author is talking about, and to assign their respective world views to their proper, distinct frames. Of course, many may disagree with my views and find it ironic that one should choose to celebrate Unamuno's centennial in this manner. If, however, you compare what follows with what Unamuno had to say about Cervantes (some of which I mention later) on the occasion of the 1905 *Don Quixote* centennial, you may conclude that this unfavorable comparison is not an entirely inappropriate way of paying homage to Unamuno. It is indeed unfortunate that we do not have the benefit of Cervantes' comments on Unamuno's writings, which, no doubt, would have made the task much easier and shed much light on the subject. As for Unamuno's comments on Cervantes' writings,[1] they mirror in sharp outline Unamuno's mind and are

---

[1] For a general bibliography and commentary, see *Obras*, IV, 9–62.

perhaps the best screen on which to observe the strange course that tormented and anguished soul was to take and then follow to the end. His writings on the greatest book of Spanish literature are one of the best records of the many ups and downs of Unamuno's personal problems and mental tortures. And, as is well known, Unamuno's inner problems are his major problems; his personal preoccupations are his main preoccupations. After his youth, his anguished, mystical fixations conditioned and determined his moods and quixotic attitudes, so the more intense his anguish was, the more extreme his quixotism was likely to be.

It is always something of an experience to compare Unamuno's early writings and his early, truly exceptional and balanced intellectual development with his most characteristic, Unamunian pronouncements and lay sermons, such as *The Agony of Christianity*. Although there are early hints of what was to come later, by and large his first writings (which he was later to repudiate) seem to be the work of a different man. The break seems to be final around his thirtieth year. It was at this time that his spiritual obsessions began to obscure all else and to develop into the most intense of his inner crises, which occurred two years later during the spring of 1897.[2] As had happened to his admired William James exactly twenty-seven years before, Unamuno fell prey to the deepest melancholy, soul-sick like him for lack of a philosophy to live by, and like him repelled by positivism. James, we are told, slowly fought his way back to health and full activity once more.[3] Unamuno could have followed his friend Ganivet into suicide (a way out that he, in fact, repeatedly considered), but he chose instead to make literature out of his inner turmoil and went on to plunge into Kierkegaard's abyss. The poet was thus greatly enriched at the expense of the thinker; and both the poet and the public figure fed, from then on, on the man himself, like a stomach that devours itself (to use Unamuno's own words). All his major books fall on this side of what might be called the "great divide" in his life.

[2] Antonio Sánchez Barbudo, *Estudios sobre Unamuno y Machado* (Madrid: Guadarrama, 1959), pp. 41–42, and *passim*.
[3] George A. Miller, *Psychology: The Science of Mental Life* (New York and Evanston: Harper and Row, 1962), pp. 70–71.

Unamuno's prototheory of quixotism straddles the divide itself. It emerges, somewhat timidly, in his celebrated essays of the spring of 1895, *En torno al casticismo*; and already in October of the same year, under the very title "Quixotism," he wrote what amounts to the first fragment of his book of nine years later on the subject. Yet, surprising as it may seem, in this article he still opposes quixotism, that impractical devotion to extravagantly chivalrous or lofty romantic, utopian fancies which no amount of ordinary prudence or common sense would restrain. For three more years he continued to advocate the death of Don Quixote. His famous article, "Down with Don Quixote!" which echoes Costa's "Down with the Cid," was published in June of the crucial year of 1898. The United States was already at war with Spain, and what was left of the Spanish Empire had only two precarious months to live. At this time, it is true, Cervantes' book was already a "gospel" for Unamuno, but it was a gospel of regeneration and reconstruction: Don Quixote was already a kindred spirit of the Spanish mystics, but Unamuno wanted him to die along with the nation (the official establishment, you might say) and, purged of his madness, to be reborn along with the people, the grassroots of Spain.

A national crisis was now dogging the footsteps of Unamuno's own crisis, and the compounded crisis was perhaps too much to withstand.[4] In November of 1898, a month before the Treaty of Paris (which would seem to put an end to Spanish quixotism forever), Unamuno reversed his position and turned against the ideas of regeneration and Europeanization, which preached a fresh start for Spain, this time with doors open to Europe. The title of this new article was, characteristically, Calderón's "Life Is a Dream," an idea that would hardly have occurred to the soldiers facing death in Cuba or the peasants confronting toil and starvation on the Peninsula.

[4] It is well to keep in mind, however, Unamuno's own words in a letter to Ilundain (dated Dec. 23, 1898): "The truth of the matter is that these national crises interest me much less than those that unfold in each individual conscience. There is in my blood a certain incurable individualism, which is what drives me to be a socialist, no matter how much of a paradox this might seem." See Hernán Benítez, *El drama religioso de Unamuno* (Buenos Aires: Universidad de Buenos Aires, 1949), p. 277.

Realizing that the Spanish people were paying for his leisure and that it was not scholarly work or good teaching that they needed most, Unamuno (so he says) decided to serve his country in the best way available to him. He considered it his sacred duty to stir what he called the "dormant" souls of Spaniards, and made a start with a series of "Evangelical Meditations" (always a boon in Spain). Then, after discarding the idea of a volume on Sancho Panza's death (maybe for the very reason that Cervantes' Sancho never really did die), he made up his mind, at the turn of the century, to write a book again of "Meditations," this time on the *Quixote*.[5] This was to be a work of mysticism, not unlike the medieval commentaries on the Bible. Indeed, Unamuno sought to establish Cervantes' book as the "Spanish National Bible." Evidently, Unamuno was unaware, or he chose to ignore, the significant remark in the prologue to *Don Quixote*, Part I, in which the author is advised by a friend to preach no sermon to anyone "by mingling the human with the divine, a kind of motley in which no Christian intellect should be willing to clothe itself."[6]

Nonetheless, Unamuno's Christian intellect clothed itself in this kind of motley and produced, in the summer of 1904, his book of quixotic meditations, strangely entitled *The Life of Don Quixote and Sancho, According to Miguel de Cervantes Saavedra, Expounded with Comment by Miguel de Unamuno*. But this lengthy title is misleading. Here is how Unamuno accounts for his stand, eight years later, at the end of his famous book *The Tragic Sense of Life*:

> That horrible Regenerationist literature, almost all of it an imposture, which the loss of our last American colonies provoked, led us into the pedantry of extolling persevering and silent effort . . . of extolling prudence, exactitude, moderation, spiritual fortitude, synteresis, equanimity, the social virtues, and the chiefest advocates of them were those of us who lacked them most. Almost all of us Spaniards fell into this ridiculous mode of literature, some more and some less. And so it befell that that arch-Spaniard Joaquín Costa, one of the least European spirits we ever had, invented his famous saying that we must

[5] *Ibid.*, pp. 258, 390, and *passim*.

[6] *The Ingenious Gentleman Don Quixote de la Mancha*, trans. Samuel Putnam (New York: Viking Press, 1949), I, 15.

Europeanize Spain, and, while proclaiming that we must lock up the sepulchre of the Cid with a sevenfold lock, Cid-like urged us to—conquer Africa! And I myself uttered the cry "Down with Don Quixote!" and from this blasphemy, which meant the very opposite of what it said—such was the fashion of the hour —sprang my *Vida de don Quijote y Sancho* and my cult of quixotism as the national religion.

I wrote that book in order to rethink Don Quixote in opposition to the Cervantists and erudite persons, in order to make a living work of what was and still is for the majority a dead letter. What does it matter to me what Cervantes intended or did not intend to put into it and what he actually did put into it? What is living in it is what I myself discover in it, whether Cervantes put it there or not, what I myself put into and under and over it, and what we all put into it. I wanted to hunt down our philosophy in it.[7]

Notice how vigorously he rejects his initial position regarding *Don Quixote*, and how emphatically he declares his indifference to what Cervantes actually put into his book. At the same time he makes explicit his intention of projecting himself into the book, which leads us to suspect that he does not seriously mean to "rethink" *Don Quixote* as he says, or to extract any philosophy from it. We might be led further to expect Unamuno himself, not Don Quixote, to emerge as the real hero; Don Quixote will only be the name of his alter ego, a sublimation of his own self. To accomplish this, he must push Cervantes out of the way. What he calls "opposition to the Cervantists" is really opposition to Cervantes himself, and to everything Cervantes represents. Unamuno persistently tries to prove Cervantes wrong, sometimes claiming misunderstanding or plain forgetfulness on the part of the narrator, although the narrator himself explicitly states, with reference to the "first" author: "He wishes it understood that he has sufficient ability and intelligence to take the entire universe for his theme, if he so desired, and he asks that his labors be not looked down upon, but that he be given credit not for what he writes, but for what he has refrained from writing."[8]

But paying no heed to this significant warning is nothing com-

[7] *TSL*, pp. 308–309 (*Obras*, XVI, 431).

[8] *The Ingenious Gentleman Don Quixote*, trans. Putnam, II, 789, (*Don Quixote*, II, chap. xliv).

pared with what Unamuno does to the text itself. On one occasion, he puts another character's words in Sancho's mouth (an error he had already committed in one of his essays of 1895),[9] and goes on triumphantly to argue from these words that Sancho, now at the summit of his faith, will alone remain after Don Quixote's death with the unshakable faith that his master supposedly gave him, all of which serves to prove his theory of the quixotization of Sancho.[10] When the error was brought to his attention, apparently for the second time, more than twenty years later (by a translator of the book, who was, incidentally, a California resident), he replied:

> It is true that the strict letter of Cervantes escaped me, but since my comment is neither literary nor tropological, but what might be called mystical, the felicitous mistake must be left as it is. It would have been really *awkward* [although writing in Spanish, he uses this English word] on my part to sacrifice the intimate impetus of my comment by sticking to Cervantes' letter.[11]

A most explicit example of Unamuno's attitude toward Cervantes and, at the same time, Unamuno's brand of logic, appears at the very end of the book:

> If the pious biographer considers Loyola's greatest miracle to be his founding of the Company of Jesus, may we not regard as Don Quixote's greatest miracle the fact that he caused his biography to be written by Cervantes, a man who in his other works showed the feebleness of his genius and how inferior he naturally was in the gifts necessary to one who should recount, as Cervantes did indeed recount, the deeds of the Ingenious Gentleman?
>
> There is no doubt that in *The Ingenious Gentleman Don Quixote of La Mancha* Miguel de Cervantes Saavedra appears far superior to anything we might have expected of him in view of his other works. He outdid himself conspicuously. This suggests the belief that the Arab historian Cide Hamete Benengeli is something more than a literary device and conceals a profound truth, which is that the story was dictated to Cervantes by another man, whom Cervantes harbored within himself, a spirit dwelling

9 *Obras*, III, 279.
10 *LDQ*, p. 311 (*Obras*, IV, 367).
11 *Obras*, IV, 29.

in the depths of his soul. . . . The immense disparity between the history of the Knight and all the other works of Cervantes, this obvious, indubitable, and splendid miracle, is the principal reason . . . for believing and confessing the history to be true and genuine, and that Don Quixote himself, enveloped in Cide Hamete Benengeli, dictated it to Cervantes. And I even suspect that while I have been expounding and commenting on this life, Don Quixote and Sancho have secretly visited me without my knowledge, and uncovered and displayed to me the inmost sanctuary of their hearts.[12]

So you see, it was a great day for Spanish literature when Don Quixote decided to pick out that man of feeble genius and make a Cervantes out of him. Unamuno's idea could not possibly be more original, and he usually had original ones. Less convincing is his opinion on Cervantes' other works.[13] Could Unamuno have seriously meant to suggest that his three *Exemplary Novels* surpass any three of the twelve written by Cervantes, or that any piece of his theater can equal *Numantia* or one of the interludes?[14] What cannot be denied is that even great men like Goethe had unreservedly admired Cervantes' novels, interludes, and plays. Friedrich Schlegel went even further to state that when it comes to Cervantes, one must read everything or nothing.[15]

[12] *LDQ*, pp. 324–325 (*Obras*, IV, 379–380).

[13] A similar opinion was expressed by, among others, Ernest Mérimée: "Let us not hesitate to say it: without *Don Quixote* and some *Novels*, all Cervantes' others works would probably not be known today save by mere erudites and specialists; none of them was such as to compel the attention of posterity. *Don Quixote* is an accident, a lucky stroke, a flash of genius, a miracle in the literary life of Cervantes" (cf. *Précis d'histoire de la littérature espagnole* [Paris: Garnier, 1908], p. 277).

[14] About Unamuno's strange literary rivalry with Cervantes, see Emilio Salcedo, "El primer asedio de Unamuno al *Quijote* (1889–1895)," *Anales Cervantinos*, VI (1957), 227–250.

[15] J.-J. A. Bertrand, *Cervantes et le romantisme allemand* (Paris: F. Alcan, 1914), p. 89. On December 17, 1795, Goethe wrote to Schiller: "I have had a real treat in the novels of Cervantes, both as regards amusement and instruction. How delightful it is to find oneself able to recognize the excellence of what is generally recognized as good, and how greatly one is encouraged by meeting with works that are based upon those very principles according to which we ourselves act, within the limit of our ability and in our own sphere" (*Correspondence between Schiller and Goethe, from 1794 to 1804*, trans. L. Dora Schmitz [London: G. Bell, 1877], I, 129).

There is, of course, some possibility that Unamuno's assess-
ment was less than wholly accurate, so the absolute stand he
takes against the creator of Don Quixote cannot be without explanation. One that comes readily to mind is that only without
Cervantes' ironical frame could Don Quixote approximate what
Unamuno wished him to be. Because the two authors held such
incompatible views of life, either Cervantes' or Unamuno's had
to go.

Let us examine for a moment what it was in Cervantes that
Unamuno found so hostile to his own inclinations. Unamuno
certainly could not find that propensity toward medieval intellectual anarchism which he applauded in himself, since Cervantes has rightly been credited with writing the epitaph of
medievalism.[16] Neither could Unamuno find the extravagant Romantic attitude that his fellow Romantics had attributed to Cervantes, or the disposition toward mysticism so deeply ingrained
in himself. An otherworldly Basque visionary could have no use
whatsoever for Cervantes' realistic down-to-earthness and lack of
concern for an afterlife, Unamuno's paramount preoccupation.

Herein, it would seem, lies the crux of the matter. Cervantes'
world view is diametrically opposed to Unamuno's, and the latter
no doubt reacted instinctively to this simple fact. The humanistic
world view of the Italian Renaissance (which was Cervantes'
own, as it was Ariosto's) had nothing in common with that of the
New Testament, and, more especially, that of Paul's epistles,
which is the one fervently advocated by Unamuno, apparently
unaware of the tremendous cleavage between these two. This
cleavage, however, is undeniable, as has been made abundantly
clear by Bishop Nygren. Paul's most genuine heir, Nygren

16 J. D. Bernal, *Science in History* (2d ed.; New York: Cameron Associ-
ates, 1957), p. 720. Cf. E. C. Riley, *Cervantes's Theory of the Novel*
(Oxford: Clarendon Press, 1962), p. 223: "*Don Quixote I* appeared in
the same year as Bacon published *The Advancement of Learning* and
Kepler finished writing the *Astronomia nova*. The event of greatest consequence during the lifetime of Cervantes was the rise of science, and the
predominant characteristic of European thought in the early seventeenth
century was its ideological ambivalence. The medieval universe was beginning to fall apart."

further argues, is clearly Luther, who stands in sharp contrast to Catholicism.[17] And Unamuno, it has been said, was, in his own peculiar way, the only Spanish Lutheran.[18] Unamuno once remarked that every man could be judged by his favorite readings. Unamuno's favorite authors included Dante, Pascal, Rousseau, Sénancour, Leopardi, Kierkegaard, and William James, a group characterized by him as "men of desperation," or malcontents at odds with the world. On the other hand, Cervantes' preference leans toward Garcilaso, Ariosto, Martorell, and Boccaccio, men always ready to rely on the "rights of nature" to vindicate the life of the senses, men irrevocably attached to the here and now.[19] It cannot be accidental that Unamuno neglected to take a copy of *Don Quixote* with him into exile, but did not forget to take the New Testament (which he knew almost by heart), the *Divine Comedy*, and the poetry of Leopardi.

It might not be too far off to assume that it was the polar opposition in world views which alienated Unamuno from Cervantes, certainly not a question of religious belief. It is hardly to be assumed that Unamuno had more faith than Cervantes; we have some assurance that, at least after his crisis of 1897, Unamuno had practically none.[20] What in fact drove them miles apart was "the undiscovered country from whose bourn no traveller returns": Cervantes worshiped life; Unamuno was obsessed with death. Cervantes was not eager to shuffle off his mortal coil, but always quick to use his inexhaustible optimism to move the melancholy to laughter and make the cheerful man merrier still; Unamuno, on the other hand, having decided that he should never die, consumed most of his mortal hours dwelling on his immor-

[17] Anders Nygren, *Agape and Eros,* trans. Philip S. Watson (2d ed., rev.; Philadelphia: Westminster Press, 1953), Part Two, chap. vi. Paul's polemic against Gnosis is echoed in Unamuno's essay of January, 1897, "¡Pistis y no gnosis!" (*Obras,* IV, 1019–1024), a few paragraphs of which he used three years later as the core of "La fe" (*Obras,* XVI, 99–113).

[18] José Luis L. Aranguren, "Sobre el talante religioso de Miguel de Unamuno," *Arbor,* XI (Sept.–Dec., 1948), 485–503.

[19] C. P. Otero, "Cervantes e Italia: Eros, industria, socarronería," *Papeles de Son Armadans,* XXXIV (July–Sept., 1964), 287–325.

[20] Sánchez Barbudo, *op. cit., passim.*

tality, meanwhile injecting his somber pessimism into melancholy and cheerful alike. Unamuno, by his own admission, lacked any sense of humor and human understanding; Cervantes could not but be ironic and benevolent.[21] These contrasting attitudes could only generate contrasting effects: Unamuno identified with his replica of Don Quixote; Cervantes, genuinely loving common people and common sense, would probably feel closer to Sancho Panza, like himself realistic, good-natured, and ironic.

But Cervantes could not totally identify with any one of his creatures, or any one of his fragments, since no single one carries the total meaning, a meaning subtly diffused throughout the complex and multidimensional world presented in his writings. If Unamuno, like many other readers before and after him, did not completely succeed in comprehending this meaning, it is hardly surprising. Prejudice aside, it is indeed not easy to detect, even when the veil of Cervantes' pervasive irony appears to be at its most transparent. In addition to the irony, there is the interplay between the "first" and the "second" author, so that what can be relatively clear in its proper context and perspective becomes opaque or radically changes when uprooted and isolated. One thing may be said with certainty: no one character, much less a single utterance, can be taken at face value as if self-contained.

On top of all this complexity, each one of Cervantes' main characters offers an additional difficulty all his own: Don Quixote, his off-and-on madness; Sancho, his simplicity. The latter is, more often than not, a wise fool; the former is, not infrequently, a wise madman. Many are the truths spoken in jest by Sancho or in a somewhat ridiculous seriousness by Don Quixote. The real difficulty is to sort out their utterances according to a finely graded scale going from sheer absurdity all the way to pure wisdom. It goes without saying, the book, as such, is never absurd. Its absurdities are there to be chided, not—as Unamuno pretends—

---

[21] See, for example, his essay of 1910, "Malhumorismo" (*Obras*, IV, 616–624). According to Ernst Robert Curtius, *Kritische Essays zur europäischen Literatur* (Bern: A. Francke, 1950), p. 231, Unamuno "treibt aus dem Roman des Cervantes den Humor bis auf die letzte Spur aus." Cf. J. Rof Carballo, "Humorismo e sociedade," *Grial*, no. 5 (July–Sept., 1964), 310.

to be exalted. More or less thinly disguised, the book contains the most subtle criticism of Spanish society and of society in general.[22]

Without these considerations it would be difficult to estimate the extent of what the German critic Ernst Robert Curtius has called "an imposing violent distortion of the authentic Don Quixote."[23] Unamuno's distortion amounts, in fact, to an unabashed "praise of madness," and a mockery of reason and common sense: "The point is," he writes, "to turn crazy without provocation, in wholehearted rebellion against logic, the implacable foe of the spirit. . . . Madness, genuine madness, is with us a crying need, and a possible cure for this pest of common sense which has inhibited the individual sense of each one of us."[24]

Unamuno's is, to say the least, a strange way of rethinking Cervantes' book and trying to extract its unique philosophy. In fact, Unamuno could not have picked a more unlikely medium for his invective. Where Cervantes seeks to efface folly, Unamuno assails reason. How can we doubt his words when he says that what Cervantes put into his book does not matter to him? Kierkegaard and James, surely not Cervantes, are the spirits that hover incessantly over Unamuno's book.

Not only does Unamuno appoint himself the supreme arbiter of Cervantes' world, he deals in like fashion with the world at large. It is typical of him to generalize his desires and emotions as if the Unamunian way were the only possible way to be human. From his own morbid obsession with death, he infers that everybody feeds on immortality; from his identifying his wife with his mother, he concludes that maternal love is the only love, that all love is maternal. Although he claims that everyone is unique and irreplaceable, he never seems to suspect that his private experience can be just that—private and idiosyncratic—and as-

[22] Cf. Ludovik Osterc, *El pensamiento social y político del Quijote* (México: De Andrea, 1963).

[23] Curtius, *op. cit.*, p. 232.

[24] *LDQ*, pp. 96–97 (*Obras*, IV, 171–172). "Esta defensa de la locura es un tema unamunesco como pocos," writes Carlos Blanco-Aguinaga, "Unamuno, Don Quijote, y España," *Cuadernos Americanos*, LXVI (Nov.–Dec., 1952), 206.

sumes instead that everybody is exactly like him. He usually takes his stream of consciousness at face value, as if there were no more to the mind than meets the inner eye. If one assumes that the world beyond his own consciousness is but a mirror image of himself, the Friday afternoon toothache (or soul ache, for that matter) of a single individual may miraculously appear in everybody's mouth, or one's puritanical disgust with sex may lead to the conclusion that sex is disgusting. Contrary to the suspicious New England farmer who would not commit himself beyond saying, "It looks like a cow on this side," Unamuno would consider himself most capable of knowing both sides at once and even of reading a genuine longing for immortality in the cow's thoughts. He is in earnest when he states that Cervantes' book is only the pretext for him to project himself.

For Unamuno, Don Quixote's madness becomes the highest level of heroism. It was heroic, he says, on the part of Don Quixote to attack the windmills, and even more heroic to have withstood the ridicule that ensued. Here again, Unamuno distorts beyond recognition. For Cervantes, ideals can bear fruit only in marriage with the world; a utopian ideal that shrinks from fact is barren, as are most of Don Quixote's ideals. But for Unamuno, Don Quixote is no longer a well-meaning idler, misled, more often than not, by his delusive wishful thinking, impotent to bring about the realization of either his noble aims or his outmoded illusions. He is, instead, a most heroic Knight of Faith (another Kierkegaardian touch) who sets out to ensure his fame and immortality. Dulcinea is none other than the Glory with a capital G he is after (although he never comes near her). As for Don Quixote's kingdom, it is not of this world. And even if elsewhere Unamuno sees chivalry to be imbued with paganism (as indeed it is in Don Quixote's tirades), he nonetheless declares the Knight the high priest of a new brand of Christianity, Spanish style. Using now the materials he had collected years before for a life of St. Ignatius of Loyola, Unamuno forces a running parallel between him and Don Quixote, who, naturally enough, becomes St. Quixote. In fact, "Life of Saint Quixote and Saint Ignatius" would have been a more appropriate title. This parallel, of course, does not prevent Unamuno from expressing violent hatred for the Society of Jesus, the natural outcome of what he calls Loyola's knight-errantry, nor does his admiration for the Basque Loyola stop him from admiring the Basque founder of Jansenism or the non-Basque founder of Lutheranism, the two main brands of anti-Jesuitism. Clearly, there is no limit to what Unamuno can bring under one cover. He even tries to bring together the world views of Calderón and Cervantes, which are totally incompatible and mutually exclusive.

Besides being compared with Loyola and Segismundo (the protagonist of *Life Is a Dream*, for Unamuno takes fictional beings to be more real than historical ones), St. Quixote is likened by Unamuno to the Cid, to Pizarro, and even to Christ himself. Unamuno's St. Quixote is, surprisingly enough, as much of an ascetic as he is a hero; he is at once the paradigm of the Spanish *conquistadores* (though he has no America to his credit) and of the Spanish mystics (even if he shows no awe for things of the Church).

Obviously, such an interpretation is conceivable only if many passages and even full chapters of Cervantes' masterpiece are completely overlooked. Unamuno is always ready to exclude anything that is not grist for his mill and to glide over anything that runs counter to his main argument. Nor is he bothered by his most obvious contradictions. (It would take us too far afield to discuss this matter in detail.) On the other hand, he is too quick in assigning arbitrary symbolism to episodes and characters alike. The windmills, for instance, represent for him "locomotives, dynamos, turbines, steamships, automobiles, telegraphy with and without wires, bombs, instruments of ovariotomy." Not even an H-bomb would stop his brave Don Quixote. "The Knight was right," says he, commenting on Don Quixote's view of Sancho's sense of reality; "fear, and fear alone, made Sancho and makes all of us poor mortals see windmills in the monstrous giants that sow evil through the world. . . . Fear, sanchopanzesque fear, alone inspires the cult and worship of steam and electricity, makes us fall on our knees and cry mercy before the monstrous giants of mechanics and chemistry."[25]

[25] *LDQ*, p. 40 (*Obras*, IV, 118).

Clearly, Unamuno had no more admiration for modern technology than he had for modern science, and he lost interest in science from the moment he discovered that the formula for water was not wet. Both science and technology were for him evils of the modern world which destroyed the mystical charm of the Dark Ages. In his view, moreover, some countries were just not made for science. Two obviously hopeless examples were, according to him, Spain and Russia, so the Spaniards, he advised, should follow the example of the Russians, "a people," he says, "not unlike ourselves."[26] With all his flair for prophecy, he could not possibly have anticipated in 1912 the ironical twist that just a few years of the very history that he, in search of things eternal, had cast aside, would soon give to his words. Would Unamuno have changed his mind by now? Would he have spontaneously retracted his "Let others invent!" It is at least doubtful. Everyday reality running against him is no more guaranty today than it was during his lifetime. It is perfectly conceivable, and even probable, that for the Spaniards he would probably still prefer a return to the Dark Ages, with a yearning no less fervent than that of Don Quixote for his illusory Golden Age—anything to escape the horrible actuality of the present, anything to lose touch with everyday life, anything to turn one's face away from reality. Most of Unamuno's intellectual pursuits after the "great divide" were cast in a strangely irrational mold of mystification and paradox. In a rare moment of genuine sincerity, he portrays himself, again taking a cue from Kierkegaard, as a Don Juan of Ideas, admonishing himself with these fitting words: "You have fed, not on truth, but on intellectual lust, which ignited that fury with which you so violently persecute reason. But reason has taken revenge for that offense, making your thinking sterile."[27]

Reason took yet further revenge, making him a witness to that unfortunate incident when the cry "Muera la inteligencia!" ("Down with intelligence!"), so much in keeping with the Civil

26 *TSL*, p. 305 (*Obras*, XVI, 427).

27 *Obras*, XIII, 618 (*Rosario de sonetos líricos*, CVII). This sonnet is probably Unamuno's most severe self-indictment, according to Sánchez Barbudo, who goes on to say: "Lo malo es que no hubiera en él enmienda tras el arrepentimiento" (*Estudios*, p. 193).

War, went up within the very walls of his own university, one of the oldest in Europe. It must have been a bitter experience for a university professor and writer to realize that the deprecation of intelligence was in Spain no longer the exclusive privilege of the intellectual elite of 1898. Unamuno, as perhaps the most extreme of them, had devoted a good number of his lines to deifying quixotism and vilifying common sense and reason; and doing so is surely a greater crime in an intellectual than it is in a general, just as it is a greater crime in an intellectual than in a general to incite civil strife in a country that had had more than its share of it and, with shocking frivolity and irresponsibility, to invite further violence and abuse. To this crime most members of the Generation of 1898 would have to plead guilty. It is no longer possible to read without dismay some of the things they wrote. Consider, for instance, Unamuno's comment on the passage where Don Quixote insists on a basin being a helmet:

> What are [the fools] afraid of? That a row will be started, and civil war kindled again? Excellent! That is what we need.
> Yes, that is what we need: a new civil war. It is urgent to declare that the basins are and ought to be helmets, and to start . . . a new civil war.[28]

Unamuno may not have gotten his kind of immortality, but he most certainly got a civil war (be it the kind he wanted or not), if only a few months of it. Fortunately for him, death, which he so abhorred, was soon to rescue him, leaving to other Spaniards the full weight of the burden.

Unamuno's unbridled hostility toward reason places him among the most extreme representatives of metaphysical mysticism, the "feelers," in opposition to the "thinkers."[29] But honorary membership, of which he is so proud, in this not so exclusive club constitutes in fact one of his severest limitations. Emotion cannot be "the inspirer of whatever is best in man" unless it is later validated by sense, analysis, reason. Otherwise, it can be irresistibly deceptive. *The Tragic Sense of Life* and one of the three volumes of *Principia Mathematica* both appeared in 1912.

28 *LDQ*, p. 133 (*Obras*, IV, 205–206).
29 Cf. Hector Hawton, *The Feast of Unreason* (London: Watts, 1952), pp. 121, 216, and *passim*.

Two years later, Unamuno's unlike contemporary, Bertrand Russell, stated concisely the dialectic of the two extremes, mysticism and logic, in the following words:

> Metaphysics, or the attempt to conceive the world as a whole by means of thought, has been developed, from the first, by the union and conflict of two very different human impulses, the one urging men towards mysticism, the other urging them towards science. Some men have achieved greatness through one of these impulses alone, others through the other alone. . . . But the greatest men who have been philosophers have felt the need both of science and of mysticism: the attempt to harmonise the two was what made their life, and what always must, for all its arduous uncertainty, make philosophy, to some minds, a greater thing than either science or religion.[30]

In closing, the contrasting figures of Unamuno and Cervantes posit, especially in a context like the present one, the much-belabored question of the so-called Spanish peculiarity. Many Spaniards and non-Spaniards alike would be in perfect agreement about assigning to the so-called Spanish character fiery, irrational, overindividualistic traits which the bullfight seems to exemplify best. In fact, this character is as much the prime allure for many students of Spanish culture and for the millions of visitors who every year flood Spain, as it was for nineteenth-century Romantics. For these incurable Romantics, Unamuno would be everything they imagine a Spaniard to be. He himself seems to have subscribed to a similar view, and he remarked more than once that, being a Basque, like Loyola, he was Spanish twice over. His anti-European Counter-Regeneration was unquestionably in keeping with Loyola's Counter-Reformation.[31] Cervantes, on the contrary, probably would claim to be Spanish only once, and Spanish European at that—or, if you prefer, Spanish Italian, since his Italy was his Europe. Nonetheless, allow me to submit, Cervantes is not a less genuine representative of the Spanish people than Unamuno. Cervantes alone would suf-

---

[30] *Mysticism and Logic* (Garden City, N.Y.: Garden Books, n.d.), p. 1.
[31] Archibald Robertson, *The Reformation* (London: Watts, 1960), pp. 141 f. In 1925 a collection of Unamuno's essays translated by Francis de Miomandre was published in Paris under the title *Vérités arbitraires* (*Espagne contre Europe*).

fice, as would Galdós, to shatter any image of Spain which would not include them.

As for Unamuno's plight, it is not easy to come to any kind of a conclusion, unless we emulate his readiness to make snap judgments, especially condemnatory ones. Was he such a tragic figure? A contemporary of his, Professor Valdecampa, who once dared suggest to him that he would have made a great comedian was taken aback when Unamuno unhesitantly retorted: "Who, me? Why, I've never been anything else."[32] But again, there is no reason to suppose that this comic view of himself was any more valid than the tragic one. Like everybody else, Unamuno was both nature and nurture. It would be vain to try to determine to what extent he had been freer from his nurture than everyone is free from his binding nature, and no one can be held responsible beyond the sphere of his actual freedom. It is true, he seems to have reveled in his morbid pet obsessions. Of one thing we can be almost sure: Had Cervantes lived long enough to learn from Unamuno what the masterpiece of Spanish literature is all about, he would probably have viewed him as an unquestionably talented and unhappy Basque Don Quixote tilting at imaginary windmills while the real battle raged elsewhere. And once more Cervantes would have been unable to contain his irrepressible smile.

[32] Cf. Francisco Madrid, *Genio e ingenio de Miguel de Unamuno* (Buenos Aires: Aniceto López, 1943), p. 137. See also *Obras*, IV, 312 (*LDQ*, p. 251).

11

UNAMUNO'S OTHER SPAIN
Aníbal Sánchez-Reulet

From his early years, Unamuno felt a peculiar attraction for the Spanish-American world. It was almost a kind of fascination. He might have emigrated to America as had many of his countrymen and friends, and even his own father. It was a possibility in his life, not unusual for a Basque, but a possibility that never became real. Instead, he migrated to Castile. Even so, as an older man in Salamanca, Unamuno seems to have given serious consideration at one time to the idea of moving to Argentina; however, he kept postponing his final decision under various pretexts.[1] Still later, he was invited four times to go to Argentina: in 1910, 1912, 1922 (on this occasion as an official guest of the Argentine government), and finally in 1936, to attend a conference of the International Pen Club. But, whatever the reasons were, the invitations were not accepted and the dream of going overseas never materialized.[2]

Unamuno had to fulfill his deep and sincere love for Spanish America in a different way, the only one open to him: through the vicarious, imaginary experience of literature. Spanish America is,

[1] In April, 1904, Unamuno wrote to his devoted friend and admirer Pedro Jiménez Ilundain, living in Buenos Aires: "Far from having abandoned the idea of my departure for America, I am more and more resolved to go" (Hernán Benítez, "Cartas inéditas de Unamuno," *Revista de la Universidad de Buenos Aires*, 4th ser., 3d yr., no. 9 [T. IV, Vol. I], p. 164). In December of the same year, Unamuno told his friend the main reason for his not leaving Salamanca: "I love this rocky castle in which I live alone among so many people" (*ibid.*, p. 168).

[2] In a letter addressed in June, 1936, to Enrique Díez Canedo, at that time Spanish ambassador to Argentina, Unamuno writes: "Parece que está de Dios que yo no logre 'ultramarinearme'" (Manuel García Blanco, *América y Unamuno* [Madrid: Gredos, 1964], p. 14).

188

of course, not unique in this respect, for many other important experiences in Unamuno's life were purely literary in nature. After all, despite the contempt for literature he often showed— one of the paradoxical traits of his personality—Unamuno was essentially a man of letters and words. He was an amazingly voracious reader in many languages, and he wrote about literature all his life. A considerable part of this tireless activity was devoted to the reading of Spanish-American authors. He read not only pure literature (poetry, fiction, drama, essays), but also historical and sociological works, and, what is more revealing of his interest, memoirs, chronicles, and collections of letters. He considered these minor genres as very rewarding, especially insofar as Spanish America was concerned.

But Unamuno's contact with Spanish-American literature was not only through books. He was himself a very active and consistent cultivator of the epistolary genre and numbered among his correspondents Spanish-American writers as notable as the Uruguayans Zorrilla de San Martín and Carlos Vaz Ferreira, the Mexican Alfonso Reyes, the Argentine Ricardo Rojas, not to mention the most famous of all, Rubén Darío. Moreover, correspondence led, in many instances, to personal contacts and friendly relations, as with Darío and Rojas.[3]

Unamuno did not leave Salamanca to go to Spanish America, but numerous Spanish-American writers went to Salamanca to meet and see him out of devotion or mere curiosity, or in quest of literary patronage. It was part of his legend, of the myth he himself had laboriously built. Salamanca became during his lifetime, and because of his presence there, a kind of literary shrine, a place of intellectual pilgrimage, especially for Argentines, since Argentina was the country with which Unamuno was most familiar and where he had most friends, readers, and admirers.

---

[3] A large part of this correspondence has already been published. Manuel García Blanco, *op. cit.*, gives an excellent and well-documented account of the epistolary relations between Unamuno and several Spanish-American writers. More comprehensive and perhaps overly ambitious is the work of Julio César Chaves, *Unamuno y América* (Madrid: Ediciones Cultura Hispánica, 1964), which discusses not only personal relations but also Unamuno's opinions and literary criticism on Spanish-American authors.

As a young, traveling apprentice writer, I was myself one of those fortunate pilgrims, going to visit him in 1934 in his home at Number 4 Bordadores Street. He received me in his book-lined studio. I could not help noticing immediately the portrait of the Argentine writer Sarmiento in a place of preference, beside a row of his works. We sat down next to the window, a table covered with a green cloth between us, the same table upon which he leaned over and died two years later. We talked for more than two hours; or, to be more precise, I should say that he did most of the talking. In fact, it was one of his "mono-dialogues." He performed his main role, the role of Miguel de Unamuno, and I was a respectful spectator. At that time Unamuno was seventy years old; but though he looked sad and tired, I was amazed at his alertness, his quick memory, his inexhaustible curiosity in asking for news of old and mutual friends. What amazed me most was the extent of his information on my own country and the detailed knowledge he had of even obscure and unimportant figures in Argentine literature. At a certain moment, for instance, he talked for a long while about the characteristics of language and the spontaneous style of the memoirs of General Aráoz de Lamadrid, a half-literate gaucho general, which I had not read and did not intend to read at that time.

Unamuno not only read (sometimes without discrimination) a large number of Spanish-American authors, he also wrote about them. For a short period, from 1901 to 1906, he was in charge of reviewing current Spanish-American publications for *La Lectura*, a Madrid literary magazine. He gave up this strenuous task, overwhelmed by the hundreds and hundreds of volumes that kept pouring in, but he continued until the end of his life to write assiduously on books and authors and on linguistic and cultural problems related to Spanish America. In all, he wrote more than one hundred articles on Spanish-American subjects, comprising almost a thousand pages. To this impressive amount of literature, we have to add the numerous letters of praise, advice, and criticism addressed to Spanish-American literati, some of which are still uncollected and unpublished.

Unamuno was right when he said that he was the European most interested in Spanish America; however, his interest was not that of a scholar or a professor of literature. He was not in pursuit of a systematic and well-organized knowledge of Spanish-American culture. Quite the contrary, his readings and his critical views were clearly arbitrary; but in their very arbitrariness, they are most revealing of Unamuno's character and aesthetic preferences. We may agree with his opinions—and I personally agree with much of what he said—but we cannot consider his essays and articles as models of literary criticism. As a matter of fact, he did not consider himself a critic at all and always looked upon critics with scorn. His articles on literary subjects served mainly as pretexts to expound his own views and always offered an opportunity to communicate his personal reactions, his predilections, and his aversions. One thing is true: he always seems sincere, whether he is eulogizing, condemning, or simply ignoring. His silences are always eloquent.[4]

When Unamuno began his brilliant literary and academic career in the early nineties, the Modernist trend in literature was gathering momentum in Spanish America. *Azul*, Rubén Darío's first work inspired in the new aesthetics, was published in 1888. But, of course, the process of profound renovation of Spanish prose and verse which the Modernist movement carried out had begun years earlier with the innovations of Martí and Gutiérrez Nájera in prose, and the poetical contributions of Casal and Silva, as well as Gutiérrez Nájera.

Unamuno disliked Modernism as a whole. He was prejudiced, and failed to recognize the positive and original aspects of the new trend. He was unable to discriminate between the real contribution and the extremes indulged in by most of the Modernist poets, especially in the first period: the exaltation of art for the sake of art or literature for the sake of literature, the cultivation of formal values, the virtuosity in the use of words and sounds, the exoticism of content, the precious and overrefined use of language and images. After all, these extremes were a necessary reaction against a literary establishment in which the leading

[4] For a general appraisal of Unamuno as a critic of Spanish-American literature, the pioneering article by John E. Englekirk, "Unamuno, crítico de la literatura hispanoamericana," *Revista Iberoamericana*, III (Feb.–May, 1941), 19–37, is still useful.

poetical figures were Campoamor and Núñez de Arce. Without question, Unamuno was also irritated at the obvious influence of French models, and the clear preference of the Modernists for contemporary French literature.

Unamuno reacted to Modernism, in some instances, by pretending that he did not understand what it meant: in others, by castigating (although usually in very general terms and without dealing in personalities) poets and prose writers who under the Parisian spell had turned into mere parrots and imitators; and at least on one occasion, by proclaiming that what he wanted was Eternalism, not Modernism. "Modernism," he said, "will be old-fashioned and grotesque ten years from now."[5]

Despite his rejection of Modernist aesthetics as a whole, Unamuno wrote several favorable and appreciative articles on individual writers who were initiators or participants in the movement. An example is his study on José Asunción Silva, who was, in Unamuno's opinion, the main originator of the Modernist trend in poetry, and perhaps one of the most influential. He wrote on Silva with sympathy and affection, although more about the man than about his poetry. He was mainly interested in discussing the motivations for Silva's suicide. One of the possible answers he suggests to the enigma is typically Unamunian, that is, paradoxical: Silva committed suicide because he loved life too much and was anxious for eternity. At the end of the essay, taking issue with Silva's opinion that Baudelaire was the greatest poet of the preceding fifty years, Unamuno wonders what kind of poetry Silva would have written if he had been more familiar with the English lyricists and with Walt Whitman. The implication that Baudelaire, or the reading of Baudelaire's poetry by Silva, was in part responsible for his suicide is tenuous, but it is there.[6]

Unamuno commented with sincere appreciation on the poetry of Amado Nervo, one of the few Modernists of whom he approved, obviously because of the religious accent of most of his themes and his preoccupation with death, and perhaps also because of the melancholic, sad tone of his poetry.

[5] Obras, IV, 913–914.
[6] Ibid., p. 782.

On the other hand, Unamuno did not truly appreciate the poetical work of Rubén Darío. They knew each other, but between them there was always a lack of communication, a distance, a reticence, embarrassing to both of them. They corresponded for several years (from 1899 to 1909), and they met personally in Madrid when Darío visited Spain for the second time in 1899. It was owing to Darío's initiative that Unamuno began to publish in the newspaper *La Nación* of Buenos Aires, an activity that lasted for more than thirty years and from which Unamuno derived a considerable part of his income. In the same newspaper, in 1909, Darío published an article entitled "Unamuno poeta," commenting on Unamuno's first volume of poetry, which had appeared two years before. Unamuno admitted later, in 1916, that Darío was "the only one who said something substantial, full of understanding" about his book, adding that this was a proof of the breadth of Darío's aesthetic appreciation.[7] He also included Darío's article as a prologue to another volume of poems (*Teresa*, 1924). Despite being so much in debt to Darío, however, Unamuno refrained during Darío's lifetime from publishing any commentary on his poetical work. The only review dealing with him in the series that Unamuno wrote for *La Lectura* was a very short one on *España contemporánea*, a volume of literary sketches. It is interesting to point out, however, that Unamuno in that book review acquits Darío of the charge, made by Rodó and others, of being Gallic to such an extent that his prose seemed "translated from the French; a good translation, but a translation nevertheless."[8] For Unamuno, on the contrary, the peculiar characteristics of Darío's prose, at least in this book, arise from a different way of thinking, a way of thinking, in his view, which is authentically Spanish American. Darío's prose, he says, creates a kind of cinematographic illusion because of the short sentences and the succession of flickering images (like those in the old movies). What Unamuno does not seem to realize is that this was precisely one of the ways the Modernists were attempting the renovation of Spanish prose. They preferred juxtaposed short sentences to phrases architecturally organized in long oratorical

[7] *Ibid.*, VIII, 582.
[8] *Ibid.*, p. 121.

paragraphs, which had been characteristic of most Spanish writers of the second half of the nineteenth century.

Darío's feelings were deeply hurt because of the silence and lack of recognition of his poetical work by Unamuno. In a letter to him in 1907 he complained of this silence and appealed for a juster and more benevolent attitude. The plea was not successful; Unamuno responded with a vague promise, but published nothing. In private conversations and letters he even went so far as to criticize his poetry as prosaic, artificial, and hollow. Only nine years later, after Darío's death, did he manifest repentance and admit that he had not been just and honest with him; but even on this occasion he spoke mostly of the man and limited himself to saying that Darío was a great poet, without ever dealing with specific aspects of his poetry. Moreover, when he quoted verses by Darío (in fact, just two), he did it to exemplify what he considered the weakest and most frivolous side of his poetry.[9]

There are different ways of explaining Unamuno's attitude toward Darío. In addition to the difference between their aesthetics, there was a strong difference between their personalities. Unamuno described Darío as a man without passion, sensual and sensitive, too tolerant, benevolent, and eager to understand and appreciate any literary work, however dissimilar it might be to his own creations. Unamuno admits that Darío was his opposite, declaring that he feels closer to men who are passionate and fanatical, and going on to say that it is easier for him to understand men of a different brand of fanaticism from his own than men who try to understand and justify everything. "The common reason of fanaticism and passion even unites opposites";[10] but for Unamuno, Darío lacked this unifying passion.

It was probably because of this dissimilarity in aesthetics and personalities that Unamuno gave scanty attention to Darío's poetical work. He evidently read *Azul* and *Prosas profanas*, which he did not like, but it is doubtful that he ever read *Cantos de vida y esperanza*. If he had, how could he have completely ignored the highly personal and original poems in that volume, in which Darío expresses, without rhetorical adornments, his mental tor-

9 *Ibid.*, p. 520.
10 *Ibid.*, p. 532.

tures and existential anguish? Yet there is no indication any-
where, either by allusion or quotation, that Unamuno knew
them.[11]

In contrast with this silent indifference to Darío's best contributions to Spanish poetry stands Unamuno's enthusiastic reaction to the work of José Martí, who, in fact, was the initiator—at
least in his prose—of the Modernist trend. Unamuno admired
the use Martí made in his *Versos libres* of blank hendecasyl-
lables, a metrical form he adopted himself in the composition
of his long religious poem *El Cristo de Velázquez*. Unamuno also
points out the poetic qualities of Martí's prose.

One of the best pieces of literary criticism Unamuno ever
wrote, to my way of thinking, is an article published in 1919
in which he discusses the prose style of Martí as found in his
letters. The short, elliptical, aphoristic, trimmed sentences seem
conversational to him and remind him of St. Teresa. He likes
the creative spontaneity of this prose, or protoprose, in which the
words are more than mere words and seem to be acts, creations.
Unamuno included a kind of anthology of the best phrases of
Martí to show their lyric and poetic essence.

Strange as it may seem, Unamuno did not write a great deal
about Martí the man. Of course, he refers here and there to his
greatness and to the circumstances of his death. He says that
Martí died as a martyr, but he never inquired as to the motivations of his readiness to face death fearlessly for an ideal cause.
Unamuno quotes, without commentary, a pathetic phrase of
Martí's: "When we are willing to die we do not think of death;
neither our own nor other people's."[12] And for Martí, as we
know, this was not a mere literary phrase.

If Unamuno was repelled by the aesthetic extravagances of

[11] This view is confirmed by the testimony of Ricardo Rojas. He visited
Unamuno in 1908 and, according to him, at that time Unamuno "knew
only a few ultramodernistic verses of the *Prosas profanas* period." He
tried unsuccessfully to convince Unamuno of the new values in Darío's
poetry by reading to him from *Cantos de vida y esperanza* (Ricardo
Rojas, *Retablo español* [Buenos Aires: Losada, 1938], p. 291). For a
brief presentation of Unamuno's views on Darío and his poetry, see Philip
Metzidakis, "Unamuno frente a la poesía de Rubén Darío," *Revista Iberoamericana*, XXV (1960), 229–249.

[12] *Obras*, VIII, 583.

the Modernists, he was conversely attracted by the best creations of the Spanish-American Romantics. For instance, he considered *Tabaré* by Zorrilla de San Martín the most beautiful poem ever written in Spanish America, a work with genuine native inspiration. Moreover, in a letter to Zorrilla in 1906, Unamuno declares that, despite their ideological differences, he is of all contemporary Spanish poets the one to whom he feels closest.[13] (Zorrilla, of course, was a practicing Catholic all his life and his *Tabaré* is a literary expression of his faith.) Zorrilla attributed this preference of Unamuno's for his work to a deep, hidden attraction which gave them a spiritual bond.[14] Unamuno promised Zorrilla to write a study on *Tabaré*; and although he never did, we cannot doubt the sincerity of his promise, because, on every possible occasion, he kept referring to *Tabaré* as one of the most significant works of Spanish-American literature. Instead of writing on *Tabaré*, Unamuno wrote at least two articles on the style of Zorrilla's speeches, in which, as in those of Martí, he found poetic qualities. They were the speeches of a poet, not those of a lawyer, like the speeches of Castelar, the acclaimed nineteenth-century Spanish orator. Unamuno also wrote a series of three articles on a historical work by Zorrilla on the national hero of Uruguay, Artigas. They were intended for publication in *La Nación*, but only the first was there printed.

Unamuno's inclination toward Romanticism is also clear in the enthusiasm he felt for so-called gaucho poetry. Early in his life, in 1892, he discovered almost by chance the poem *Martín Fierro* by the Argentine José Hernández. The effect of its reading was instantaneous: Unamuno fell in love with the work. He confessed later that he went mad over it. As a consequence, he began a personal campaign to make the book known, which he carried so far that his devotion became an easy target for many jokes, even practical ones, on the part of his friends. His first article on the poem, calling the attention of the Spanish public to its importance, was published in the *Revista Española* in 1894,

---

[13] Arturo Sergio Visca, ed., *Correspondencia de Zorrilla de San Martín y Unamuno* (Montevideo: Instituto Nacional de Investigaciones y Archivos Literarios, 1955), p. 26.

[14] *Ibid.*, p. 28.

and his devotion was to last for years. Writing on other subjects, he often alluded to and commented on the significance of Hernández' work, and even quoted verses from it in his book *Vida de don Quijote y Sancho.*

What Unamuno most admired in *Martín Fierro* was the kind of language used by the author, the so-called gaucho dialect (*el lenguaje gauchesco*). In Unamuno's view this language was essentially Spanish, and strict Castilian—rude and rural, but Castilian nevertheless. He found in it archaic expressions, idioms, proverbs, colloquialisms, and peculiarities of pronunciation common in the spoken language of many regions of Castile. Basically, it was the language of the sixteenth-century Spanish colonizers as preserved in the Argentine pampas.

For Unamuno *Martín Fierro* was "a poem that has almost no meaning at all outside the context of Spanish literature."[15] He praised its primitive and popular character, which reminded him of the old Spanish ballads and, in this respect, preferred the first part to the second, because of its freshness and spontaneity. Finally, he exalted the literary significance of the work, which in his opinion combined both epic and lyric elements. According to Unamuno, there were more poetic values in *Martín Fierro* than in most of the cultivated and refined poetry of the day, an obvious critical allusion to that of the Modernists. Because of the popular character of the sources from which it took its inspiration, *Martín Fierro* was for him a genuine representative work of both native Argentine and Spanish spirit.

I agree with Unamuno in considering *Martín Fierro* an important and significant work of Spanish literature, perhaps the most original of the nineteenth century, but I cannot help but feel that, in some of his judgments, Unamuno reveals himself to be the victim of a Romantic delusion, like many other critics before and after him. *Martín Fierro* is not an epic poem and has very few things in common with the traditional Spanish ballads. Moreover, despite its popular inspiration, *Martín Fierro* is more literary than Unamuno believed, or wished to believe. He did not realize the process of identification of José Hernández with his

15 *Obras,* VIII, 58.

character Martín Fierro, which is, ironically, further proof of his ideas of the simultaneous self-creation of author and character.

We may agree with Unamuno that the language used in *Martín Fierro* is basically Spanish; with the exception of a few words, its vocabulary is Spanish, and its grammatical structure is also Spanish. It is a dialect not too far from standard Spanish, but it possesses a distinctive characteristic that Unamuno did not, and probably could not, detect. It is a difference in accent which is clear when the poem is read aloud. Long sections of the poem cannot be recited with the standard Spanish intonation used in the reading of poetry. If we do so, we destroy the main effect. This is to me the most important distinctive characteristic of the language of *Martín Fierro*, and it is too bad that it escaped Unamuno, who used to say that in order fully to understand a text, we must always read with our ears, never with our eyes alone. However that may be, what is important now is to point out that Unamuno's enthusiasm for *Martín Fierro* is most revealing of his aesthetic preferences; and also that he was the only one who had the courage to express his feelings in a period when the poem was being neglected by most Argentine critics because of the rising Modernist tide.

Another figure of Spanish-American literature for whom Unamuno professed an admiration without limits was also a Romantic, the Argentine Sarmiento. Unamuno felt, for the man and for his work, a deep, strong attachment. In his view, Sarmiento's significance as a writer transcended the limits of any regional literature. On one occasion, somebody asked Unamuno who, in his opinion, was the most important writer in the Spanish language in the nineteenth century. Despite the fact that the question, as he remarked, was "too Spanish, that is, too simplistic," he answered without hesitation that it was Sarmiento.[16]

Sarmiento, Unamuno affirms, is the only Spanish writer of the nineteenth century who had real genius. He particularly acknowledges Sarmiento's distinctive style. Although emphatic and oratorical at times, as the man himself was in real life, the prose of

[16] *Ibid.*, p. 367.

Sarmiento is always colorful, vigorous, personal, original. His style did not derive from previous literature. "He has nothing in common with the irritating classics of the sixteenth and seventeenth centuries."[17] His prose was not made of artificial words and expressions picked up in books, but came directly out of the man himself and a living tradition of the spoken language learned in his childhood in his home in the remote Argentine province of San Juan. This characteristic alone would be enough to endear him to Unamuno, who was always preaching the virtues of the living language, insisting on the richness and value of spoken words in contrast with the ghostly existence of written words (signs without sound of which "literature," in a derogatory sense, is made). To Unamuno, Sarmiento's was a spoken prose (*prosa hablada*), and sometimes it was even more than that: it was a shouted prose (*prosa gritada*).[18] It looks almost like a literal transcription of oral language and retains the syntactic structure of speech. "If there are men," Unamuno says, "who are disgusting because they speak like a book, in considering Sarmiento we have to admit that his books speak like a man."[19]

Unamuno makes a point of Sarmiento's talent for creating types and archetypes, and his extraordinary ability to enlarge and to give a peculiar and, at times, epic relief to even the most obscure of his characters, who are all taken from real life. Sarmiento makes giants of simple people. Unamuno mentions, for instance, the singular portrait of Father Castro, the humble priest who was the teacher of Sarmiento's mother, carrying the Gospels in his hand but at the same time hiding a volume of Rousseau under his cassock. Unamuno also observes that through the creative power of Sarmiento the figures of the Argentine *caudillos* Rosas and Quiroga reach the proportions of Miltonian Satans. Sarmiento re-creates history like a novelist. His most famous book, *Facundo*, is a kind of novelized history.[20]

On the other hand, according to Unamuno, Sarmiento was a

---

[17] *Ibid.*, p. 371.
[18] *Contra esto y aquello* (Madrid: Renacimiento, 1912), p. 252. Owing to a misprint, the text in *Obras*, IV, 945, reads *prosa agitada*.
[19] *Obras*, VIII, 371.
[20] *Ibid.*, IV, 929.

truly lyrical writer, with a strong compulsion to express his emotions. He was immodest to the very limits of vanity and spoke too much about himself, but when he spoke about his country or the events of his time, whether describing the wild vastness of the pampas, or the primitive battles of Facundo Quiroga, or a bullfight he attended while in Madrid, Sarmiento always did so with a powerful lyricism.

Nevertheless, whatever Sarmiento's merits as a writer, what Unamuno perhaps liked most in him was his personality. My impression is that he admired the man much more than the writer, or he admired the writer because of the man. Sarmiento, says Unamuno, was above all a man; and as a result of being just a man, but no less than a man, he was a great writer.[21] Moreover, in Unamuno's interpretation, Sarmiento the man was deeply and truly Spanish by virtue of his linguistic and cultural background. He also was Spanish by temperament: passionate, aggressive, arrogant, contradictory, fond of extremes. Indeed, Sarmiento was an extremist, though there is no vice in extremism like his, which was positive and constructive, and aimed at promoting reforms.

Unamuno points out correctly that when Sarmiento criticizes Spain, he does so as a true Spaniard; just as any Spaniard who really feels Spain in his heart and in his blood and who sincerely wishes to change the image of Spain must criticize his country. Sarmiento criticized Spanish defects and vices with the same voice and the same tone that Unamuno himself did. Yet, there is, concurrently, in both Sarmiento and Unamuno, a concealed admiration for some of the negative traits of Spanish character which they attack. Unamuno liked to say that in some instances we must defend our own defects.

But if Sarmiento and Unamuno were congenial and similar in many respects, they were not exactly twin souls. Sarmiento tended to simplify; Unamuno, to complicate. Sarmiento was a man of action; Unamuno, a man of ideas. I wonder if Unamuno did not have a secret longing, a kind of generous envy, for some of Sarmiento's accomplishments as a man of action—the envy born of the frustration that the intellectual, the writer, the poet (a

[21] *Ibid.*, VIII, 371–372.

virtual prisoner in a pure realm of words and ideas), sometimes experiences. Unamuno was essentially an intellectual, despite his protests to the contrary. His creative talent, original and powerful as it was, never crossed the limits of literary fiction. On the other hand, Sarmiento was a practical, unsophisticated, solid, one-piece man who used literature, words, and ideas literally to promote social reforms and to create institutions, that is to say, to carry out a different type of fiction of supposedly more historical consequence. In any event, Unamuno, from the vantage point of the intellectual, could fully understand and appreciate Sarmiento the man and the writer. I doubt very much if Sarmiento would really have understood Unamuno.[22]

The interest of Unamuno in Spanish-American literature was not the result of mere curiosity or polite condescension, as with many other Spanish writers and critics before and after him, when dealing with books and authors of Spanish America. Unamuno, of course, in some instances, used a diplomatic approach, or preferred to remain silent; but his interest was always active and sincere, with a feeling of real participation, as is proved by his strong devotions and rejections.

Unamuno's interest in the literature of Spanish America parallels his concern with the destiny of the Spanish language. And when he said *Spanish language*, he was thinking about something more than the language of Castile. A Basque by birth, he became a Castilian by adoption, but he was always dreaming of a universal Spain, a greater Spain. In his view, the language of Castile was the best instrument for forging that greater, universal Spain, with one condition: that the Castilian language become real Spanish by a progressive enlargement and enrichment through the contributions of all the people who speak Spanish beyond the limits of the Peninsula, all over the world. He referred on many occasions, and always with peculiar emotion, to José Rizal, the national hero of the Philippines, half Tagalog and half Chinese, who was condemned to death by the Spanish colonial regime, but who said good-bye to life in Spanish in his last memorable poem.

---

[22] On the relationship, literary and otherwise, between Sarmiento and Unamuno, see Dardo Cúneo, *Sarmiento y Unamuno* (2d ed.; Buenos Aires, Ediciones Transición, 1955).

And he also recalled the great Benito Juárez, a pure Mexican Indian who lived and thought in Spanish.

The idea of a Greater Spain, as Unamuno thought of it, had nothing to do with either race or geographical expansion. He conceived it mainly as a process of spiritual growth through a common linguistic experience. Words, he would say, are the flesh of the soul, and the spiritual fatherland of men is the language they speak. Having a common language, however, would not preclude variety. On the contrary, the process of enrichment of a language requires a variety of voices with different accents. It is a process of integration through diversification. What Unamuno was looking for in Spanish-American literature was a real response, not an echo. He was looking for new and original voices, which precisely through being new and original might express the genuine spirit of both Spanish America and Spain. And this spirit, he thought, could best be expressed by writers deeply rooted in a living, popular tradition of spoken Spanish.

Spanish America, for Unamuno, was the Other Spain (*la otra España*), a different Spain but also an integral part of the greater, universal Spain of his dreams. He was hoping that Spanish America could eventually restore, bring back, the ideal Spain that could have been and should have been, but never has been.

12

UNAMUNO'S POLITICS
Stanley Payne

In writings on twentieth-century Spanish affairs, it is not uncommon to come across statements declaring that the members of the so-called Generation of 1898 reawakened the spirit of critical thought in Spain, or in some fashion encouraged Spaniards to make a new analysis of national political or cultural problems. The accuracy of this generalization in the broader sense is doubtful, but of all the Spanish littérateurs of the early twentieth century, the most persistently didactic was Miguel de Unamuno. If more concerned with poetry than with sociology, Unamuno was even more devoted to his self-chosen role of stinging gadfly of Spanish mores. Julián Marías has written that

> Unamuno did not want to amuse, nor instruct, nor convince. He wanted two things: to exist for others, to be irreplaceable and unforgettable, to continue living in their memory—this was the first thing; the second, "to cause everyone to live restless with longings."[1]

Thus, although Unamuno explicitly, if not consistently, rejected active participation in the mundane affairs of government and politics, a not inconsiderable portion of his thousands of pages of commentary, criticism, and exhortation touched directly or indirectly on the world of politics. Spanish politics in turn intervened brutally and directly in his personal life, eventually causing him six years of painful and lonely exile—perhaps the most difficult period of his life—and possibly even hastening his death at the end of 1936.

[1] Miguel de Unamuno, *Obras selectas* (3d ed.; Madrid: Plenitud, 1956), prologue, p. 23.

203

Unamuno's birthplace, Bilbao, was one of the most politically conscious provincial capitals in Spain, and became much more so during Don Miguel's lifetime. It was a coveted objective for both liberals and traditionalists during the two main Carlist Wars, the latter of which was fought during Unamuno's childhood and early adolescence. Though Bilbao and most other cities of the region were liberal, Carlism was in general terms the regional political movement of the Basques. Unamuno was hardly attracted to Carlism per se, but appreciated the Carlists' intense loyalty and spiritual devotion to the traditionalist cause, their attachment to historic values of their region, and the repulsion inspired in them by the negative aspects of bourgeois liberalism. Some of this appreciation for Carlist sentiments was reflected in Unamuno's first and longest novel, *Paz en la guerra* (1897), which brought some critics to label him pro-Carlist. Unamuno naturally forswore any such identity, but even later had a few sympathetic words for certain of the spiritual aspects of the Carlist movement.[2]

In the later nineteenth century, as Unamuno was growing up, Carlism lost ground in his native province of Vizcaya to a more modern form of regionalist traditionalism, which emerged as Basque nationalism. Unamuno always felt a deep identity with the Basque customs and regions of his forebears and could not remain unaffected by the ideological pressures of Basque ethnocentrism. His doctoral dissertation at the University of Madrid in 1884 was "Crítica del problema sobre el origen y prehistoria de la raza vasca" ("A Critical Study of the Problem of the Origin and Prehistory of the Basque Race"). This study concluded, however, that virtually nothing was known for certain about the origins and prehistory of the Basques. Even though almost all the literary efforts made by Unamuno until the age of twenty-five were written on Basque themes, he early rejected any sort of Basque exclusiveness which would have isolated his native region and its culture from the broader Spanish scene.

While always warm in his praise of the Basque virtues, especially the hard work and industrious enterprise of his native

---

[2] Cf. his remarks in "La crisis actual del patriotismo español" (Dec., 1905), *Obras*, III, 950–951.

Bilbao, Unamuno unfailingly spoke out in his mature years against Basque nationalism and separatist proclivities. He urged Basque reformers to achieve their goals in the broader context of Spain, to apply their energy to the larger task of raising Spanish cultural and moral standards, to Basque-ize Spain rather than try to withdraw within their own small region. In 1901 the Basque leaders organized an art festival, the Juegos Florales, in imitation of the Catalan culture festival which had been reorganized in 1859. As the leading Basque writer, Unamuno was invited to be guest of honor and to deliver the central address on August 26, 1901. His speech hailed the principal glory of the Basques as lying not in their separateness but in their diffusion throughout the Hispanic world.[3] In his youth he had been a candidate for the first academic chair of the Basque language, but throughout his mature career Unamuno combated efforts to impose Basque as the official language of the region, pointing always to the obvious fact that the Basque language was dying out, urging Basques and all other Spaniards to develop their aspirations in the common cultural tongue, Castilian.

If Unamuno's rejection of the Basque ideology was always tempered by strong affection for his native region and appreciation of Basque qualities, he gave Catalan nationalism somewhat less gentle treatment. Widely read in Catalan literature, which, up to a point, he admired, Unamuno recognized the greater strength of the Catalan language in its native provinces, but he had no patience for the transformation of the Catalan cultural revival into a regionalist political movement. His capsule dismissal of Catalan nationalism was expressed in the famous epithet:

> ¡Seréis siempre unos niños, levantinos!
> ¡Os ahoga la estética![4]
>
> (You will never grow up, East-Coasters!
> Aesthetics is drowning the life out of you!).

Yet Unamuno's own intellectual vocation did not find its proper channel immediately, and he too went through a phase of

---

[3] *Obras*, VI, 326–343.
[4] *Ibid.*, XIII, 249.

youthful radicalism before arriving at his adult philosophy. During his early twenties, Unamuno was temporarily influenced by scientific positivism. Without full-time professional employment, he and other poor young intellectuals founded a short-lived weekly journal, *La Lucha de Clases,* in the mid-80's. It was "the first socialistic organ in Bilbao aimed at creating a revolutionary party."[5] Young Unamuno published a number of anonymous articles in this ephemeral review, and for some time had the reputation of being a social radical; however, his brief bout of protosocialism stemmed from personal, emotional, and intellectual conflicts. It had little or nothing to do with Marxism and was not formed along doctrinaire ideological lines. As Unamuno's literary ambitions became fixed, he abandoned such journalistic agitation altogether.

The mature Unamuno's commentary on Spanish affairs took shape in his first major work, the collection of essays entitled *En torno al casticismo* (1895). The first essays were an interpretation of Spanish history and of the essence of traditional Spanish culture and values. They were neither political diatribes nor attempts to rally patriotic opinion, but in them Unamuno drew attention to the basic qualities that had endured through Spanish history, while criticizing some of their negative features. For most of the nineteenth century, Spanish intellectuals had been highly critical of their national heritage. Unamuno attempted to adjust the focus, so that some twentieth-century historians have referred to this work as an anticipation and encouragement of twentieth-century Spanish nationalism. Laín Entralgo has pointed out that it was Unamuno and certain of his contemporaries who created the twentieth-century sense of the Castilian landscape.[6] What had earlier been ignored or dismissed as barren and sterile was now seen as full of positive characteristics, molding the values and feelings of the peoples of Spain.

[5] Hernán Benítez, "La crisis religiosa de Unamuno," *Revista de la Universidad de Buenos Aires,* 4th ser., IV (Jan.–June, 1949), 51; quoted in Margaret T. Rudd, *The Lone Heretic* (Austin: University of Texas Press, 1963), p. 62.

[6] Pedro Laín Entralgo, *La generación del noventa y ocho* (Madrid: Diana, 1945), pp. 21–42.

Part Five of *En torno al casticismo*, entitled "On the Current Morass of Spain," expressed some of Unamuno's fundamental criticism of the Spanish scene. Spaniards were sunk in a routine conformity, divided against one another by cliques. There was little genuine concern to make laws, parties, or government stand for fresh, new, living goals. Spontaneous, creative association of self-responsible individuals was rare. Constant opposition between stubborn cliques was not accompanied by the cultivation of individual cultural personality. The herd instinct, brute force, abstract law, and government decrees were invoked, instead of civic education being encouraged.

> In this society, composed of camarillas who abhor one another without knowing one another, it is saddening to watch savage atomism from which there is no escape other than iron, disciplinary organization of committees, commissions, subcommissions, graphed programs, and similar trivia. And as in earlier ages, this atomism is accompanied by faith in the above and beyond, in external law, in the government, which is seen either as God or as the Devil, the two persons of the divinity in which our "intra-official" Manicheanism believes.
>
> Beside the great external liberty that we think we enjoy because no one denies it to us, the lack of internal freedom stands out in sharper contrast. Enormous monotony spreads throughout all contemporary Spanish society and dissolves in numbness, the dull uniformity of all-pervasive vulgarity.[7]

Unamuno's social and political critcism was customarily apolitical, centering on the absence of education, imagination, and free creative personalities in Spanish society, of which the political morass was merely the consequence, not the cause; but he did on occasion denounce specific groups or measures. In 1905–1906 he spoke out a number of times against the passage of the new Law of Jurisdictions by which the regime turned control of civil disorder over to the army.[8] As the above quotation indicates, he had no respect whatever for the established political parties or the great majority of the Cortes deputies. Not incorrectly, he saw Spanish political life of the late nineteenth and

[7] *Obras*, III, 284.
[8] *Ibid.*, pp. 937–956, 975–991.

early twentieth centuries as based on negativism. In a pointed
essay on "Los antipoliticistas," he wrote:

> I am accustomed to saying that in the small towns and rural
> districts of this Spain of ours there are always at least two
> parties, which are the anti-Xists, who follow Z against X, and
> the anti-Zists, who follow X against Z. And note that I do not
> call them Xists and Zists, because they are essentially and funda-
> mentally negative. More than following one leader, they are
> against the other. And in general it can be said that our Re-
> publicans are no more than anti-Monarchists, while our Mon-
> archists are merely anti-Republicans.[9]

On the pretext of reviewing Azorín's booklet *Un discurso de la
Cierva comentado por Azorín,* in December, 1914, Unamuno denounced the Spanish parliamentary system in the following terms:

> In Spain it cannot be said that the parliamentary regime is
> based on public opinion. There is very little political opinion
> in Spain; one of our greatest national misfortunes is the weak-
> ness and penury of our national public conscience, but it can
> be affirmed that what little opinion there is, is not represented
> in the parliament. I know one rural district whose truly domi-
> nant opinion, however feeble that may be, tends toward agrarian
> reform and suppression of the evils of the latifundia; but it is
> represented by a great landowning proprietor, a fierce political
> boss who tyrannizes the very people who vote for him. Either
> because of fear or greed, his greatest enemies either give him
> or sell him their votes. And so it turns out that our parliament
> does not even represent the average level of Spanish intelligence,
> but something rather lower.
> . . . Recently I repeated once more in Madrid—and being
> said in Madrid it was much more widely heard, reaching even
> parliament itself—that our parliament is composed in general
> of the wealthy, who are the best; of servants of the wealthy,
> who are a hundred times worse, and of the lawyers of the
> wealthy, who constitute the lowest level of the moral order.[10]

There is no evidence that Unamuno found a single redeeming
feature in the contemporary Spanish political system, but as these
passages indicate, he also castigated the indifference and irresponsibility of most of the public, the apolitical quality of

[9] *Ibid.,* IV, 730.
[10] *Ibid.,* V, 406–408.

Spanish life which he properly equated with its fundamental lack of intellectualism and its cultural anomie. Though at this time he himself had not yet participated in regular politics, he considered cultural education the indispensable basis of politics, and so with his customary egotism could refer to himself as Spain's number one civic activist—or, as he put it on one occasion,

> I shall not tire of repeating . . . that politics is one of the best viewpoints from which to consider any problem.
> Further, it is clear that one can be interested in politics and even be politically active without joining any of the organized parties. . . . Myself, for example . . .
> I believe that I am one of the Spaniards who has done most in the politics of the fatherland, yet without belonging to any party, which I do not consider recommendable in every instance, but to me it gives great liberty of movement.
> What we must all attempt to bring to an end is the antisocial or at least unsocial sentiment hidden beneath the phrase: "The government does nothing for me." . . . Where there is not intense political life, culture is superficial and without roots.[11]

The interpretation of such remarks has, however, sometimes led commentators astray. Certain lingering traces of his youthful radicalism, his rejection of official Spain, the oft-repeated phrase about the need to delve deeply into the common people (*chapuzarnos en pueblo*),[12] certain remarks of the 1890's and afterward about the need to "Europeanize" or "Japanize" Spain— these have caused some to label Unamuno a supporter of political progressivism. In fact, he never showed much enthusiasm for social reforms and sometimes even opposed the official standard-bearers of political liberalism and republicanism.

After about 1905, Unamuno was very chary of recommending the improvement of Spain by merely technical means or economic advances. As early as 1897 he had written to Azorín: "I expect nothing from the Japanization of Spain. . . . What the people of Spain need is to gain confidence in themselves, to think and feel for themselves."[13] He later came to emphasize that

---

[11] *Ibid.*, IV, 734–735.
[12] "En torno al casticismo," *ibid.*, III, 300.
[13] Quoted in Laín Entralgo, *op. cit.*, p. 333.

the Spaniards' defects were their virtues;[14] and, since Unamuno found truth and meaning within the inner self rather than in the affairs of the world, he looked to the regeneration of Spain from cultivation of the preexisting values and characteristics developed by the Spanish people in their history, refined and adapted to the needs of the twentieth century. If Spain had difficulty competing with the ideas or the technology of the rest of the Western world, the best defense was a good offense. Rather than Europeanizing Spain, he came to recommend Hispanizing the West, applying Spanish ideas and Spanish solutions to twentieth-century problems. The secret of Spanish culture, Unamuno was sure, lay hidden in the collective subconscious of the Spanish people, and he was certain that constitutional reform alone would no nothing to vitalize it.

Melchor Fernández Almagro[15] was perhaps the first to point out that the aesthetes of the *noventayochista* varieties ought not to be confused or identified with the Regenerationist movement of critics, sociologists, and political commentators who, in the years immediately after 1898, tried to analyze the causes of Spain's disaster and search for political, social, and economic remedies. The Regenerationists were led by such men as Joaquín Costa, Francisco Macías Picavea, Damián Isern, Luis Morote, and Julio Senador. They were concerned particularly and almost exclusively with political and social problems.

Unamuno at no time associated himself with the Regenerationists. On the contrary, though he had in the 1890's made criticisms quite similar to theirs, he later censured the Regenerationists and particularly Joaquín Costa for grossly mistaken emphasis, for concocting intellectual recipes to solve what were at bottom, he believed, moral and spiritual problems.

Nor had he anything better to say of the progressivist politicians. In one of the essays included in *Contra esto y aquello* (1912), he condemned the venerable Republican former president Salmerón for remarks

---

[14] "Sobre la europeización," *Obras*, III, 1119.
[15] *Vida y obra de Angel Ganivet* (new ed.; Madrid: Revista de Occidente, 1953), p. 192.

in which this dreariest of statesmen once again calumniated his
fatherland saying that it is hostile to progress—to what progress?—words that are reminiscent of a dismal speech he gave
in the congress on June 9, 1902, in which he asked that we line
up at the service of France [in the Moroccan question], contenting ourselves with whatever might be given us, "not anything like a bone, since we don't even have teeth with which to
gnaw, but something whose expense is compensated by its bene-
fits," and recalling, with the opportuneness that always distinguished him, the expulsion of the Moriscos.[16]

Though a champion of representative government, Unamuno
was no proponent of mass democracy. As Arturo Barea has
written,

> In 1904, when politicians, particularly Conservatives, extolled
> the uneducated masses to whom they owed their electoral vic-
> tories, Unamuno declared in an article on "Public Opinion" that
> the alleged democracy was a rule of illiterates, at that time 49
> percent of the adult population, who voted like sheep. He went
> so far as to demand that they should be deprived of their votes
> because they "had neither opinions nor any social understanding
> of their own, outside the immediate needs of their existence,
> outside their struggle for their daily bread."[17]

Unamuno also took exception to the idiosyncratic ethical conduct he noted in Spanish self-styled "progressives" and "conservatives," respectively. In his 1907 essay "Sobre la lujuria," he
intoned,

> In other nations the so-called advanced or progressive parties
> are the ones that take most care to maintain a certain tone of
> austerity, part-Christian or part-Stoic, in public customs, while
> the conservatives are the ones who give free rein to ethical
> license, which favors their designs. Here the conservatives are
> not distinguished by their ethical rigor, for they limit themselves
> to keeping up appearances; but, on the other hand, the parties
> that call themselves advanced defend license in one form or an-
> other, which is accompanied by that special tone of grossness
> and vulgarity that has always distinguished our progressivism.[18]

[16] *Obras*, IV, 862–863.
[17] Arturo Barea, *Unamuno* (New Haven: Yale University Press, 1952),
p. 25.
[18] *Obras*, IV, 473 (*PEP*, p. 148).

The prime exponent of paradox could perhaps hardly be expected to develop a consistent and practical political attitude, nor did he feel that to be his responsibility. The vocation of the moralist and poet he understood to be quite distinct. Unamuno was well aware of the dangers inherent in what Julien Benda later called the *trahison des clercs*.[19] The function of the righteous was not to form a political program, but to bear witness against evil, to "cry in the desert." Since Unamuno's kingdom was not of this world—at least not of this political world—he reserved the right to denounce everyone without necessarily endorsing anyone or offering an explicit alternative.

As he grew older, Unamuno continued his fulminations "against this and that." He took issue with the government's educational system and wrote a number of diatribes denouncing its narrowness and inadequacy. After World War I began, he came out strongly on the side of the Anglo-French Entente, despite official Spanish policy. Government circles strongly resented Unamuno's peculiar combination of pedagogy and politics, saying that it was improper for the president of the University of Salamanca to speak out so loudly in public lectures and newspaper articles against official positions and institutions.

It appears that during the summer of 1914 the minister of education, José Bergamín, attempted several maneuvers either to silence Unamuno or buy him off. According to one version, Unamuno refused to resign from the university presidency in exchange for a lifetime seat in the Senate.[20] At any rate, other means unavailing, the government dismissed Unamuno from his post as president in August, 1914, immediately after the controversy over participation in the war began.

During the course of the war, Unamuno continued to speak out strongly for the western Allies and also waged a personal campaign against Alfonso XIII, whom he denounced privately

[19] He was especially aware of this in connection with the Catalan intellectuals who were responsible to such a great degree for promoting Catalan nationalism. Cf. "Política y cultura" (July, 1908), *ibid.*, IV, 441–446 (*PEP*, pp. 36–41).

[20] According to Manuel García Blanco, in Rudd, *op. cit.*, p. 219. For a somewhat different explanation, see Bernardo Villarrazo, *Miguel de Unamuno: Glosa de una vida* (Barcelona: Aedos, 1959), pp. 79–80.

and criticized publicly. In 1920 he participated directly in politics for the first time when he permitted himself to be nominated for election to the Cortes by liberal groups in Madrid and his native Bilbao. The subsequent electoral defeat may not have been too sharp a disappointment. He was named vice-president of the University of Salamanca shortly afterward.

When the King allowed General Miguel Primo de Rivera to install a military dictatorship in September, 1923, Unamuno's personal reaction was immediate and extreme. Despite all the flaws of the preceding parliamentary regime, outright dictatorship he could only regard as even more artificial and fraudulent. During the very week that Primo de Rivera took over, Unamuno was writing in Palencia that he considered all his own cultural activity pervaded by a personal brand of "metapolitics."[21] He could not allow this to be silenced, and in the next few months made sharply critical remarks about the political situation in public speeches at Bilbao and Valladolid. Even more resented by the new dictator was a letter that Unamuno wrote to a friend in Buenos Aires commenting on the *Caoba* affair, the first major scandal of the Primo de Rivera regime. Unamuno's supporters have said that the letter was not written for public consumption; but, like numerous others of his criticisms of the Spanish government and king, it was published in the Buenos Aires daily, *La Nación*. Primo de Rivera was not disposed to endure any more. On February 21, 1924, the government once again removed Unamuno from his university post, and this time he was exiled to the island of Fuerteventura in the Canaries.

Primo de Rivera's pardon was rarely difficult to obtain, but Unamuno had no intention of asking favors from a dictator. Since he found existence on Fuerteventura uncomfortable in the extreme, his eldest son and friends in France easily arranged his "escape" on an ocean steamer in June, 1924. The day that he escaped, a pardon arrived from the dictatorship, but Unamuno's resentment had reached overwhelming proportions. He refused to return to Spain so long as Primo de Rivera remained in power. Unamuno's antiroyalism became even more pronounced, and he

---

[21] "Despedida" to *Teresa: Rimas de un poeta desconocido,* in *Obras,* XIV, 466.

identified Alfonso XIII with Primo de Rivera, declaring they both must go. And yet, during these long and lonely years, Unamuno did not engage in any direct political activity other than to write a series of essays and newspaper articles. He adhered to his own definition of metapolitics, and refused to be drawn into the plans and conspiracies of exile activists.[22]

The nature of Unamuno's opposition was made clear in an article entitled "Mi pleito personal," written in Hendaye in January, 1928. The monarchist-military dictatorship was, he said, the expression of "Spanish animal force, its infrahumanity, its bestiality," the lack of education, culture, or spiritual reflection and self-consciousness, the absence of internal tension and discipline, the very embodiment of all those things that Unamuno had struggled against all his life. He continued the struggle from exile because his literary activities and his ostracism from official Spain only increased his personal fame and the renown of his work. In that way Unamuno could be much more influential in Spanish affairs than he could be by trying to lead political forces. "I do not aspire to govern: I govern!"—at least in the realm of mind and spirit.[23]

Unamuno's long and dreary exile finally came to an end in February, 1930, after the Dictator's resignation. He returned to Spain amid great acclamations and addressed large meetings of admirers in Irún, Bilbao, Valladolid, and Salamanca. After the second republic was installed, Unamuno was restored to his old post as president of the University of Salamanca and then was elected to a seat in the Constituent Cortes. At the age of sixty-seven, he had reached the apex of his life. The object of widespread adulation for his writings, he had the satisfaction of seeing the elimination of the king, the old political cliques, and the militarist oligarchy. It seemed as though the values and attitudes that he had preached for four decades were, at least in some respects, being realized in Spanish affairs.

Yet he was now an old man with flagging energy. His topical

22 Carlos Esplá, *Unamuno, Blasco Ibáñez y Sánchez Guerra en París* (Buenos Aires: Araujo, 1940), pp. 21–49.

23 *Dos discursos y dos artículos* (Madrid: Historia Nueva, 1930), pp. 13–24.

comments became less frequent and less biting. His only Cortes speech of any consequence was a long and eloquent address of September 18 urging that Castilian be written into the constitution as the language of all Spain despite the clamor of Basques, Catalans, and Galicians.[24]

During the last five years of his life, Unamuno withdrew increasingly into his private thoughts and feelings. His sister died in 1932; one of his daughters, in 1933; his wife, in 1934. By that time it had become apparent that the Spanish people had not at all achieved the plateau of civic responsibility and rule of law which Unamuno and many others had thought they saw in 1931. Perhaps it had been a mistake to seek the education and regeneration of the Spanish people. Perhaps it would be better to "let them dream for they really do not want to know the truth, nor would they understand it if it were explained to them."[25]

During the years of mounting political tension and polarization from 1933 to 1936, some thought that Unamuno deserved more than ever Ortega's earlier epithet of *el morabito máximo* ("the supreme Marabout").[26] As Ferrater Mora has written,[27] Unamuno was frequently exhorted in those years to "define his position," but this was precisely what he could not do. He had always avoided any specific political position regarding parties and programs, believing that the moralist and philosopher dare not form partisan commitments. Those who did not line up with one group or another were increasingly ignored during the Spanish political crisis, and the newspaper articles of Unamuno's last years reflected his personal bitterness over this refusal to listen to a voice above the storm.

The breakup of public order in the spring and summer of 1936 to some extent jolted him out of the shell into which he had been withdrawing. He was appalled by the excesses of the working-class movement on the one hand and of the reactionary forces

[24] *Obras*, V, 686–703.

[25] Quoted in Rudd, *op. cit.*, p. 284.

[26] José Ortega y Gasset, *Obras completas* (5th ed.; Madrid: Revista de Occidente, 1961), I, 461.

[27] José Ferrater Mora, *Unamuno: A Philosophy of Tragedy*, trans. from Spanish by Philip Silver (Berkeley and Los Angeles: University of California Press, 1962), pp. 22–23.

on the other, among them, the Falangists, whom he had condemned in Salamanca in 1934 for the "de-mentalization of
youth."[28] At first he was not so apprehensive over the possibility
of an authoritarian Rightist reaction as he was over the possible
collapse of responsible government under Leftist assault. His
public statements in the spring of 1936, or those attributed to
him, were mostly devoted to condemning the senseless irration-
ality of the Anarchists and Left Socialists.

When the military rebellion occurred in July, Unamuno at
first accepted it as the only means of sustaining civilized order.
During the summer and fall, a number of statements attributed
to him were printed in the Nationalist zone, some of them possibly the work of other hands. On September 26 he signed as
lifetime president of the University of Salamanca a formal "Message from the University of Salamanca to the universities and
academies of the world concerning the Spanish Civil War." It
protested Leftist terrorism and was printed in *La Gaceta Regional* of Salamanca on October 4.

There is little doubt that Unamuno desired the defeat of the
Leftist groups then dominating the Republican zone, but there
is no more doubt regarding his fundamental distrust concerning
the forces that promoted the "Glorioso Movimiento Nacional."
If at first he accepted the necessity of an army-led reaction to
control the Anarchists, Left Socialists, and Communists, the
prospect of a regular military dictatorship he considered just as
disastrous in 1936 as ten years earlier, and he made this clear
in conversation with private visitors.[29]

Even at the time that Unamuno signed the university protest
message, the emotional atmosphere of the Nationalist zone—
laden with hysterical anti-intellectualism, calls to blind devotion
for the movement, and vengeful hatred against Leftists and liberals—was becoming unbearable for him. It was only a matter
of time before he would speak out directly, and the moment finally

[28] Francisco Bravo [Martínez], *Historia de Falange Española de las
J.O.N.S.* (Madrid: Editora Nacional, 1940), p. 87.
[29] Cf. "Entrevista del hispanista holandés Dr. J. Brouwer con don
Miguel de Unamuno, en el mes de setiembre de 1936," *Repertorio ameri-
cano*, XXXIII (1937), 217–218; quoted in Rudd, *op. cit.*, pp. 10, 295.

arrived at the large "Día de la Raza" meeting held in Salamanca on October 12. Less than two weeks earlier Franco had become chief of state of the Nationalist regime. He had established his headquarters in Salamanca, making the city of which Unamuno two years earlier had been named perpetual mayor the capital and propaganda center of Nationalist Spain. A considerable number of the leading intellectual figures supporting the new regime attended the annual event held in the Ceremonial Hall of the university. Doña Carmen Polo de Franco, wife of the new dictator, occupied a place of honor on the rostrum next to Unamuno.

There is no absolutely reliable record of what transpired on that occasion; but the principal speeches have been paraphrased by several commentators, and there is at least general agreement on the tenor of the remarks. Introductory statements by several university professors preceded a major speech by General José Millán Astray, organizer of the Legion, the elite unit of the Spanish Army, and temporarily chief of propaganda for Franco's government. Millán Astray was no mere anti-intellectual caveman, having attended the Spanish Staff College for nearly five years as a young man and written four training manuals, but he had a great dramatic flair and had long cultivated his histrionic talents. He had been wounded in battle half a dozen times, had lost an arm and an eye, and made an impressive figure in his calls for unity and sacrifice. He specialized in rousing his troops to feats of blind, death-defying heroism, and had given the Legionnaires their motto of "Long live death!" He was not concerned with rational discourse, but with rousing his audience to a pitch of violent hatred against the Loyalist forces. His speech contained vicious denunciations of the Basque and Catalan movements, and produced an emotional response among some of the university audience, until, as was common with Millán Astray, he began to talk too long and wander.

Unamuno found such emotionally pitched, hate-filled propaganda repellent in the extreme, and was doubly incensed that Millán Astray had delivered this kind of speech within university confines. When Unamuno arose to deliver the closing remarks, he denounced the whole tenor of the preceding address, praising the positive accomplishments of the Basques and Catalans, rejecting the effort to create through mass psychology a mood of unthinking hatred against the Republicans, and questioning the Legion's slogan of "Viva la muerte!" as a repudiation of life itself. Most accounts agree that Millán Astray finally cried out, to silence Unamuno, "Muera la inteligencia!" and that in the hubbub that followed, the ultraconservative rhetorician from Cádiz, José María Pemán, tried to correct him: "No, ¡viva la inteligencia, y mueran los malos intelectuales!"[30]

The meeting ended amid considerable confusion. It has been reported that the "Unamuno case" was discussed the next day at Franco's headquarters, and that from that time forward an armed guard was maintained outside Unamuno's residence to keep him under house arrest. When he died of a stroke on December 31, 1936, it was announced in the Republican zone that he had been poisoned or otherwise disposed of by Nationalists, but the evidence points to a natural death.[31]

Since that time, both Republicans and Nationalists have claimed Unamuno as a supporter. The former point to his outspoken remarks of October 12 and private declarations to visitors; the latter, to his university protest of September 26 and his earlier critical remarks about the Loyalists, adding that a Falangist honor guard was present at his burial. But of course Unamuno was for neither the Republicans nor the Nationalists, any more than before 1923 he had been for the Conservatives or the Liberals, for the super-Catholics or the radical anticlericals. Unamuno's metapolitics could never be committed to any single faction, however "Spanish" or "progressive" or "intellectual" it might be. Unamuno's politics were intended only to bear witness

[30] The fullest account is an article by Luis Portillo, widely distributed in manuscript and published in *The Golden Horizon* (London: Weidenfeld and Nicolson, 1953), pp. 397–403; reprinted in Robert Payne, ed., *The Civil War in Spain, 1936–1939* (New York: Putnam, 1962), pp. 111–117. A great many journalistic versions have been given, differing in minor details.

[31] The last person to talk with Unamuno, and in whose presence he evidently suffered his stroke and died, was a young economics professor at Salamanca, Bartolomé Aragón Gómez. See José María Ramos y Loscertales' prologue to Aragón's *Síntesis de economía corporativa* (Salamanca: Librería "La Facultad," 1937), pp. 13–16.

against the evils of his time, "crying in the wilderness," as he said, but also with the hope that, as he once wrote,

> the desert hears, though men may not, and will one day be transformed into a resonant forest, and that solitary voice that falls in the desert like a seed will produce a giant cedar whose hundred thousand tongues will sing an eternal hosanna to the Lord of life and death.[32]

32 *Obras*, XVI, 450 (*TSL*, p. 329).

13

UNAMUNO TODAY
José Ferrater Mora

What can we add today to what has already been said about Unamuno? Has not everything imaginable, and even a few things unimaginable, already been said? We have delved into his life and his papers (which were so intimate a part of his life); we have disinterred texts (although not all of them); we have scrutinized his novels, his theater, his poetry; we have expounded, explained, justified, criticized, exalted, and reviled his philosophy, theology, anthropology, and even his aesthetics and his theory of knowledge; we have made an exegesis of his political ideas (or his lack of them); we have even psychoanalyzed him (that alone would have been enough to make him furious, although the truth is he did not need psychoanalysis to make him furious). It has been exhaustively demonstrated that he was essentially a polemicist or, as he himself said, an "agonist"; that he was, at bottom, a contemplator; that he was a "protestant" and, needless to say, a "protester"; that he was, after all, a conformist; that he was a Rightist, a Leftist, a Centrist, an Anarchist, a Carlist. With all this, one wonders what there is left to say about Unamuno today.

Fortunately, we are dealing with one of those "authors" (for lack of a better word) who may be called inexhaustible. And this is true not, or not *only*, because he was interested in a great variety of subjects or because his works are rich in what are usually called "themes." Naturally, there are in Unamuno (or, if you will, in his works) many themes and many topics, to the extent that in spite of the abundant bibliography on him, no one has made, or perhaps even attempted to make, a reasonably complete inventory of these themes and topics. Besides, the simple truth is that Unamuno was an essayist, a journalist, a playwright,

220

a poet, a thinker, a polemicist—all of which contributes to making our "author" not easily exhaustible. But if Unamuno is, or continues to be, inexhaustible, it is not merely because of the diversity of the genres he cultivated or the variety of the topics and themes that he treated. An author is not inexhaustible because he has said, or tried to say, many things, for it would be possible to make a list for oneself of the "things said" and proceed to study, exhaustively of course, each one of them. Once we had the list and the pertinent studies at our disposal, it would be merely a question of adding details, as odd as they are boring. Rather, an author is inexhaustible because he has said, or attempted to say, something, one single thing, of real substance which, to be sure, is then no longer a "thing," because it can never be identified completely with a topic, a theme, or even an idea.

Say "one single thing"? Could it possibly be an "intuition" of a more or less Bergsonian stamp which cannot be discussed without falsifying it? The idea is tempting. To affirm that an idea, a thought, an intuition, a feeling, or whatever, is inexhaustible seems to be the same as situating it beyond all language, changing it, then, into the object of a mystical or ineffable experience. Now, if there is in an author or, in general, in a man, something that we can declare inexhaustible, it is not necessarily something of which we cannot speak. The opposite could very well be true: that "inexhaustible" is an attributive especially applicable to something that can be discussed endlessly, without ever reaching the very heart, or the end, of it.

If that inexhaustible "thing" is, therefore, neither a topic, theme, idea, nor even an intuition, what is it? It is personality. But then, why speak particularly of Unamuno? Whether he liked it or not, he neither had nor exercised any monopoly on personality. If it is a question of personality, we might talk of any human being and discover that he is also inexhaustible; after saying many, many "things" about him, there would always be some further "thing" left to say. As Sartre wrote, laying hold (probably without realizing it) of a typically Unamunian expression, any human being is *tout un homme* ("every inch a man"), that is, "composed of all men and as good as all of them and no better than any."[1] Because he was just a human being and, consequently, "every inch a man," Unamuno was no different from any other human being: Unamuno was Unamuno, and he was Sartre, and he was each and everyone of us. Today, as will be true twenty years from now, it would be possible to talk endlessly about Unamuno—and about anybody else as well.

Now, in every human being there is what Unamuno, long before Gabriel Marcel, called a "mystery," rather than a problem: the mystery of being like everybody else (consequently, "every inch a man") and, at the same time, fundamentally different from all the rest (therefore, "this man"). The mystery of the human being consists largely of the fact that to speak of a human being is, at the same time, to speak of some human being or other, without speaking of "just anybody." Every human being is at one and the same time himself and everybody else. This, then, is a mystery. I am well aware that there are people who chafe at the word "mystery." For them, I suggest other words, for example, "perplexity," which is not such a bad word, since it is in fact perplexing to face another person and, even more, to try to understand what we are dealing with. But whether perplexity or mystery, the human being is "something" we can talk about, and talk about, furthermore, incessantly, so he is "something" of an effable or even rational kind. Reason is not to blame for the things that not a few rationalists have done with her: that is, to suppose that whatever is rational is exhaustible because it is perfectly clear and transparent. Everything that can be talked about, wrote Wittgenstein (the "first Wittgenstein," of course), can be talked about clearly. This supposition would quickly take us to the conclusion that everything that is inexhaustible is necessarily irrational. Now, I am often inclined to think that reason is not beyond, or, if you like, this side of, the realm of the mysterious, the opaque, and the inexhaustible. I believe that Unamuno would have agreed with this view; after all, his irrationalistic frenzies never kept him from recognizing the fact that you cannot lightly dismiss reason, for reason will always turn on her attacker and take what Unamuno called "reprisals."

---

[1] Jean-Paul Sartre, *The Words* (New York: Braziller, 1964), p. 255.

Our "subject" (in both senses of the word) is, at one and the same time, rational (in being effable) and mysterious (in being inexhaustible), which is fine with me, for otherwise I would have nothing more to say. But it also makes me uneasy, for we never know how to begin with such subjects; when there is too *much* to say, the first problem we come up against is *what* to say. Our subject is inexhaustible since it is personality, but what is it exactly? A man? His philosophy? Let us say both, taken together. Whoever knows his Unamuno knows that his philosophy of personality is at the same time the philosophy of *his* personality. Here, then, at last, is our subject: a philosophy of personality that is personal through and through.

In many ways the Unamunian philosophy of personality is linked to other philosophies and, needless to say, to other personalities. Unamuno was well aware of this when he said he had "been" St. Augustine and Pascal and Kierkegaard—and, we might add, Plato and Kant and Hegel, for all *these* philosophers and, as a matter of fact, *all* philosophers have been men whose philosophy, whether they liked it or not, whether they knew it or not, was of a "personal" nature. But here it is not exactly a question of ideas but of how one, or rather someone, uses them. While bound up with other philosophies and to a great extent dependent upon them, Unamuno's philosophy still has its own personal stamp—as Unamuno would say, its own "tone" and its own "accent." Unamuno's philosophy of personality is his personal property, since it is an original way of feeling and therefore of expressing ideas, be these invented or merely borrowed.

I have said "original," and so it is, provided, however, that by "original" we mean "that which is at the origin." "Original" means here, or rather also means, "originary." Thus the Unamunian philosophy of personality is original because it is originary, that is, it is at the origin or fountainhead of everything Unamuno has thought, done, and dreamed. In any event, it is not a question of what is often called "personalism," if by this we mean the doctrine according to which all reality is, at bottom, personal in nature or, more precisely, the doctrine according to which everything that exists is real only so far as it comes close to the "personal being," that is, "the person." If the Unamunian philosophy of personality were a variety of the usual personalism, we might study it as a metaphysical thesis on the nature of reality. Now, Unamuno does not begin with theses, metaphysical or otherwise; he begins (even when he expresses himself, more or less skillfully, in the language of the philosophers) with an experience, the experience that to exist as a person, far from being a reality, is a problem, and even, as we have already noted, a mystery. The personalists do not have to bother too much with the possibility of existence as personal existence; for them, the reality of the person (or what approaches that reality) is, as Bergson would say, something "given"—even when their "being" consists of a constant "becoming." In short, for the personalists, *esse est personare*, "to be" in every instance means "to be personal" or "personable."

Unamuno felt the mystery of the personality more than anything else as that which exists "against" ("counter to," "contra"). Much has been said of the stubbornly negative attitude of Unamuno, of his incessant and tireless "against this and that." It is (and why shouldn't it be?) an irritating attitude. What does this man, who talks and writes endlessly, want? This man who hurls words at us as if they were stones, who never agrees with anyone on anything, not even himself? So many words and, what's worse, so many plays on words! He doesn't seem to be serious. It is sheer "energumenism" (to adopt the term Ortega y Gasset applied in a moment of ill humor),[2] a desire to get himself talked about, intellectual histrionics. These and other explosions against Unamuno's perpetual explosions are not entirely unjustified. Unamuno carried to its extreme and exacerbated an attitude that was characteristic of certain intellectuals and especially of certain writers at the end of the nineteenth century and the beginning of the twentieth. These men seemed to concentrate on playing with ideas; they made them turn flips, they showed them off, they made them disappear—tricks designed to dazzle the audience, the small audience they had left which, through a kind of continuous miracle, kept renewing itself, the same audience,

---

[2] José Ortega y Gasset, *Obras completas* (5th ed.; Madrid: Revista de Occidente, 1961), I, 461.

we might say in passing, which let itself be fascinated and hum-
bugged some years later by all kinds of vanguardists. These intellectuals seemed to be putting on a show, but what they were
actually doing was making a show of themselves, incapable as
they were of living without stage and spotlight.

But now, after having frankly recognized all there is in Unamuno of theatricality, of juggling with ideas, one must confess
that "no, no; it wasn't the same thing." If Unamuno was invet-
erately against, if he repeated himself, contradicted and recon-
tradicted himself, it was not because, or not just because, he loved
to hear the sound of his own voice. He was "against everything"
because he could find nothing to fill the void that opens up the
moment one perceives what we have called "the mystery of personality"—nothing, that is, no idea, no theory, no doctrine. One
might argue, of course, that it is not legitimate to identify "nothing" with "no idea," and this is true; but one must try to understand the personal and historical situation of Unamuno. He was
born and, more importantly, grew up in an age in which it was
usual to think that ideas would, in the end, settle everything; one
had only to discover which were the "true" ideas. It was the age
of ideologies, and even some of those who most persistently denounced them as masquerades succumbed to them. It is perfectly understandable and even natural that Unamuno (like
Nietzsche, for that matter) would play with ideas. His "prag-
matism" came from the realization that one could do anything
with ideas, even play with them; but he did not believe in them.

Let us not, then, always interpret the negativism of Unamuno
as mere exhibitionism. Such negativism was, rather, his personal
way of showing that one can put little confidence in ideas (and,
by the same token, in doctrines as systems of ideas), and that
one must turn to something else.

Some have thought that this "something else" was, or might
have been, a belief. Did not Unamuno delight in quoting the
title of William James's *The Will To Believe*? But it would be a
mistake, actually, to confine ourselves to this title; if there were
a real title, and if it was complete, it would be, instead, "The
Will To Believe . . . and Its Impossibility." Certainly it would
be much simpler to infer that since Unamuno could not believe

in ideas, he embraced, willy-nilly, belief *itself*, and even a *single* belief. Since Unamuno was not, as they say, "a good Catholic," why not make him "a bad Catholic"? Good or bad, we would still be left with a Catholic. Since he was a *sui generis* Christian, why not make him "a doubtful Christian," but after all (and this would be a bit more sensible) still "a man of Christ"? If we get started down this path, there is no reason not to go on and on. Unamuno, one could say, played with ideas and, needless to say, with words, because he was searching for a belief. Too bad that he knew little or nothing of Marxism, since it would not have been hard for him to find there the solution to his problems and his anguish, and so on.

Let us skip hastily over the by no means evident idea that Catholicism, Christianity, Marxism, and the like are beliefs and only beliefs. And Unamuno would have refused to embrace (or, as he would have said, to take as his mistress) any single such belief, or set of beliefs, because he would not have found in any of them anything with which to fulfill his personality.

We have already said that Unamuno felt the mystery of personality as, more than anything else, something negative. We have tried to show that neither ideas nor beliefs were able to fill for him what Hegel would have called "the abyss of negativity." Now we must see if there is not, or if there is not also, something positive in the mystery of personality.

Let us go back for a few moments to the words "existing against." "Against" is a preposition that functions only in a context. Up to this point we have interpreted "against" as "opposed to." If personality exists "against," it is, then, because it is opposed to everything that is not itself, to things, to the world, to ideas, to doctrines. And this is exactly what allows us to understand Unamunian negativity: Unamuno was "against" in the sense that he was not in agreement with anything. But "being against" ("counter to") also means "leaning upon," as exemplified in the words counterport, countermure, and counterfort. Now, I have the impression that the perpetual and almost obsessive Unamunian "against" has, along with its negative aspect, a positive sense; in any event, it is the negative aspect of the positive, and the one would be inconceivable without the other.

Let us recall what has been said about personalist doctrines. According to them, reality is basically personal in nature, or rather it more and more approaches the "realm of personality," which is, at the same time, the "realm of personal community." Unamuno seems at times to subscribe to these doctrines. He not only spoke of human beings as "persons and nothing but persons," but he also described landscapes, cities, and ideas as if they exhibited a "personal" profile. He wrote novels, or at least some novels (strictly speaking, all except the first, *Paz en la guerra*, and the last, *San Manuel Bueno, mártir*) in which the circumstances ("Night fell"; "They knocked at the door") were used or, more precisely, misused, as if they were purely stage settings. He found very annoying and bothersome what he used to refer to as "stage borders" (*bambalinas*) and even the plots themselves. All these would hinder, weaken, and impair the eclosion of personality, which for him does not seem to consist of living in a world where night falls and where there are people (but, are they really "people"?) who knock at the door! We have taken seriously the Unamunian invectives against "stage borders" (Unamuno himself took them seriously) in order to show that the Unamunian vision of the world emerges from a kind of exclusive, and even exclusivistic, disjuncture: "Either the person or nothing." Unamuno the poet, Unamuno the philosopher, Unamuno the polemicist, Unamuno the contemplative, Unamuno the dreamer—all these "Unamunos," which are so diverse and so contradictory, seem to join harmoniously together in the above disjuncture. The solution, then, seems very simple: "Either the person or nothing? Very well then, the person!" But I have my doubts that such a solution is truly or fully Unamunian. It is based, in fact, on the merely negative sense of the "against." The positive sense of this preposition is still left dangling.

To a certain extent, as we already have mentioned, one cannot be against something without leaning upon it. And this is exactly what personality does (or what it *also* does). If personality were capable of existing by itself, it would be self-sufficient. There would be no problem and, a fortiori, no mystery. Personality would be "what is." Like everything else, it would be a "thing," a subtle, vehement, and turbulent thing, but, after all, a thing; but it is not. Whatever personality may be, it is not a thing, it is not what is. Could it be then, like the Bergsonian "what is real," "what is becoming," a ceaseless and tireless *devenir*? Could it be, like the Sartrian "conscience," "what is not" at the same time that it is not "what is"? To the same extent that these philosophers have talked of "things" that are not things, it could be said that Unamuno was a Bergsonian without knowing it and a very *avant la lettre* Sartrian. But let us not fool ourselves. Unamuno was no quasi-Bergsonian or pre-Sartrian any more than he was, for example, a post-Augustinian or a post-Fichtean. Yes, of course, Unamuno tended to see personality initially as a kind of void and therefore as "what is not." Consequently, personality would "make itself" and "become." But how does it make itself? It makes itself "against things," and to the extent that it leans against them for the purpose of struggling with them for ground, that is, for existence. Here is one of the aspects of the "mystery of personality": there is no personality except insofar as there are things against which and in which personality constitutes itself.

It is tempting to hasten to the formulation of conclusions that are more or less philosophical: if personality exists insofar as it leans on things, they are, so to speak, the reverse or counterparts of personality. It seems, then, that Unamuno was a personalist. Did he not frequently write that things, all things (trees, stones, landscapes, flesh, words) had "insides"? And the insides of which he was speaking (insides that, according to what he said, vibrate, beat, palpitate), are they not the most "personal" aspect of things? There is no doubt that in a certain sense we have to do here with a kind of pan-personalism. In another study[3] I attempt to show that the Unamunian vision of the world is expressed by means of a system of linguistic preferences (and, no less, by linguistic repugnances). Unamuno showed an undeniable predilection for such terms as "insides," "soul," "viscera," "medulla," "marrow,"

---

[3] In the book *Unamuno: Bosquejo de una filosofía* (2d ed.; Buenos Aires: Editorial Sudamericana, 1957), chap. vii. Some revisions and additions have been made in the English translation of the same work: *Unamuno: A Philosophy of Tragedy*, trans. Philip Silver (Berkeley and Los Angeles: University of California Press, 1962).

"depth," "fountainhead," "overflow," "grave," "substantial," and "inexhaustible," and a no less undeniable scorn for such words as "skin," "surface," "frivolity," "lightness," "neat," "perfect," "polished." It seems, then, that the prefered terms are like key words by means of which one can describe or, better still, feel what is deep, intimate, in short, personal, not just in man but in everything. But we must proceed cautiously. Say what he will, Unamuno is far from thinking that the world is made up in greater or less proportion of personal realities, nor does he think that it is made up simply of "souls," of "viscera," of "insides." If it were, the person, as human being, would live in a universe that would be his own, and even exclusively his own; man would live in this world like a fish in water, submerged and immersed, comfortable. Now, the world is not in itself necessarily "deep"; it does not necessarily have "soul" or "insides." Actually, the world does not seem to have been made for the person, but rather against the grain of the person. It seems to be an opaque and indistinct mass always on the verge of pressing the life out of personality.

And nevertheless, this is precisely the world (in principle, hostile to the person) where personality develops and affirms itself. Personality affirms itself, and reaffirms itself, in short, against the world, which is not limited to being impersonal but is often even depersonalizing. But if this world so foreign to the person did not exist, the person would not know what to do with himself. He would be limited to staying, so to speak, "at home," in his own universe, wearily cultivating his own garden, and, in the end, vegetating—all of which is a thousand miles from personal reality because saying "personal reality" or "personality" is like saying "that which is not self-sufficient." In Unamunian terms, it is saying something like "struggling," meaning "struggling against any possibility of depersonalization." For that reason, and precisely for that reason, the person tends to push himself forward willfully as if he were the standard-bearer of the whole universe. Unamuno throws this tendency into relief in many different ways. One has been noted all too frequently: to be a person means not only to exist as one is but also, and especially, to exist as one wants to be. Unamuno's celebrated jokes about personality (there is the

John who is, the one he wants to be, the one others want him to be, etc.) are not merely more or less ingenious witticisms. Personality cannot even be reduced to the will to be what it is; it consists also of dreaming that it is what it is and, of course, of being dreamed. Unamuno repeated it to satiety: the human being is, at very bottom, a dream—a dream of God's, a dream of others', a dream of his own self. These three dreams are subsumed in one, the dream par excellence, the substance with which, or out of which, we have been engendered. And in this way the person becomes a reality, a supreme reality, but at the same time essentially indigent.

In this way Unamuno felt and lived his own personality: as the hardest, roughest, most stubborn and impenetrable of all realities, and at the same time as the most needy reality, since it needs all the others, including the most "frivolous" and "superficial." It needs them so much that it takes possession of them. Unamuno "unamunized" the universe, but he did not for this reason keep from making himself the universe or "universalizing" himself. "To be every inch a man" and, as he said, "to be everything to the limit" (*serlo todo en todo*) meant for him simply this: *to be*.

One may wonder now if, and to what extent, this Unamunian philosophy of personality (which was at the same time, and apparently in high degree, the philosophy of *his* personality) can help us to live and make out our own personalities. If Unamuno had been asked this question, he would have answered that it was not to the point, that it is not a question of helping anyone to live or even to understand himself. All that is something for the psychologists and the psychoanalysts, who, he would surely have added, do not belong to the "every inch a man" species. He would have said, moreover, that the question is an idle one, for what we here call "his" philosophy of personality was not, strictly speaking, "his" and, in addition, was not a "philosophy." It was, and will ever be, everybody's, universal for the very reason that it is strictly individual. This other witty remark of Unamuno's is now clear as crystal: we are "like everybody else" only when we strip ourselves of everything and are left with only our personality. Everything is superfluous; only the man is essential. This becomes quite clear without further explanation at the moment of death, and would be clear, if we were conscious of it, at the moment of birth. Birth and death—these are the moments of truth, when mankind is, or becomes, purely and simply a man. It is what Antonio Machado, twin soul of Unamuno, said, in the way he knew how to say those things, poetically and simply:

> And when the day comes for the last voyage outward
> and the boat that will not come back is just about to sail,
> you will find me on deck with little luggage, to windward,
> and almost naked, like the sons of the sea and the gale.[4]

In closing, I would like to add a few words on a question that may be running through the minds of some of my readers and, it goes without saying, that it would not have occurred to me to include if it had not been running through mine, too. It is this. Unamuno's personality, and the vision of the world which emanates from it, are they not, today, antiquated matters? Isn't it a question, after all, of preoccupations, not to say obsessions, which are too subjective and, Unamuno to the contrary, downright "exquisite" and "minoritarian"? Of drifting excrescences of a philosophy of intellectuals, and bourgeois intellectuals to boot, who have no more nourishing matters with which to occupy themselves? In a world like today's, which is getting every day more and more impersonal, economic, technical, and massive, who can take any interest in the problems of personality? Three-fourths of humanity hungers for bread, and more than three-fourths hungers for justice. Doesn't it seem like utter nonsense to wrack one's brains over mere nothings? Let the dead bury the dead.

One could, of course, take up the challenge and defend Unamuno, saying that he by no means neglected social questions; that he broke his heart in political struggles; that at one time or another he was a political hero; and that, if an accounting is made, it will show that more than once he gave proof of a courage that many of my hypothetical contradictors might well wish for. One could even exhume old texts in which Unamuno does not seem as Unamunian as we have painted him. This essay is free of quotes from Unamuno, but I have them in abundance for those

[4] Cf. Angel Flores, ed., *An Anthology of Spanish Poetry* (New York: Doubleday, 1961), p. 239.

who crave them. If need be, I could bring in some quite curious ones. For example, in an article written in 1901 in a magazine that is not easy to find today, Unamuno, campaigning, oddly enough, for "world citizenship" wrote: "The only firm barrier to the barbarianism of local exclusivism is Socialism."[5] In another article, in 1903, in a magazine that is now all but unavailable, Unamuno wrote: "What Socialism actually does is not so much to destroy patriotic feeling . . . as to transform and modify it, and I hope that by making use of what will remain of it—as something eternally human—[Socialism] will lay the foundation for future universal solidarity."[6] Yes, of course, all this is not very far from what was called in his time "social patriotism," reinforced by an attack on what the author called "*bizkaitarrismo*" ("Basque nationalism"); but it at least shows that Unamuno (and not in those days alone) did not spend all his time ruminating about personality.

Nevertheless, it is not necessary to defend Unamuno by showing that he was not, or was not *always,* exactly what we have said he was, for I am confident that he was, when all is said and done, what I have said. Let us limit ourselves here to our problem, the mystery of personality. To be sure, to those who live, as they say (by the light of Hegel, let us not forget), "detached" or "alienated," questions relative to personality seem to be pure nonsense; but let us be wary. People who live in the kind of poverty which is pure and simple degradation are too alienated even to have a consciousness of their own alienation. In such instances, it is not a question of making them forget the question of personality for good, but rather of doing whatever is possible to put them on the road to this question through a consciousness of their alienation. As for those who have come to think that once they have eliminated alienation the question of personality will vanish for good, we would remind them of this fact: human anxieties, which are personal anxieties and which are closely linked with the mystery of personality, are not like a mask that one can tear off quickly and on the run; when one tears off one of those masks, it is frequently to replace it with another, the

---

[5] *La Nueva Era* (Madrid), I (1901), 584.
[6] *La Revista Socialista* (Madrid), I (1903), 360.

mask of clear conscience. Now, "clear conscience" you can have at many prices. Granted, Unamuno frequently went too far with his "personalistic energumenism." Not once but many times one is tempted to burst out: "How exaggerated!" But only truths can be exaggerated; the rest is not even worth bothering to talk about.

14

EPILOGUE
Walter Starkie

I have many pictures of Miguel de Unamuno y Jugo in my mind's eye, before exile and after exile, but the most vivid of all is of when I met him for the first time in Salamanca in the summer of 1921. Certainly he was the symbol of that august university, "Mother of all the sciences," and when in the evening we used to sit with him in a café in the Plaza Mayor, one of the noblest in Spain, his table was surrounded by disciples and admirers who had come from all parts to pay court to him. I listened to the master firing off paradox after paradox, pulling the beards of solemn old professors and adopting the Socratic method of pretending at first to be ignorant until he saw an opportunity to clinch his argument with a sledgehammer, aphoristic blow. He also discussed the plots of his novels and plays while making strange little paper birds with extraordinary agility. He called this *cocotología*, or "the art of paper bird making," and it was an art that made him popular with children as well as adults. To the children he would make the little paper birds speak of their dreams, and to adults he would say: "Birds from time immemorial have symbolized divinity and the spirit, hence poets have always worshiped them."

Unamuno was in those days the "enfant terrible" of Spain, in spite of his air of puritanical austerity which made him resemble a Welsh elder at an Eisteddfod. His appearance was as ragged as that of the primeval oak tree of the Basque race, and was made somewhat severe by his white beard of formal cut. His gold-spectacled, peering eyes and his hooked nose, however, gave him the air of an owl and justified the nickname Tiresias which he received from the novelist Ramón Pérez de Ayala. He shunned personal adornment. He wore no tie, and his coat was buttoned up to his white collar. His gestures were brusque, and he emphasized his speech with gesticulations. From time to time he would peer from side to side through his glasses, as though expecting an attack from some quarter. At first I was somewhat repelled by his blunt aggressiveness, and I resented his contemptuous and petulant references to Benito Pérez Galdós, who had passed away the preceding year, as a mere *jornalero* or day laborer in literature. Such references toward one whom most Spaniards considered the greatest novelist since Cervantes seemed at least ungenerous.

As I listened to Unamuno's conversation, I came to the conclusion that he had, like Bernard Shaw or Pirandello, created for himself an outer mask, a second aggressive personality that enabled him to face the world; and in Unamuno, this second personality came to the fore the moment he rose to his feet and harangued the crowd. The presence of the crowd so excited him that he would throw all caution to the winds and deliberately trail his coat and make a speech of blatant provocation. As he spoke his eyes blazed, his gestures became more violent, and his voice became so prophetically intense that everyone in the audience discovered hints of deeper and more sinister implications in his strictures against the government. This was true, for instance, of his celebrated speech years before in the Teatro de la Zarzuela in Madrid against the Law of Jurisdictions which granted special power to the military in Spain. Unamuno, however, once he descended from the public rostrum, generally shed his mask of aggressiveness and returned to his normal personality, that of a philosopher and humanist. By nature he was cautious and circumspect, and his conscience often pricked him for having succumbed to the temptation of playing the demagogue or anarchist. For this reason, after one of his periodic outbursts as the "enfant terrible," he would slip quietly away to his refuge in Salamanca.

His habit as a public figure in Spain was first of all to provoke the people, then to deny that he had done so; thus advance was always followed by retreat, for he never believed that his paradoxes would find an echo in men's hearts. Gómez de la Serna, however, held that Unamuno was a tower of strength in a national emergency, and that once he had taken his stand fearlessly, he would go back without a word to his home, to the university presidency, or into exile.

In Unamuno's study at Salamanca, there were no dimmed lights or mysterious corners: all was sunny, and from the broad window we could see in the distance the graceful tower of the Duke of Alba's palace of Monterrey, which Unamuno called the symbol of Salamanca's beauty. At sunset he would take us for walks along the banks of the river Tormes, where once Lazarillo, the picaresque knave, used to loiter. Not a sound could be heard, save the occasional booming of church bells in the distance, as the shadows of evening descended rapidly over the broad, parched plain of Castile. Here and there the ghostly shadow of a cypress tree reached toward night, while across the river the cathedral tower loomed like a giant. At such moments Unamuno would become reflective and ponder the destiny of Spain. He gloried in pointing out the warring tensions in the Spanish soul: the mystery of the Arab, the steadfastness of the Germanic race, and the fierce independence of the Iberians. It was at such moments that he would give vent to intense quixotism, after quoting the lines of Calderón:

> Cada vez que considero
> Que me tengo de morir
> Tiendo la capa en el suelo
> Y no me harto de dormir.

Perhaps he would soliloquize in a slow, rhythmic voice: "Death immortalizes us. Nothing passes, nothing disappears into emptiness. The smallest particles of matter, the weakest blow given is made eternal." As the master rambled on, voicing his thoughts on death and immortality, his twin obsessions, I reflected that he had been predestined by his allegorical name, Miguel de Unamuno y Jugo, for Unamuno in the Basque language means "hill of asphodels," the pallid flowers that the specters, flitting through the shadowy Elysian fields, nibbled when they wished to become invisible. But, as his disciples used to point out, his second name, the name of his mother's family, Jugo ("juice," or "sap"), contradicts the funereal and gives a note of earthly antithesis to modern Spain's apostle of quixotism.

Unamuno, meanwhile, continued his soliloquy in a dreamy voice: "Spanish literature has forever been obsessed with the idea of death. Death permeates the dramas of Calderón, especially the early 'Autos Sacramentales.' What is the whole mass of poetry of St. Teresa and St. John of the Cross, but an invocation to death? At times we reach Nirvana with Miguel Molinos, the quietist in the seventeenth century."

Unamuno's greatest work, *The Tragic Sense of Life*, the continuation of *The Life of Don Quixote and Sancho*, is a long monologue on the subject of death and immortality. His central idea is that man is all the more man, that is to say, the more divine, the greater capacity he has for suffering; and because he sees us all plunged in materialism with our eyes turned away from death, he preaches unceasingly his gospel of the Middle Ages and Don Quixote. If *The Life of Don Quixote and Sancho* is, as Aubrey Bell called it, a kind of lay sermon grafted onto the text of *Don Quixote,* with parallels from the life of St. Ignatius de Loyola, *The Tragic Sense of Life* is the author's attempt to construct a systematic treatise on philosophy. Rather than a methodical treatise, however, it is the passionate autobiography of a soul in anguish. It should be considered an appendage to Unamuno's poetry, especially to the poems "Aldebarán" and "The Christ of Velázquez." Christ is, for Unamuno, not the dead Christ but the Christ of Pascal who lives in a passion of suffering to the end of the world, and he has summed up his Dostoevskian message in these lines from his greatest sonnet, *Siémbrate* ("Sow Yourself") :

> You, as you pass, your very self must sow,
> Not looking back, not looking on death's strife,
> Lest the past weigh upon the path to go.

Unamuno finds proof of immortality less in reason than in his passionate longing for immortality, his longing to "live and live forever."

At the end of *The Tragic Sense of Life*, Unamuno evidently was aware that he still had not succeeded in composing a system of philosophy, for he referred to the finished book tentatively as *estos ensayos,* "these essays," "these attempts." That statement gives us a clue not only to the personality of Unamuno, but to that of his companion authors of the Generation of 1898, of which he was the acknowledged patriarch.

In the last sixty years of troubled Spanish history, some of the most striking utterances by Spanish thinkers have been in the form of essays. The *ensayo,* or "essay," has been the most significant literary form in modern Spanish as well as Italian literature because it embodies concisely and dramatically the dominant ideas of the day. Sometimes the essay may be a passionate appeal by a seer to his people, and modern Spanish history has had a number of prophetic essays that, in their day, summed up the thoughts that seethed in the minds of the thinking minority. Many in Spain today still remember Larra's celebrated essay, *El Día de Difuntos de 1836* ("All Souls' Day, 1836"), written in the tragic mood of one who saw the first Carlist War extend all over Spain and found nothing but death and tombs on both sides of the "two Spains." "Here lies half Spain," he cries. "It died at the hands of the other half." Again the suicide of Angel Ganivet (Unamuno's contemporary) in 1898, the year of the Spanish-American War, seemed symbolic, a gesture of despair in the face of disaster recalling that of Larra. As Shakespeare said, "The tongues of dying men / Enforce attention like deep harmony," and Ganivet's swan song on the eve of the "disaster" was a call to his countrymen to rouse themselves from their decadence and *abulia,* or "lack of will."

Unamuno, too, became the great master of the dramatic essay, and he used it as a means for expressing his own philosophy and his quixotic self-communings. And the philosophic qualities of Unamuno the novelist and dramatist, which fail to achieve their object in the novels *Niebla* and *Abel Sánchez,* or in the dramas *El Otro* and *El hermano Juan,* become more deeply significant when we discover them in the seven volumes of essays and the soliloquies. In the essays we feel that Unamuno is as much at his ease as Socrates was in the streets of Athens. So eager is his mind, so keen and persistent his curiosity, that we see him forever in our mind's eye gesticulating, questioning, warning, and laying down the law to all and sundry. As Ortega y Gasset said:

"The moment Unamuno appears in company, he installs his ego, just as a feudal baron plants his standard in the middle of the field."

As Unamuno was tireless in his excursions through the whole of modern and ancient thought, so he enriched his personality by his eagerness to absorb new ideas and impressions. Many of his essays are random commentaries on incidents in his gospel of Don Quixote, some of them written in 1895, ten years before the publication of *The Life of Don Quixote and Sancho*. They are of interest to the devotees because they are rough sketches of themes that would in time be treated in greater detail in larger works. Of particular significance is the essay entitled *Don Quixote and Bolivar* in which Unamuno calls "the Liberator" one of the most faithful adepts of quixotism and quotes a remark of the latter to his doctor when he was dying. "Who," Bolivar asked, "have been the three greatest fools the world has ever known?" When the doctor shook his head, Bolivar replied, "The three greatest fools in the world have been Jesus Christ, Don Quixote, and myself!" So thrilled was Unamuno by Bolivar's remark that he resolved to incorporate in a later edition of *The Life of Don Quixote and Sancho* a selection of parallels from the life of the Liberator, just as he had done for Bolivar's fellow Basque, St. Ignatius de Loyola. The parallel between Bolivar and Don Quixote was a close one, for if the latter's shy courtship of the rustic Aldonza Lorenzo launched him into his craze for chivalry, certainly the former's despair at the death of his wife María drove him at once into a whirlwind of activity and restless journeying which lasted three years, during which time he tried to drown his sorrow in a series of violent and ephemeral love affairs. Then, at last, calm came when he visualized the crusade for the liberty of his country; and so the shy and gentle María Teresa Rodríguez, the Spanish girl whom he had married in Bilbao in 1801, the Aldonza Lorenzo of that American Don Quixote, by her death, became transfigured into Dulcinea, that is to say, into Glory.

Each one of the essays illustrates the unceasing struggle between Unamuno's personality as a writer and his personality as a man. More than once I have heard him say: "I cannot live without discussions or contradictions, and when nobody outside discusses with me, or contradicts me, I invent someone within myself who does it." His brain, as a critic said, was like a parliament in permanent session, and he could say of himself in the words of Alfred de Vigny: "Je ne suis toujours de mon opinion."

And now as a further illustration of Unamuno's agonistic personality, I shall quote from his most revealing letter to me, dated October 15, 1921:

> I wish I could write to you with peace and serenity of mind, but it is impossible. The affairs of this Spain of mine have reached so critical a state that we who feel acutely all the shame that has come upon our country cannot dedicate ourselves to higher things. We cannot breathe in the ether of pure, speculative contemplation because we are stifled by the dust of battle. For some time past I have not written a single line of art or philosophy. I have to write articles of battle. Who knows—perhaps those articles will in the end become more permanent than all the rest! The Gospels were written for an occasion, and the Epistles of St. Paul were really newspaper articles. I do not know when I shall rest; perhaps never. And that will be for the best, for to rest is to die. One must leave oneself in the hands of God, that He may carry us whither He destines us. Who knows? "Life is a dream," said Calderón; "We are such stuff as dreams are made on," said Shakespeare; "Dream of a shadow," said Pindar. And I say that we are a dream of God. God is dreaming us, and woe to that day when He awakes! God is dreaming. It is better not to think of that, but continue to dream that God is dreaming. Farewell.

One day in the spring of 1936, only a short time before the Spanish Civil War, when I was walking with him down the Gran Vía in Madrid, Unamuno, after declaiming bitterly against the theories of Marx and Lenin as followed by their Spanish devotees, said: "There is no tyranny in the world more hateful than that of ideas. Ideas bring ideophobia, and the consequence is that people begin to persecute their neighbors in the name of ideas. I loathe and detest all labels, and the only label that I could now tolerate would be that of ideoclast or idea breaker." All his life Unamuno was a modern Don Quixote riding full tilt against hypocrisy, smug consciences, dogmatism, and shibboleths. His critics tried to lay him low by calling him "paradoxical"; but paradoxes are necessary as weapons against routine of thought, and Unamuno's function in modern Spain had been to make men probe and sift ideas. "My painful duty," he said once, "is to irritate people. We must sow in men the seeds of doubt, of distrust, of disquiet, and even of despair." I cannot imagine a more dangerous ally than Unamuno because he was always the incarnation of the Spanish spirit of anarchy. For him, the ego was everything. In one of his works he says:

> There is no other I in the world. Each one of us is absolute. If there is a God who has made and maintains the world, he made it and maintains it for me. There is no other I. There are greater ones and less, better and worse, but no other I. I am something entirely new: in me is summoned up a past eternity, and with me a future eternity starts.

If Unamuno had lived at Athens, he would have been made to drink the hemlock on the plea that such a man was a danger to the state. One Unamuno is a benefit to Spain, but dozens of little Unamunos pullulating in the universities and colleges would bring libertarian anarchy. And yet Count Keyserling said in his book *Europe* that Unamuno was the most important Spaniard who had lived since Goya because he unswervingly proclaimed out of the wholeness of primal man the very few but very deep things that he had grasped and knew: the significance of faith, of blood, of the tragic, of Don Quixote as the highest symbol of man. What the European in this hour needed more than all else was to win through again to an immediate relationship to these basic problems of life. Spain was supremely important in the modern world precisely because of the indestructible traditions springing from her past. Unamuno was a traditional Spaniard, hence he was most illuminating when he spoke to Europe.

Unamuno's death in December, 1936, at the tragic moment in the Spanish Civil War, was a warning and a reminder. It was a warning to those who thought that Spain, "the pentagonal island" set at the junction between two continents, was fated to be the prey of Russia, Germany, or Italy. Few peoples had passed through so many racial changes as those of the Iberian Peninsula, but none of those changes had modified the eternal substance of Spain. And Unamuno's death was a reminder that the spirit of the Saguntines and of Viriathus still burned as brightly as it did two thousand years ago.

SELECTED BIBLIOGRAPHY FOR ENGLISH-SPEAKING READERS

(*Only titles published by the end of 1964 are listed.*)

WORKS OF MIGUEL DE UNAMUNO

Abel Sanchez and Other Stories ["Abel Sánchez"; "The Madness of Doctor Montarco"; "Saint Emmanuel the Good, Martyr"]. Trans., with introduction, by Anthony Kerrigan. Chicago: Regnery, 1956. 216 pp.

The Agony of Christianity. Trans., with introduction, by Kurt F. Reinhardt. New York: Ungar, 1960. 155 pp.

The Christ of Velazquez. Trans. Eleanor L. Turnbull. Baltimore: Johns Hopkins Press, 1951. 132 pp.

Essays and Soliloquies. Trans., with introductory essay, by J. E. Crawford Flitch. New York: Knopf, 1925. 244 pp.

"How To Write a Novel" (extracts). Trans. S. Putnam (from a then unpublished manuscript). In Samuel Putnam *et al., The European Caravan* (New York: Brewer, Warren and Putnam, 1931), pp. 310–320.

The Life of Don Quixote and Sancho According to Miguel de Cervantes Saavedra Expounded with Comment by Miguel de Unamuno. Trans. Homer P. Earle. New York: Knopf, 1927. 327 pp.

Mist (Niebla): A Tragicomic Novel. Trans. Warner Fite. New York: Knopf, 1928. 332 pp.

Nothing Less Than Every Inch a Man [*Nada menos que todo un hombre*]. In *The Best Continental Short Stories of 1924–1925,* ed. Richard Eaton (Boston: Small, Maynard and Co., 1925), pp. 452–494.

Perplexities and Paradoxes. Trans. Stuart Gross. New York: Philosophical Library, 1945. 165 pp.

Poems. Trans. Eleanor L. Turnbull. Foreword by John A. Mackay. Baltimore: Johns Hopkins Press, 1952. 225 pp.

Three Exemplary Novels and a Prologue. Trans. A. Flores. New York: Boni, 1930. 228 pp. (Reproduced without the prologue and with an introduction by Angel Flores in *Three Exemplary Novels.* New York: Grove, 1956. 228 pp.)

Tragic Sense of Life. Trans. J. E. Crawford Flitch. Introductory essay by Salvador de Madariaga. 2d ed. New York: Dover, 1954. 332 pp.

243

BOOKS AND PAMPHLETS ON MIGUEL DE UNAMUNO AND HIS WORKS

Barea, Arturo. *Unamuno*. Trans. Ilsa Barea. New Haven: Yale University Press, 1952. 61 pp.
Brenes, Edin. *The Tragic Sense of Life in Miguel de Unamuno*. Toulouse: Figarola Maurin, 1931. 87 pp.
Earle, Peter G. *Unamuno and English Literature*. New York: Hispanic Institute, 1960. 160 pp.
Ferrater Mora, José. *Unamuno: A Philosophy of Tragedy*. Trans. Philip Silver. Berkeley and Los Angeles: University of California Press, 1962. 136 pp.
Huertas-Jourda, José. *The Existentialism of Miguel de Unamuno*. Gainesville: University of Florida Press, 1963. 70 pp.
Rudd, Margaret T. *The Lone Heretic: A Biography of Miguel de Unamuno y Jugo*. Introduction by Federico de Onís. Austin: University of Texas Press, 1963. 349 pp.
Trend, John B. *Unamuno*. Oxford: Dolphin, 1952. 20 pp.
Valdés, Mario J. *Death in the Literature of Unamuno*. Urbana: University of Illinois Press, 1964. 173 pp.

ESSAYS AND ARTICLES ON MIGUEL DE UNAMUNO AND HIS WORKS

Abrams, Fred. "Sartre, Unamuno and the 'Hole Theory,'" *Romance Notes*, V (1963–1964), 6–11.
Alluntis, Felix, O.F.M. "The Philosophical Mythology of Miguel de Unamuno," *New Scholasticism*, XXIX (1955), 278–317.
Aranguren, José Luis L. "Unamuno in Person and in Faith," *Texas Quarterly*, IV (Spring, 1961), 25–31.
Balseiro, José A. "The Quixote of Contemporary Spain: Miguel de Unamuno," *PMLA*, XLIX (1934), 645–656.
Baquero, Gastón. "Spain, Unamuno, and Hispanic America," *Américas*, XVI (1964), 8–14.
Beardsley, W. A. "Don Miguel," *Modern Language Journal*, IX (1924–1925), 353–362.
Berkowitz, H. Chonon. "Unamuno's Relations with Galdós," *Hispanic Review*, VIII (1940), 321–338.
Blanco-Aguinaga, Carlos. "Unamuno's *Niebla*: Existence and the Game of Fiction," *Modern Language Notes*, LXXIX (1964), 188–205.
Brennan, Gerald. "The Twentieth Century," in *The Literature of the Spanish People* (Cleveland and New York: Meridian, 1961), pp. 421–427.
Cannon, Calvin. "The Mythic Cosmology of Unamuno's *El Cristo de Velázquez*," *Hispanic Review*, XXVIII (1960), 28–39.

Clyne, Anthony. "Miguel de Unamuno," *London Quarterly Review*, CXLI (Jan.–April, 1924), 205–214.

Curtius, Ernst Robert. "Unamuno at Seventy," *Living Age*, CCCXLVII (1934–1935), 324–328.

Dos Passos, John. "A Funeral in Madrid: II," in *Rosinante to the Road Again* (New York: Doran, 1922), pp. 219–229.

Earle, Peter G. "Emerson and Unamuno: Notes on a Congeniality," *Symposium*, X (1956), 189–203.

––––––. "Unamuno and the Theme of History," *Hispanic Review*, XXXII (1964), 319–339.

Ellis, Havelock. "Spanish Ideals of Today," in *The Soul of Spain* (Boston and New York: Houghton Mifflin, [1908]), pp. 401 ff.

Fasel, Oscar A. "Observations on Unamuno and Kierkegaard," *Hispania*, XXXVIII (1955), 443–450.

Frank, Rachel. "Unamuno: Existentialism and the Spanish Novel," *Accent*, IX (1948–1949), 80–88.

Hammitt, Gene M. "Poetic Antecedents of Unamuno's Philosophy," *Hispania*, XLV (1962), 679–682.

Hilton, Ronald. "Unamuno, Spain, and the World," *Bulletin of Spanish Studies*, XIV (1937), 60–74, 123–137.

Housman, John E. "Izaak Walton and Unamuno," *English*, VI (1946–1947), 130–133.

Hyslop, T. "Miguel de Unamuno as a Religious Philosopher," *Modern Churchman*, XXVII (1937–1938), 646–652.

Ilie, Paul. "Unamuno, Gorky, and the Cain Myth: Toward a Theory of Personality," *Hispanic Review*, XXIX (1961), 310–323.

Jones, Geraint V. "Miguel de Unamuno: I. The Man. II. His Philosophy," *Expository Times*, LV (1943–1944), 134–138, 162–166.

Kerrigan, Anthony. "Sorrow or Nothingness," *New Mexico Quarterly*, XXIV (1954), 330–340.

Kinney, Arthur F. "The Multiple Heroes of *Abel Sánchez*," *Studies in Short Fiction*, I (1963–1964), 251–257.

Krause, Anna. "Unamuno and Tennyson," *Comparative Literature*, VIII (1956), 122–135.

Levi, Albert William. "The Quixotic Quest for Being," *Ethics*, LXVI (1955–1956), 132–136.

Livingstone, L. "Unamuno and the Aesthetic of the Novel," *Hispania*, XXIV (1941), 442–450.

López-Morillas, Juan. "Unamuno and Pascal: Notes on the Concept of Agony," *PMLA*, LXV (1950), 998–1010.

Madariaga, Salvador de. "Miguel de Unamuno," in *The Genius of Spain and Other Essays on Spanish Contemporary Literature* (London: Humphrey Milford, 1930), pp. 87–110.

––––––. "Unamuno, the Don Quixote of Salamanca," *Atlantic Monthly*, 207 (Jan., 1961), 95–98.

Marías, Julián. "The Novel as a Means of Knowledge," *Confluence*, III (1954), 207–219.

Martin, F. R. "Pascal and Miguel de Unamuno," *Modern Language Review*, XXXIX (1944), 138–145.

Masur, Gerhard. "Miguel de Unamuno," *The Americas*, XII (1955–1956), 139–156.

Moore, Sydney H. "Miguel de Unamuno," *Hibbert Journal*, XXXV (1936–1937), 349–355.

Nozick, Martin. "Unamuno, Ortega and Don Juan," *Romanic Review*, XL (1949), 268–274.

———. "Unamuno and His God," *South Atlantic Quarterly*, XLIX (1950), 332–344.

———. "Unamuno, Gallophobe," *Romanic Review*, LIV (1963), 30–48.

Ortega, Juan B. "Quixotism in the Spanish Revolution: Don Miguel de Unamuno," *Colosseum*, III (1937), 130–142.

Predmore, R. L. "Flesh and Spirit in the Works of Unamuno," *PMLA*, LXX (1955), 587–605.

Ribbans, Geoffrey. "Unamuno and Antonio Machado," *Bulletin of Hispanic Studies*, XXXIV (1957), 10–28.

———. "Unamuno and the Younger Writers in 1904," *Bulletin of Hispanic Studies*, XXXV (1958), 83–100.

———. "The Development of Unamuno's Novels *Amor y Pedagogía* and *Niebla*," in *Hispanic Studies in Honour of I. González Llubera* (Oxford, 1959), pp. 269–285.

Rudd, Margaret T. "Unamuno's Hunger for Immortality," *Christian Century*, LXXXI (1964), 1589–1592.

Sarmiento, E. "Considerations towards a Revaluation of Unamuno: I. *El Sentimiento Trágico de la Vida*. II. The Poetry. III. The Novels and Plays," *Bulletin of Spanish Studies*, XIX (1942), 201–209; XX (1943), 35–48, 84–105.

Schuster, Edward James. "Existentialist Resolution of Conflicts in Unamuno," *Kentucky Foreign Language Quarterly*, VIII (1961), 134–139.

Sedwick, Frank. "Theses on Miguel de Unamuno at North American Universities (to February, 1955)," *Kentucky Foreign Language Quarterly*, III (1956), 192–196. (For later theses, see "Dissertations in the Hispanic Languages and Literatures," published yearly in the May issue of *Hispania*.)

———. "Unamuno and Pirandello Revisited," *Italica*, XXXIII (1956), 40–51.

———. "Unamuno the Essayist and his Detractors," *Modern Language Forum*, XLII (1957), 101–112.

———. "Unamuno, the Third Self and *Lucha*," *Studies in Philology*, LIV (1957), 464–479.

Starkie, Walter. "Modern Spain and Its Literature: III. A Modern Don Quixote," *Rice Institute Pamphlet*, XVI (1929), 87–110.

―――. "A Modern Don Quixote: Miguel de Unamuno, 1854–1936," *Fortnightly*, n.s., CXLI (Jan.–June, 1937), 217–223.

Stern, Alfred. "Unamuno and Ortega: The Revival of Philosophy in Spain," *Pacific Spectator*, VIII (1954), 310–324.

Torre, Guillermo de. "The Agony of Unamuno," *New Mexico Quarterly Review*, XVIII (1948), 141–151.

Walker, Leslie J. "A Spanish Humanist," *Dublin Review*, CLXXII (1922), 32–43.

Wardropper, Bruce W. "Unamuno's Struggle with Words," *Hispanic Review*, XII (1944), 183–195.

Webber, Ruth House. "Kierkegaard and the Elaboration of Unamuno's *Niebla*," *Hispanic Review*, XXXII (1964), 118–134.

Young, Howard T. "Miguel de Unamuno," in *The Victorious Expression: A Study of Four Contemporary Spanish Poets: Miguel de Unamuno, Antonio Machado, Juan Ramón Jiménez, Federico García Lorca* (Madison: University of Wisconsin Press, 1964), pp. 1–31.

INDEX

DATE DUE

		DEC 1 5 '80
NOV 89	FEB 7	
APR 2 1 1970	DEC 1 8 '7	APR 1 6 1984
	APR 2 2 1985	
	MAR 3 1986	
8:30PM Tues	OCT 3 1 1988	
11:00 AM WED.	DEC 1 9 1988	
FEB 1 2 71 NOV 2 8 1988		SEP 2 4 1990
FEB 2 6 71		
MAR 5 71		
FEB 1 0 1972		
SEP 9 1972		
NOV 6 1972		
DEC 8 72		